THE MIRACLES OF
OUR LADY OF ROCAMADOUR

ANALYSIS AND TRANSLATION

THE MIRACLES OF
OUR LADY OF ROCAMADOUR

ANALYSIS AND TRANSLATION

Marcus Bull

THE BOYDELL PRESS

First published 1999
The Boydell Press, Woodbridge

ISBN 0 85115 765 3

The Boydell Press is an imprint of Boydell & Brewer Ltd
PO Box 9, Woodbridge, Suffolk IP12 3DF, UK
and of Boydell & Brewer Inc.
PO Box 41026, Rochester, NY 14604–4126, USA
website: http://www.boydell.co.uk

A catalogue record for this book is available
from the British Library

Library of Congress Cataloging-in-Publication Data

Bull, Marcus Graham.
  The miracles of Our Lady of Rocamadour : analysis and translation / Marcus Bull.
     p. cm.
  Includes bibliographical references and index.
  ISBN 0-85115-765-3 (hbk. : alk. paper)
    1. Rocamadour, Our Lady of.   2. Mary, Blessed Virgin, Saint – Apparitions and
  miracles – France – Rocamadour.   3. Christian pilgrims and
  pilgrimages – France – Rocamadour.   4. Rocamadour (France) – Religious life and
  customs.   I. Title.
  BT660.R54 B85 2000
  232.91′7′094473–dc2   99-037959

This publication is printed on acid-free paper

Printed in Great Britain by
St Edmundsbury Press Ltd, Bury St Edmunds, Suffolk

Contents

For Tania

ACKNOWLEDGEMENTS

In the process of planning and writing this book I have relied in various ways on a number of individuals and institutions, and it is a pleasure to be able to acknowledge my debt to them and to express my deepest appreciation. The more I pondered a text that I hoped would prove of interest to students, among others, the more I found myself reflecting on how much I had gained in my own undergraduate days from the teaching of Hugh Lawrence and Brenda Bolton, who introduced me to the rich history of medieval monasticism. In addition, I am mindful of how much I owe to the inspirational teaching that I received at both undergraduate and postgraduate level from Jonathan Riley-Smith. In more recent years I have benefited enormously from the advice and support of my fellow medievalists in the Department of Historical Studies at Bristol: Penny Galloway, John Moore, Brendan Smith and Ian Wei. I have gained much from the stimulating research and teaching environment created by Bristol's Centre for Medieval Studies. And I would also like to thank my postgraduate students: even though their research is not always directly concerned with themes addressed in this book, they have done much to shape my thoughts on many aspects of the nature and significance of primary source material. Frank Shaw and Carolyn Muessig generously responded to requests for bibliographical guidance in ways that helped me much more than they perhaps realised. Jonathan Phillips has been an unfailing source of help and advice. To all these people I offer my warmest thanks. They have saved me from numerous errors. Those that remain are, of course, solely my responsibility. My thanks must also go out to the staff of those institutions in which I conducted my research: the University of Bristol Library, the British Library, the Bibliothèque Nationale, the Warburg Institute, and the Institute of Historical Research. My editor at Boydell and Brewer, Caroline Palmer, has been a source of constant support and sound advice, which is much appreciated. Finally, my greatest debt of gratitude is to my wife, Tania. Only she knows how much I owe her. This book is dedicated to her with love.

A Note on Translation

This translation is of the version of the Miracles of Our Lady of Rocamadour that forms part of Bibliothèque Nationale MS lat.16565. One reason for this choice is that this version is very probably the oldest surviving copy of the miracle collection (possibly produced within 20–30 years of the composition of the original). In the absence of a manuscript that can be placed at Rocamadour itself – our knowledge of the text is principally reliant on copies produced in northern France – closeness to the time of writing seems a suitable principle of selection. In addition, this manuscript was the base text (designated 'B') for Edmond Albe's 1907 edition (now made much more readily available than before thanks to a reissue, with supplementary material by Jean Rocacher, in 1996). To help those who might wish to consult the edition alongside this translation, therefore, it made sense to share the same manuscript base. One of the greatest challenges facing anyone reading this text is the identification of the many place names mentioned in it. I have generally been more cautious than Albe in identifying places, and have therefore not attempted to locate the most problematic or obscure instances. I have accepted his identifications in those cases where independent supporting evidence can be found, and in some instances I have offered different suggestions. These are signalled in the notes.

ABBREVIATIONS

AASS   *Acta Sanctorum Bollandiana*, ed. Société des Bollandistes, 3rd edn, 62 vols. (Brussels, 1863–1925).

Albe   *Les Miracles de Notre-Dame de Rocamadour au XIIe siècle*, ed. and trans. E. Albe, rev. intro. and notes J. Rocacher (Toulouse, 1996).

Cottineau   L. H. Cottineau, *Répertoire topo-bibliographique des abbayes et prieurés*, 1 vol. in 2 (Mâcon, 1935–37).

DHGE   *Dictionnaire d'histoire et de géographie ecclésiastiques* (Paris, 1912–)

GC   *Gallia Christiana in provincias ecclesiasticas distributas*, ed. D. Sammarthanus, P. Piolin and B. Hauréau, 16 vols. (Paris, 1739–1877).

HGL   *Histoire générale de Languedoc*, ed. C. Devic and J. Vaissete, rev. E. Roschach, A. Molinier *et al.*, 16 vols. (Toulouse, 1872–1904).

MGH SS   *Monumenta Germaniae Historica, Scriptores.*

PL   *Patrologiae cursus completus, series Latina*, ed. J.-P. Migne, 221 vols. (Paris, 1844–64).

Rocacher   Extra editorial matter by Jean Rocacher in Albe (above).

RHGF   *Recueil des historiens des Gaules et de la France*, ed. M. Bouquet, rev. L. Delisle, 24 vols. in 25 (Paris, 1840–1904).

Tulle   *Cartulaire des abbayes de Tulle et de Roc-Amadour*, ed. J.-B. Champeval (Brive, 1903).

ANALYSIS

1

Introduction: Issues and Questions

This translation of the collection of miracle stories produced at Rocamadour in Quercy in 1172–73 has been inspired by the recognition that the text, an important example of a sometimes overlooked genre, has enormous potential. Its value lies in the fact that it can be used to address a wide range of issues bearing on how the availability of various types of source material from different times and places affects our understanding of the past. In particular, there are three important areas of investigation to which the Rocamadour collection contributes: the role of modern translations of primary sources in the study of medieval history; the ways in which miracle stories can be approached by historians; and the possibility of using miracle collections to compensate for the lack of more mainstream narrative history from areas such as the twelfth-century Midi.

The value of translated sources

The first area to consider is the imbalance in the sorts of medieval source material which are available in modern translations.[1] In recent years there has been a remarkable growth in the number of sources available in English. In the context of the British university system, at least, this has largely been a response to the needs of students and teachers, as many undergraduate, and increasingly postgraduate, courses are geared towards the study of primary materials in translation. This is a very salutary development: medievalists are responding to the expectations of students, who usually come to the subject with a background in looking at sources at school level. And they are carving out a niche for medieval history as a discipline, in that its source-driven character enables it to depart qualitatively as well as simply chronologically from the teaching of later periods. In a sense, the relative paucity of source material for the medieval period becomes a pedagogical asset. Whereas modernists can expose their students to only a small part of the abundant sources available to them, medievalists – especially those whose specialisms

---

[1] Compendia of translated sources are a growing genre: see e.g. *Readings in Medieval History*, ed. P. J. Geary (New York, 1989); *Medieval Popular Religion, 1000–1500: A Reader*, ed. J. R. Shinners (Peterborough, Ontario, 1997); *Medieval Iberia: Readings from Christian, Muslim, and Jewish Sources*, ed. O. R. Constable (Philadelphia, 1997).

are before the thirteenth century, when the amount of surviving material begins to increase substantially – can aspire to mobilizing a meaningful sample of the sources to hand in their teaching. As is often the case, moreover, trends evident in the formal, institutional teaching of history are reflected, and sometimes anticipated, in the interests and expectations of the general reader. More and more, books aimed at this market use translated extracts from sources as well as the more traditional use of images in order to draw the reader into a lively appreciation of the Middle Ages.[2]

The result of this shift is that a good range of source types have become available: for example, law codes,[3] letter collections[4] and theological works.[5] But amongst the different types of material available there is a particular trend towards the translation of historical narratives, predominantly chronicles and annals.[6] The attraction of this sort of material is evident on a number of levels. A text such as a chronicle or set of annals is often long enough to repay close attention to questions of structure and form. It will often contain a wealth of information on a wide variety of different themes

---

[2] E.g. *Chronicles of the Age of Chivalry*, ed. E. M. Hallam (London, 1987); *Chronicles of the Crusades*, ed. E. M. Hallam (New York, 1989).

[3] E.g. *The Coutumes de Beauvaisis of Philippe de Beaumanoir*, trans. F. R. P. Akehurst (Philadelphia, 1992); *The Usatges of Barcelona: The Fundamental Law of Catalonia*, trans. D. J. Kagay (Philadelphia, 1994); *The Etablissements de Saint Louis: Thirteenth-Century Law Texts from Tours, Orléans, and Paris*, trans. F. R. P. Akehurst (Philadelphia, 1996).

[4] E.g. Fulbert of Chartres, *The Letters and Poems*, ed. and trans. F. Behrends (Oxford, 1976); Bernard of Clairvaux, *The Letters of St Bernard of Clairvaux*, trans. B. Scott James, new intro. B. M. Kienzle (Stroud, 1998); John of Salisbury, *The Letters*, ed. and trans. W. J. Millor, H. E. Butler and C. N. L. Brooke, 2 vols. (Oxford, 1979–86).

[5] Among recent translations particular mention may be made of Thomas Aquinas, *Selected Writings*, trans. R. McInerny (Harmondsworth, 1998).

[6] E.g. *The Capture of Constantinople: The 'Historia Constantinopolitana' of Gunther of Pairis*, trans. A. J. Jaeger (Philadelphia, 1997); *Chronicle of the Third Crusade: A Translation of the* Itinerarium Peregrinorum et Gesta Regis Ricardi, trans. H. J. Nicholson (Aldershot, 1997); Dudo of St Quentin, *History of the Normans*, trans. E. Christiansen (Woodbridge, 1998); Galbert of Bruges, *The Murder of Charles the Good*, trans. J. B. Ross (New York, 1959; repr. Toronto, 1982); Herman of Tournai, *The Restoration of the Monastery of Saint Martin of Tournai*, trans. L. H. Nelson (Washington, DC, 1996); Orderic Vitalis, *The Ecclesiastical History*, ed. and trans. M. Chibnall, 6 vols. (Oxford, 1969–80); 'The Old French Continuation of William of Tyre, 1184–97', in *The Conquest of Jerusalem and the Third Crusade: Sources in Translation*, trans. P. W. Edbury (Aldershot, 1996), pp. 11–145; Suger, *The Deeds of Louis the Fat*, trans. R. C. Cusimano and J. Moorhead (Washington, DC, 1992); William of Jumièges, Orderic Vitalis, and Robert of Torigni, *Gesta Normannorum Ducum*, ed. and trans. E. M. C. van Houts, 2 vols. (Oxford, 1992–95); William of Poitiers, *Gesta Guillelmi*, ed. and trans. R. H. C. Davis and M. Chibnall (Oxford, 1998); William of Tudela and an Anonymous Successor, *The Song of the Cathar Wars: A History of the Albigensian Crusade*, trans. J. Shirley (Aldershot, 1996).

and issues, thereby aiding group, as well as individual, study. And it often holds out the possibility – however illusory in practice – of discovering something of the actions and motivations of historical actors. Texts of this sort typically offer a version of events which can be followed as a more or less ordered narration, with identifiable *dramatis personae* interacting in a world governed by chronological sequence.

It is important to qualify this picture by remembering that the narrative power of chronicles and other historiographical works can introduce distortions in terms of what sources are favoured against others. To take one example, the *Gesta Francorum*, an anonymous eye-witness account of the First Crusade, which has been available in a first-class parallel edition and translation since 1962, has long enjoyed an unofficial status as the definitive point of entry for those wishing to study that expedition in detail.[7] The text's seemingly uncomplicated style, its chronological ordering and its vividness – together with the fact that it has been attributed, probably incorrectly, to a lay author – have established its credentials as a piece of raw and reliable reportage.[8] In reality, of course, the *Gesta Francorum* is a very partial, complex and uneven account of just some aspects of the experience of going on the First Crusade, as is made clear not least by the availability of other versions of events, eye-witness and otherwise.[9] The moral here is that one narrative source cannot do the work of many; a full analysis of each requires close comparison of the different pieces of available evidence. Nonetheless, the study of historical topics can be enriched by an attractive and evocative starting point. It is not an exaggeration to say that Rosalind Hill's translation of the *Gesta Francorum* has done more than any other publication to stimulate the growth in English-language study of the crusades that has been evident in recent decades.

A further attraction of historiographical source material is that it permits, and indeed requires, those using it to engage with the persona of the author more fully than is the case with many other types of primary source. A fruitful dialogue between text and reader can be built up from a considera-tion of issues such as when and where the text was produced, its intended readership, the sorts of information it drew upon, and the author's biases,

---

[7] *Gesta Francorum et aliorum Hierosolimitanorum*, ed. and trans. R. M. T. Hill (London, 1962).

[8] For a recent analysis see C. Morris, 'The *Gesta Francorum* as Narrative History', *Reading Medieval Studies*, 19 (1993), pp. 55–71.

[9] The principal texts available in English are Peter Tudebode, *Historia de Hierosolymitano Itinere*, trans. J. H. Hill and L. L. Hill (Philadelphia, 1974); Raymond of Aguilers, *Historia*, trans. J. H. Hill and L. L. Hill (Philadelphia, 1968); Fulcher of Chartres, *A History of the Expedition to Jerusalem 1099–1127*, trans. F. R. Ryan, ed. H. S. Fink (Knoxville, Tennessee, 1969); Guibert of Nogent, *The Deeds of God through the Franks*, trans. R. Levine (Woodbridge, 1997). See also William of Tyre, *A History of Deeds Done Beyond the Sea*, trans. E. A. Babcock and A. C. Krey, 2 vols. (New York, 1943); Anna Comnena, *The Alexiad*, trans. E. R. A. Sewter (Harmondsworth, 1969).

preconceptions and principles of selection. This is true whether or not the author is known to us by name, and whether or not he (or more rarely she) is attested in the historical record independently of the text under consideration. Translated chronicles and other types of histories therefore offer readers an excellent medium through which to develop a range of analytical skills rooted in close attention to the text itself. To this extent, some of the approaches which may be used – for instance, examinations of narrative structure, motifs and tropes, rhetorical devices, characterization, and the use of imagery – shade into perspectives traditionally applied to literary texts. In this context, it is worth observing that there has been a recent trend – observable in the teaching of medieval culture and society at postgraduate level in particular but also informing undergraduate courses – towards challenging the barriers between academic disciplines and encouraging multi- and interdisciplinary approaches. Just as medieval historians are becoming more interested in using literary texts in both teaching and research, so they are developing new techniques in their study of chronicle material, which is no longer seen as a repository of factual information existing independently of the record in which it is preserved. The still important questions of who, what, where, when and why – the stuff of trying to recreate events and processes in the past – can be enriched by an appreciation of issues such as language, form and reception when pondering historical narratives. Having this sort of material in translation has its pitfalls, in that many issues relating to authorial use of language and style are necessarily obscured, but it still allows more people to share in many aspects of the process of exploration.

One problem worth noting is that a focus on historical narrative translations – however much it chimes with certain trends in the study of source material, as we have just seen – runs counter to important shifts in historical methodology in recent decades. Put very simply, there has been a move away from what has been seen as an old-fashioned reliance on narrative sources towards a more pluralistic approach which seeks to exploit the widest possible range of source survivals, from documentary material, such as charters, writs and financial records, to artefacts and art. To illustrate this, it is useful to return to the example of the First Crusade. Up to the 1950s, and sometimes beyond, historians recreated this event largely on the basis of chronicle accounts, which survive in unusual abundance for this particular campaign. The finest and most influential example of this methodology is the first part of Steven Runciman's celebrated three-volume history of the crusades, which appeared in 1951 but continues to be much read.[10] Runciman's absorbing account of the First Crusade, which dominates the first volume, succeeds as a quasi-Homeric epic narration

[10] S. Runciman, *A History of the Crusades, I: The First Crusade and the Foundation of the Kingdom of Jerusalem* (Cambridge, 1951).

because of the author's skill in adapting the narrative flow and vividness of the contemporary histories on which he mostly drew. More recently, however, scholars have asked whether privileging the narrative sources distorts our perspectives and limits the range of questions which can be asked of the evidence. They have therefore explored other types of source, most notably the many charters that record property transactions entered into by some of those leaving on the crusade.[11] An individual charter cannot, of course, convey the wealth of detail to be found in a chronicle account of the expedition – though a number contain interesting vignettes – but their cumulative value is immense. The fact that they survive in large numbers and their wide geographical distribution permit the historian to detect trends that would not have been spotted by an individual chronicler, however well informed. New questions can be asked about how contemporaries understood the crusade, why some wanted to go on it, and how they organized and funded themselves. The narrative evidence is still regarded as important, but it now operates in a much fuller evidential landscape.

The example of methodological shifts in the study of the early crusade movement is an extreme case, but it has wider lessons. *Mutatis mutandis*, the change from the use of set-piece classics of narrative history, where available, to the mobilization of a more variegated array of sources has characterized the study of a wide range of topics in recent decades, as well as opening up many hitherto unexplored areas in relation to, for example, women's history, cultural history and the history of ideas. So far, so good. But the complexity of the source base now within medievalists' horizons has not yet fully come across in terms of what is readily available in translation. This is often for very good logistical reasons. It would be impracticable, for example, to translate anything more than a tiny percentage of the surviving charter material; the translations which are available can only offer 'taster' samples of a type of text that usually needs to be studied in bulk for patterns and questions to emerge properly.[12] But the problem of practicalities is not the whole explanation for the very uneven distribution of translated sources; there is still a good deal of material that lends itself to this treatment waiting to be made available.

The sorts of imbalances we are considering are evident in the particular context of the medieval cult of the saints. If we limit ourselves to the written remains of this important element of medieval religious practice and thought

---

[11] See G. Constable, 'Medieval Charters as a Source for the History of the Crusades', in *Crusade and Settlement*, ed. P. W. Edbury (Cardiff, 1985), pp. 73–89; J. S. C. Riley-Smith, *The First Crusaders, 1095–1131* (Cambridge, 1997); M. G. Bull, 'The Diplomatic of the First Crusade', in *The First Crusade: Origins and Impact*, ed. J. P. Phillips (Manchester, 1997), pp. 35–54.

[12] For an excellent anthology, which includes much useful diplomatic material, see *Feudal Society in Medieval France: Documents from the County of Champagne*, trans. T. Evergates (Philadelphia, 1993).

– there was also an enormous impact, of course, in other media such as art, architecture and music – we find that a wide range of text types is available: for example, lectionaries (collections of liturgical readings), *inventiones* (accounts of the discovery of a relic or relics), *translationes* (accounts of the movement of relics to a new location) and vernacular lyrics.[13] But measured in terms of the volume of literary effort, the two main staples of written hagiographical culture were *vitae*, the accounts of a saint's life, merits, works and death, and *miracula*, miracle stories which sought to document how a saint's post-mortem intercessory power was made evident in this world.[14] It is important to note that the distinction between the two types of text was not hard and fast, for they were often run together. To take just one example, which we shall be considering in other contexts later, the Life of St Stephen of Obazine (d.1159) comprises three books, the third of which moves from an account of its principal's death and burial to a description of various miracles that took place in the following decades.[15] The miracles serve to reinforce the message of what may loosely be termed the 'biographical' record, which accounts for the majority of the text as a whole. At the end of the work the author observes that he wished to bear witness to St Stephen's virtues by writing something of his 'life, actions and miracles'.[16] Thus the post-mortem miracles form a continuum with the preceding narrative, reinforcing ideas evident in the presentation of Stephen's career. The link is reinforced by the inclusion of miracle stories which describe visions experienced by some of the monks and nuns in the religious communities that Stephen founded, and reassert some of the prescriptions for discipline and devotional behaviour that he had instilled as a monastic leader.[17]

The close textual and thematic juxtaposition of Life and miracles seen in the Obazine example was very common, but this was not the only possible

---

[13] For an excellent bibliography and survey of hagiographical materials, see J. Dubois and J.-L. Lemaître, *Sources et méthodes de l'hagiographie médiévale* (Paris, 1993). Despite its age R. Aigrain, *L'hagiographie, ses sources, ses méthodes, son histoire* (Paris, 1953) remains of value. See also G. Philippart, *Les légendiers latins et autres manuscrits hagiographiques* (Typologie des sources du moyen âge occidental, 24–5; Turnhout, 1977).

[14] For miracle collections see M. Heinzelmann, 'Une source de base de la littérature hagiographique latine: Le recueil de miracles', *Hagiographie, cultures et sociétés, IVe–XIIe siècles: Actes du Colloque organisé à Nanterre et à Paris (2–5 mai 1979)* (Paris, 1981), pp. 235–59; P.-A. Sigal, 'Miracle in vita et miracle posthume aux XIe et XIIe siècles', in *Histoire des miracles* (Publications du Centre de Recherches d'Histoire Religieuse et d'Histoire des Idées, 6; Angers, 1983), pp. 41–9; A. Dierkens, 'Réflexions sur le miracle au haut moyen âge', in *Miracles, prodiges et merveilles au moyen âge: XXVe Congrès de la Société des Historiens Médiévistes de l'Enseignement Supérieur Public (Orléans, juin 1994)* (Série Histoire Ancienne et Médiévale, 34; Paris, 1995), pp. 9–30.

[15] *Vie de Saint Etienne d'Obazine*, ed. and trans. M. Aubrun (Publications de l'Institut d'Études du Massif Central, 6; Clermont-Ferrand, 1970).

[16] *Ibid.*, III.34, p. 244.

[17] *Ibid.*, III.11–12, 14–19, pp. 214–16, 218–26.

approach available to writers wishing to record a series of miracle stories. There also survive many more-or-less free-standing collections of post-humous miracles. This suggests that the miracle story as a literary form and as a medium for certain types of material and messages enjoyed a level of prestige that made it more than an optional addendum to a saint's Life.[18] The collection of miracles from Rocamadour is one example of this genre. More specifically, it falls within the tradition of anthologies of *miracula* written at pilgrimage centres in order to record miracles attributed to the saint or saints venerated there. This type of collection enjoyed a particular vogue between the tenth and thirteenth centuries, especially in the area roughly corresponding to modern-day France and Belgium. Thereafter site-specific anthologies lost something of their status as a literary exercise as other forms of material that addressed similar processes and ideas emerged. Two factors were particularly important in this shift. First, in the case of new cults, papal canonization procedures developed from the thirteenth century onwards and stimulated the pro-duction of miracle dossiers arranged more systematically and internally consistently than *miracula* of the older type: while the basic subject matter was similar, the difference was that between material assembled as part of a legal brief and texts produced in more disparate ways to meet a range of devotional, didactic and commemorative needs.[19] Second, the greater organization and sophistication of the Church's preaching from the thirteenth century created a need for didactic material that old-style *miracula* could only meet in part. Many *exempla*, model stories deployed by preachers to illustrate and explain points that they wished to convey in their sermons, were built around a description of a miracle, and to this extent closely resemble the sorts of stories recorded at cult centres. But preachers' mobility, their need to be flexible in relation to the messages they could insert into an anecdote, the variety of their audiences, and the fact that acting as promoters of a given saint's cult was only one part of their remit, all meant that the miracle stories they used tended to work best if not anchored to a particular site and a specific time. One therefore sees in the later Middle Ages a trend towards miracle stories that were detached from the constraints of time and place: the very popular corpus of stories about the Virgin Mary, to which the Rocamadour collection supplied some of the raw material, is a case in point.[20]

---

[18] For the uses which hagiographical texts, including miracle stories, served, see B. de Gaiffier, 'L'hagiographie et son public au XIe siècle', in *Miscellanea Historica in honorem Leonis van der Essen*, 1 vol. in 2 (Brussels and Paris, 1947), i.135–66.

[19] See A. Vauchez, *La sainteté en Occident aux derniers siècles du moyen âge d'après les procès de canonisation et les documents hagiographiques*, 2nd edn (Bibliothèque des Écoles Françaises d'Athènes et de Rome, 241; Rome, 1988), esp. pp. 25–67.

[20] R. W. Southern, *The Making of the Middle Ages* (London, 1953), pp. 234–41; *idem*, 'The English Origins of the "Miracles of the Virgin"', *Medieval and Renaissance*

The development of formalized canonization procedures and the system-ization of preaching are two symptoms of the later medieval Church's emphasis upon centralization and consistency. In contrast, the miracle collections of earlier centuries are symptomatic of a more atomized and particularistic religious landscape in which institutions had greater oppor-tunities to create particular identities for themselves and to make strategic choices about how they projected their status and prestige onto the wider world. The collections survive in substantial numbers and constitute an important resource. But with a few notable exceptions they have not been the subject of modern translations.[21] This contrasts with the good number of Lives available in English and other modern languages, with the result that a student or general reader beginning to explore the hagiographical culture of the Middle Ages risks gaining a lop-sided view both of the forms in which that culture was given written expression and of the ways in which the cult of the saints functioned in the lives of medieval men and women.[22] Without pushing the analogy too far, it may be said that miracle stories stand in relation to saints' Lives as documentary sources such as charters do in relation to chronicles. They permit us to move the focus of inquiry to some extent away from the behaviour and ideas of an elite of prominent individuals or small groups. Like charters, an individual miracle story can only provide a limited amount of information, but the formulaic and often repetitive quality of the stories, as well as the fact that they mostly engage with a quite limited range of human experiences, means that they lend themselves to comparative analysis. And, as is the case with many charters, miracle stories often feature lay people – sometimes those who would otherwise be very unlikely to enter the historical record – coming into contact with the institutions of the Church. Consequently they can throw valuable light on the religious aspirations, needs and instincts of people on the ground level of medieval Christianity, even though the experiences described come to us mediated by the monastic or clerical authors. It is

---

Studies, 4 (1958), pp. 176–216; B. Ward, Miracles and the Medieval Mind: Theory, Record and Event 1000–1215, rev. edn (Aldershot, 1987), pp. 155–65.

[21] The most important recent translation is The Book of Sainte Foy, trans. P. Sheingorn (Philadelphia, 1995), which deals with the eleventh-century collection from Conques. For important twelfth-century collections from England see 'The Miracles of the Hand of St James', trans. B. Kemp, Berkshire Archaeological Journal, 65 (1970), pp. 1–19; Thomas of Monmouth, The Life and Miracles of St William of Norwich, ed. and trans. A. Jessopp and M. R. James (Cambridge, 1896). Also of interest is The Life and Miracles of St Ivo, trans. S. B. Edgington (St Ives, 1985).

[22] For translations of twelfth-century vitae see e.g. Eadmer, The Life of St Anselm, Archbishop of Canterbury, ed. and trans. R. W. Southern (Oxford, 1972); Walter Daniel, The Life of Ailred of Rievaulx, ed. and trans. F. M. Powicke (London, 1950); The Life of Christina of Markyate, ed. and trans. C. H. Talbot (Oxford, 1959). See also The Cistercian World: Monastic Writings of the Twelfth Century, trans. P. Matarasso (Harmondsworth, 1993), pp. 19–41, 59–64, 229–71.

therefore important to make more texts of this type available in translation in order to raise the profile of a valuable source base which will repay more widespread attention.

The importance of miracula as part of medieval hagiographical culture

This brings us to the second set of trends mentioned earlier: the different ways in which scholars have exploited the potential of miracle stories in their researches into various aspects of medieval culture. There is a wariness on the part of some historians as to what uses *miracula* serve: the miracle story is rooted in understandings of phenomenology that are fundamentally different from modern analyses of how and why things happen, and it occupies an imprecise and shifting ground between 'hard' historical data and imaginative literature.[23] Nonetheless various strategies have been developed in recent decades to mobilize the material fully. Perhaps the most straightforward technique is one of circumvention. Here the basic assumption is that however much an author of a miracle story was in the very nature of the exercise writing about an event that departed from normal experience, he was not necessarily engaged in creating a fantasy world. On the contrary, the essence of a miracle was that it represented a stark juxtaposition between the exceptional and the mundane. In order to draw out what exactly was miraculous about an episode, therefore, a sensible authorial strategy was to include details of routine life which readers or listeners would be able to recognize without difficulty; the more commonplace the setting, the greater the contrast to be made in identifying what constituted the miracle.

One scholarly approach, therefore, has been to sift the 'miraculous bits' out of stories in the expectation that what will be left is a residue of incidental material about social, cultural, religious and economic conditions in the medieval West. This methodology has much to commend it, and the results can be very exciting, especially when the focus is on recurrent and narrowly defined themes. For example, Pierre Bonnassie has drawn on the eleventh-century miracles of St Faith (Foy) from Conques in south-central France to explore the form and function of castles at a time when they were beginning to make a significant social and political impact.[24] A number of St Faith's miracles involve prisoners escaping from captivity, and in the process a wealth of information is provided about the places in which they were held. Details emerge that would be more difficult to glean from other written

---

[23] See the useful comments of R. Van Dam, *Saints and their Miracles in Late Antique Gaul* (Princeton, 1993), p. 84. See also W. D. McCready, *Signs of Sanctity: Miracles in the Thought of Gregory the Great* (Toronto, 1989), pp. 117–25.

[24] P. Bonnassie, 'Descriptions of Fortresses in the Book of Miracles of Sainte-Foy of Conques', in his *From Slavery to Feudalism in South-Western Europe*, trans. J. Birrell (Cambridge, 1991), pp. 132–48.

11

records or architectural evidence. More generally, many treatments of daily life in the Middle Ages have used the circumvention technique to recreate aspects of people's lives.[25] The attraction of miracle stories as evidence is clear in this context: they mention routine and habitual activities; and many of them foreground members of social groups – for example women, the poor and those marginalized by disease or disfigurement – who seldom appear prominently in other types of evidence, particularly before the thirteenth century.[26]

In addition, this way of exploiting miracle material is validated by the fact that it often sits comfortably with a significant feature of many *miracula*: their clear visual quality. Many groups of people and many of the things they did are, so to speak, invisible to historians, and miracles can appear to fill some of the gap. The visual quality of the stories flows from a number of factors. They are often structurally straightforward: a central figure or group of people is introduced at the beginning, and their experiences move the narrative forward. Chronological sequence is usually maintained; there is little retrospection or anticipation (other than, of course, the expectation on the part of the reader that a miraculous resolution will eventually take place). Also, many stories deal with situations that have a clear, sometimes graphic, visual or tangible dimension. This is revealed by its presence in stories that might not at first glance seem to require it: thus, mental disorders were routinely described in terms of their physical effects on the sufferer, and the cure of conditions that might not obviously manifest themselves externally could be signalled by noticeable markers such as convulsions, haemorrhaging or vomiting.[27] The writers of miracle stories encouraged their readers or listeners to recreate events in their mind's eye. The result is a wealth of visual detail. Any material that helps to compensate for the paucity of evidence about what medieval life looked like is therefore welcome, even if the vignettes offered by miracles can individually appear quite trivial or mundane.

On the other hand, some notes of caution need to be entered regarding a methodology that bisects *miracula* into historically valid data and the purely

---

[25] See e.g. R. Latouche, 'Sainte-Foy de Conques et le problème d'or aux temps carolingiens', *Annales du Midi*, 68 (1956), pp. 209–15; P. Bonnassie, 'La monnaie et les échanges en Auvergne et Rouergue aux Xe et XIe siècles d'après les sources hagiographiques', *Annales du Midi*, 90 (1978), pp. 275–88; C. Caitucoli, 'Nobles et chevaliers dans le *Livre des miracles de sainte Foy*', *Annales du Midi*, 107 (1995), pp. 401–16. For an excellent study based on a miracle text which takes the form of an account of a relic tour, see G. Koziol, 'Monks, Feuds, and the Making of Peace in Eleventh-Century Flanders', in *The Peace of God: Social Violence and Religious Response in France around the Year 1000*, ed. T. Head and R. Landes (Ithaca, 1992), pp. 239–58.

[26] For a stimulating study based on later medieval material see M. E. Goodich, *Violence and Miracle in the Fourteenth Century: Private Grief and Public Salvation* (Chicago, 1995).

[27] See e.g. I.5; I.23; II.7; II.10.

miraculous. First, it is deceptively easy to be drawn by the wealth of intimate, incidental detail contained in the stories, and by the knowledge that much of this sort of detail is not to be found elsewhere, into the assumption that they cumulatively create a full picture of medieval people's circumstances and activities. This is far from being the case. The great majority of *miracula* describe episodes that could be slotted into one or more of a range of categories that added up to an unofficial but widely recognized typological 'canon'. The significance of this canon, and its limiting effect on what was recorded, can be detected in those instances in which the authors were conscious that they were departing from it and consequently believed that they needed to justify themselves carefully. To take an extreme but revealing example, the author who wrote the first part of the miracle collection of St Faith, Bernard of Angers, wished to include two stories about mules brought back from death, as well as two others about unlikely restorations of people's sight. He was so sensitive to the potential criticism that this was an irregular way to illustrate Faith's power that he included a lengthy, and laboured, justification.[28] The canon also governed the selection and presentation of mainstream miracles. In particular, many instances of the most common type of miracle story, the cure of illness, were clearly influenced by the models found in the accounts in the Gospels of cures effected by Christ.[29] (The correspondence is not complete, however: cures of leprosy are infrequent in medieval *miracula*, perhaps a consequence of the segregation of lepers from the rest of society.) The basic terminology most commonly used – *surdus, mutus, caecus, paralyticus* and so on – is essentially that of the Bible. What these stories do not amount to, then, is a comprehensive catalogue of the medical conditions that afflicted medieval men and women, nor even a list of most of the symptoms that ill people would have presented. Rather, *miracula* represent a particular discourse – a way of perceiving, ordering and describing experiences – that was not predicated on the need to address the full variety of human ailments. In addition this discourse was detached from – although not completely unaffected by – contemporary medical learning, diagnostics and practice.

The implications of this for our ability to use the stories in the context of medical history become clear when we consider analyses which attempt to apply modern diagnostic techniques to the conditions described in miracle stories. While very valuable in opening up insights into the sorts of medical problems that affected medieval men and women and into aspects of their material circumstances such as diet and living conditions, this approach runs up against the problem that the medieval authors' discourse is not easily

---

[28] *Liber Miraculorum Sancte Fidis*, I.7, ed. L. Robertini (Biblioteca di medioevo latino, 10; Spoleto, 1994), pp. 98–103; *Book of Sainte Foy*, pp. 63–8.

[29] See M. Rouche, 'Miracles, maladies et psychologie de la foi à l'époque carolingienne en Francie', in *Hagiographie, cultures et sociétés, IVe–XIIe siècles: Actes du Colloque organisé à Nanterre et à Paris (2–5 mai 1979)* (Paris, 1981), pp. 322–3.

translated into modern methods of explaining and categorizing physical and mental disorders.[30] Certainly some writers of *miracula* were more expansive than others in their efforts to describe the symptoms they observed or heard about, and this can ease diagnostic analysis. But overall they were little concerned with aetiology – what causes disease[31] – and concentrated much more on describing symptoms that, as we have seen, were governed by a fairly blunt and limited typological schema which privileged certain categories such as blindness, lameness, paralysis and deafness.

Similarly, other types of miracle story present at best a partial picture of the anxieties and problems that medieval people would have faced. For example, accounts of members of the military aristocracy escaping captivity outnumber descriptions of miraculous protection from the more immediate dangers of armed conflict and other crises associated with knightly activities. But it would be hasty to conclude from this that fear of imprisonment was the main anxiety experienced by men of this class.[32] If we turn to people lower down the social scale we again find that miracle stories could not have addressed the full range of difficulties that they must have had to confront: there are, for instance, relatively few stories that deal with the problems faced by those working the land, even though this was the main occupation of the great majority of the population. By the time that the Rocamadour collection was being written, many models existed to circumscribe what was considered appropriate material for a miracle collection: in addition to biblical precedents, early writers such as St Augustine, Sulpicius Severus, Pope Gregory the Great, Gregory of Tours and Bede had cumulatively created a body of language and imagery that was highly influential.[33] In other words, a

---

[30] See T. d'Angomont, 'Sur les miracles de saint Privat véneré à Mende', *Revue du moyen âge latin*, 23 (1976), pp. 13–26. For a more cautious analysis see E. C. Gordon, 'Child Health in the Middle Ages as Seen in the Miracles of Five English Saints, A.D. 1150–1220', *Bulletin of the History of Medicine*, 60 (1986), pp. 502–22.

[31] Cf. Van Dam, *Saints and their Miracles*, pp. 86–7.

[32] See the statistical analysis in P.-A. Sigal, *L'homme et le miracle dans la France médiévale (XIe–XIIe siècle)* (Paris, 1985), pp. 288–310; cf. D. Gonthier and C. Le Bas, 'Analyse socio-économique de quelques recueils de miracles dans la Normandie du XIe au XIIIe siècle', *Annales de Normandie*, 24 (1974), pp. 3–36.

[33] See Ward, *Miracles and the Medieval Mind*, pp. 3–32. A number of the most influential works from the late antique and early medieval periods are available in good English translations: St Augustine, *The City of God against the Pagans*, trans. H. Bettenson, intro. J. O'Meara (Harmondsworth, 1984); Sulpicius Severus, 'The Life of Saint Martin of Tours', in *Soldiers of Christ: Saints and Saints' Lives from Antiquity and the Early Middle Ages*, ed. T. F. X. Noble and T. Head (London, 1995), pp. 1–29; Gregory the Great, 'Life of Benedict' [i.e. Book II of the *Dialogues*], trans. C. White, *Early Christian Lives* (Harmondsworth, 1998), pp. 161–204; Gregory of Tours, *Life of the Fathers*, trans. E. James (Translated Texts for Historians, Latin Series, 1; Liverpool, 1985); *idem*, *Glory of the Martyrs*, trans. R. Van Dam (Translated Texts for Historians, Latin Series, 3; Liverpool, 1988); *idem*, *Glory of the Confessors*, trans. R. Van Dam (Translated Texts for Historians, Latin Series, 4; Liverpool, 1988); Bede, *The Ecclesiastical History of the English People*, trans. B. Colgrave, ed. J. McClure and R. Collins (Oxford, 1994).

writer setting about recording miracle stories would be locating himself in that tradition at least as much as he would be engaged in contemporary 'reportage' of events known to him. That is not to say that the medium of *miracula* was inflexible and unable to respond to changing circumstances and needs. For one thing, competition from other shrines, and the wish to lend one's own saint a distinctive identity, could introduce a note of difference into a collection.[34] And the enthusiasm with which writers often greeted a miracle that they could present as *inauditum* – unheard of – reveals that there was a cachet to be enjoyed if a cult centre could be presented as departing from the norm. But on the other hand, the very value attached to 'unheard-of' miracles demonstrates that stories that were in fact *audita* – in the sense of resembling earlier instances of the same sort of thing happening – were the common currency. Moreover, the expectations of pilgrims as much as the learning of the monks or clerics who ran cult centres would have perpetuated this typological conservatism.

The second note of caution is that there are limits to how far the overtly miraculous elements of a given *miraculum* can be detached from the story as a coherent whole without unravelling the narrative so completely that its value as a source is undermined. Miracle stories were not conceived as, or written in the form of, neutral descriptions of unusual things happening to everyday folk upon which a particular miraculous 'spin' was then placed by way of authorial postscript.[35] The miraculous is embedded in the whole narrative, shaping the story's structure, plot development, description and characterization, language and imagery. The creation of this whole owed a good deal to those who experienced what they interpreted as a miraculous event and shaped the way in which they recounted what had happened, as well as to the authors who produced the written version. As we shall see when we consider the issue of the veracity of the Rocamadour stories, the people who brought news of miraculous episodes to the monks were responsible for much of the interpretative process that turned initial occurrence into 'official' miracle. And this responsibility would have influenced how they constructed, and reconstructed, their versions of events. To this extent, then, no detail, however trivial or superfluous it might seem, was completely incidental to the story. This consideration does not invalidate the potential of miracle stories as evidence for a wide range of social, political, cultural and

---

[34] For competition between shrines played out in miracle collections, see C. Hofmann-Rendtel, 'Wallfahrt und Konkurrenz im Spiegel hochmittelalterlicher Mirakelberichte', in *Wallfahrt und Alltag in Mittelalter und früher Neuzeit* (Veröffentlichungen des Instituts für Realienkunde des Mittelalters und der frühen Neuzeit, 14; Vienna, 1992), pp. 115–31.

[35] For a useful discussion which emphasizes the constructedness of miracle collections, see G. Signori, 'The Miracle Kitchen and its Ingredients: A Methodical [sic] and Critical Approach to Marian Shrine Wonders (10th to 13th Century)', *Hagiographica*, 3 (1996), pp. 277–303.

economic issues; as noted earlier, their authors were anchoring what they were constructing in a 'real' world of the routine and familiar. But this problem needs to be borne in mind whenever one uses the material to extract the sorts of information that it was not the authors' main concern to record for posterity.

These problems are to some extent addressed by another analytical strategy that has been adopted by scholars studying *miracula*, one that has the merit of working with the grain of the notions of the miraculous embedded in stories. In this case the stories are treated less as snippets of medieval life than as expressions of the social and cultural values and assumptions both of the people who believed that they had become involved in the operation of the miraculous and of the writers who recorded their experiences. For example, in the context of the most common type of miracle, the cure, historians have drawn on the language of anthropology to make a useful distinction between 'disease' – what is wrong with someone in an objectively observable way – and 'illness', a concept that takes in the broader cultural system governing how people think and behave when affected by a medical problem, how other people react towards them, and the symbols, rituals and language through which disease is expressed and, in the process, controlled.[36] A particular benefit of this sort of approach is that it takes us away from treating physiological and psychological disorders in terms of what was happening clinically to the sufferer – ultimately an irretrievable detail and almost always one which cannot be checked against another piece of corroborative evidence. Instead it focuses on the social experience of both those affected and others around them. In this way miracle stories become an important source for the self-perception and functioning of different types of community within medieval society.

To take an example of one such community – the family – from the Rocamadour miracles: Book I includes the story of a couple who had been on pilgrimage to pray for a child and had subsequently had a baby boy. He was, however, born blind.[37] Later the mother decided to return to Rocamadour, with the boy, in the hope that he would gain his sight. At a village close to their destination the woman dropped to her knees to pray by a roadside cross, whereupon the boy's eyes began to bleed. When the bleeding stopped he was able to see. Then some of the local villagers accompanied the mother and child on the remainder of their journey to Rocamadour, praising the Virgin Mary. This is a straightforward narrative, but it has a number of interesting features. As one would expect, the author does not dwell on medical detail: the boy is simply 'blind', and the description of the haemorrhaging that signals the moment of the miraculous cure is undeveloped relative to the mother's prayer that immediately precedes it in the

---

[36] Cf. Van Dam, *Saints and their Miracles*, pp. 84–5.
[37] I.23.

16

text. On the other hand, the story reveals a good deal about the boy's importance to his family: the couple's urgent wish to have a child is used to introduce the tale; and there is a stark juxtaposition of the mother's joy at giving birth and her desolation when the baby's blindness is discovered. In addition, the bond between parent and child is asserted in the author's statement that the mother clung to the hope that he would be cured all the time that she was bringing him up. Significantly this story, like many others involving the cures of children, departs from the standard narrative form whereby the beneficiary (or victim) of the miraculous is the one made to dominate and propel the action.[38] Here it is the parent who is constructed as the principal figure, and the miracle is as much about effecting a change in her morale as it is about the boy's eyesight. A family community has been repaired by the Virgin's actions as restorer (*reformatrix*). Moreover, it is noteworthy that other communities and relationships come into play in this story. The miracle cure results from a reassertion of the couple's earlier links to Rocamadour as a devotional centre and, by extension, to the community of its devotees. The mother's plea by the cross is prompted, we are told, by the sound of a church bell summoning the faithful to prayer. And mother and child find themselves absorbed into the community of the villagers, who identify with them to the extent that they participate in the communal acts of thanksgiving, in the process sharing in and reinforcing the attachment of particular meaning to what had happened to the boy.

The value of miracle stories as evidence for social behaviour and for ideas and aspirations played out in group contexts is not only apparent in accounts of cures. Other crises resolved by miraculous intervention throw light on similar issues. For example, a story from Conques relates how a local knight named Gerald borrowed a prize falcon from his lord on condition that he would forfeit his property if the bird were lost.[39] (We are informed that in fact the lord was avariciously scheming to find a pretext that would allow him to get control of Gerald's property.) Sure enough, the bird disappeared as soon as Gerald released it. Terrified at the prospect of having to tell his cruel lord, Gerald made his way home, bemoaning the imminent loss of his property, honour and social status. Members of his household could not console him until his wife suggested that he make a vow to go on barefoot pilgrimage to Conques. This fortified Gerald enough to allow him to join his companions at the meal table. As they all ate, the lost falcon flew in through the window in pursuit of a goose, whereupon there was an outpouring of thanks. The following day Gerald made the journey to Conques. As with the earlier example, the central figure's actions and reactions have a communal setting and impact. The bond between lord and knight, which should be one of mutual support, is threatened by the lord's attempts at manipulation, but

---

[38] See e.g. I.16; I.22; I.33; I.35; I.44; II.16; II.29; II.31; II.40; II.46.
[39] *Liber Miraculorum Sancte Fidis*, I.23, pp. 123–5; *Book of Sainte Foy*, pp. 88–90.

the calamitous repercussions for the knight, innocently exposed to danger by engaging in a social exchange typical of his class, are averted. Although it is Gerald's vow which triggers the miraculous return of the bird, it is presented as the consequence of his relationship with his wife and his acknowledgement of the moral authority she brings to their marriage. In addition, the chronological and spatial connection between the making of the vow and the miraculous effect – which in many other stories is very compressed – is here attenuated enough to draw attention to the fact that Gerald is not the sole beneficiary: his household stood to suffer as result of his impoverishment and social downgrading, and this is effectively asserted by the author in his inclusion of the detail that the falcon returned as all were gathered to eat, the occasion par excellence of aristocratic communal behaviour in its domestic setting. A community in peril is thus made good, and in the process joins the wider devotional community formed around St Faith and her cult at Conques.

The stories of the blind boy and the lost falcon are just two examples among many of culturally determined reactions to personal and collective crisis, and of the assumptions and expectations that people like the anxious mother and Gerald brought to their relationship with institutional religion in the form of the cult of the saints. Their significance lies in the fact that they are part of larger patterns of ideas and behaviours which emerge from a reading of substantial numbers of miracle stories. The search for these patterns has been a central objective of many scholars working on *miracula* in recent decades, and has done much to shape our understanding of the material.[40] In this, the recurrence of language, motifs and topoi across a range of stories written at different times in a variety of locations becomes the main analytical resource. Lost birds, for example, are not a major subject of miracle stories, but they crop up in a number of collections, and their interest increases if they are seen as part of a broader category of stories that deal with the fracturing and reintegration of aristocratic communities: for example, those that describe prisoners restored to their families, or mother and child surviving a difficult labour. Stories of children being cured are more numerous; indeed they are one of the most common types of miracle recorded and are consequently rich in potential for comparative analysis. A recent study by Ronald Finucane has drawn attention to how miracles can aid our understanding of children's illnesses and other dangers that they

---

[40] Two studies stand out: Finucane, *Miracles and Pilgrims*; Sigal, *L'homme et le miracle*. See also the excellent study by C. Rendtel, *Hochmittelalterliche Mirakelberichte als Quelle zur Sozial- und Mentalitätsgeschichte und zur Geschichte der Heiligenverehrung untersucht aus Texten insbesondere aus Frankreich*, 1 vol. in 2 (Düsseldorf, 1985). There is much of interest in P. Morison, 'The Miraculous and French Society, circa 950–1150', unpublished D. Phil. thesis (Oxford, 1984). For the later Middle Ages see C. Krötzl, *Pilger, Mirakel und Alltag: Formen des Verhaltens im skandinavischen Mittelalter (12.–15. Jahrhundert)* (Studia Historica, 46; Helsinki, 1994).

faced.[41] By extension they throw valuable light on family relationships and the attitudes of parents towards their offspring. Finucane's data is taken from 600 stories drawn from eight substantial miracle collections written between the twelfth and fifteenth centuries in various parts of Europe.[42] Although rightly cautious about generalizing on the basis of a sample that is chronologically and geographically dispersed, Finucane has identified an important corpus of material which opens a window on themes such as parental emotionalism and the social restraints acting on it, the differences between the attitudes of mothers and fathers towards their children, and the different social values attached to boys and girls. In opening up these insights, it is the volume of the source material which is the key to its value. Similarly, the abundance of miracle stories has made possible research into a number of different aspects of medieval life. In particular, because the *miracula* are centred on the idea of the intercession of saints associated with specific cult centres, scholars have been able to examine the dynamics of the relationships between the faithful and those whom Peter Brown has memorably termed the 'impresarios' of cults,[43] the monks and clerics who ran shrines, staged their rituals, directed the participation of outsiders in devotional acts, and propagated the power of the saints with whom they identified.

There are drawbacks, however, to a methodology that relies on collating information from a wide range of texts. Attention tends to be drawn more to issues and questions where various miracle collections converge and reinforce one another rather than to where they differ. And it can become difficult not to lose sight of the particular historical circumstances and experiences that informed each individual text.[44] There is consequently a danger of subordinating what happened at cult centres to a constructed model, based on the most recurrent patterns, to which specific examples only more or less approximate (for reasons which might not be readily apparent). Yet however much those who produced miracle collections were consciously

---

[41] R. C. Finucane, *The Rescue of the Innocents: Endangered Children in Medieval Miracles* (London, 1997).

[42] See *ibid.*, pp. 3–6.

[43] P. R. L. Brown, *The Cult of the Saints: Its Rise and Function in Latin Christianity* (Chicago, 1981).

[44] For useful studies of individual shrines and cults drawing on *miracula* see P.-A. Sigal, 'Maladie, pèlerinage et guérison au XIIe siècle: Les miracles de saint Gibrien à Reims', *Annales: Économies, Sociétés, Civilisations*, 24 (1969), pp. 1522–39; R. Foreville, 'Les "Miracula S. Thomae Cantuariensis"', in *Actes du 97e Congrès National des Sociétés Savantes, 1972: Section de philologie et d'histoire jusqu'à 1610* (Paris, 1979), pp. 444–68; R. C. Finucane, 'Pilgrimage in Daily Life: Aspects of Medieval Communication Reflected in the Newly-Established Cult of Thomas Cantilupe (d.1282), its Dissemination and Effects upon Outlying Herefordshire Villages', in *Wallfahrt und Alltag in Mittelalter und frühen Neuzeit* (Veröffentlichungen des Instituts für Realienkunde des Mittelalters und der frühen Neuzeit, 14; Vienna, 1992), pp. 165–217.

conforming to the forms and methods of a widespread and well-practised genre, drawing inspiration from shared exemplars and from each other, each text was necessarily shaped by the particular circumstances of where, when and why it was brought into being. This is so even if – as is the case with many miracle collections – the author did not expressly address these issues himself. It follows, therefore, that comparative analyses based on a wide range of different collections need to be supplemented by close attention to the individual features of each example approached as a discrete entity, for this can help to refine the questions that can be asked of the material when treated en masse. With this in mind, part of the remainder of this Introduction will explore how we can ask questions of the Rocamadour miracles in order to build up a picture of their value as a source. As we shall see, part of the challenge posed by this text is the fact that it is not at all forthcoming about important issues such as what prompted the decision to write it and how its creators regarded it in the context of the development of the cult it celebrated. This reticence about purpose and timing is a common feature among *miracula* collections. The intention is, therefore, that the Rocamadour material should form the basis of a case study that can help to suggest questions that others can adapt and improve upon when investigating other examples of the genre.

The paucity of chronicle sources for southern France in the twelfth century

The value of looking at some of the specific features of the Rocamadour miracles also emerges in relation to the third of the issues mentioned at the beginning: the extent to which miracle collections can be used by historians in identifying the sorts of problems and framing the questions that are normally associated with the analysis of 'traditional' narrative sources such as chronicles. The Rocamadour collection commends itself in this context because there is a dearth of historiographical output from southern France in the central medieval period. In a very important and stimulating study of this problem, Thomas Bisson has observed that Mediterranean France was not noted for the writing of history between the Carolingian era and the time of the Albigensian Crusade.[45] One reason suggested by Bisson is that this relative lack of interest in history was not a sign of cultural impoverishment but an indication of the social and professional priorities felt by the literate elites and those to whom their writings were directed: the sophisticated legal culture of the Midi encouraged functionalist rather than more imaginative and self-consciously creative literary approaches when writers made decisions about what in the past needed to be recorded and the form that the

---

[45] T. N. Bisson, 'Unheroed Pasts: History and Commemoration in South Frankland before the Albigensian Crusades', *Speculum*, 65 (1990), pp. 281–308.

record should take. This argument is not altogether convincing, because it was not uncommon for a developed legal culture and interest in the writing of history to work in tandem: twelfth-century England is an obvious example, the Latin East another. But another of Bisson's observations carries greater weight: that the fragmented political scene in southern France militated against the presence of dominant leaders around whose dynastic identities and accomplishments historiographical writings could be constructed. Significantly, much of the interest in texts such as annals and ruler-lists that is detectable is found in Catalonia, where the eleventh- and twelfth-century counts were able to entrench themselves at the centre of military and political affairs more successfully than their counterparts to the north of the Pyrenees.

While not a historiographical desert, the Midi offers little compared to the abundance of material which survives from the linked political and cultural zones of England, northern France and the western regions of the Empire. In a sense the comparison is unfair, especially with respect to England; the 150 or so years after the Norman Conquest saw a remarkable growth of historiographical output which was unmatched in western Europe for its volume and range. It has been well observed that historical writing was one of the country's foremost contributions to the so-called 'Twelfth-Century Renaissance'.[46] Areas of northern France linked to England after 1066, in particular Normandy, shared to some extent in this heightened activity. And from around the middle decades of the twelfth century the areas directly controlled by the Capetian kings had in the abbey of Saint-Denis near Paris an important centre of historiographical effort, encouraged by the ruling dynasty's close ties to the monastery and its sensitivity to the creation and propagation of its prestige.[47] It is therefore unrealistic to set up north-western Europe as the norm against which other parts of western Christendom will inevitably appear to fall short. Southern French society was not dysfunctional in failing to produce its own versions of writers such as William of Malmesbury, Galbert of Bruges, Orderic Vitalis, Suger of Saint-Denis, Otto of Freising, Henry of Huntingdon, Gervase of Canterbury or Ralph Diceto.

Nonetheless, the paucity of historiographical evidence from the Midi does matter in the practical sense that it influences the sorts of historical reconstructions that can be attempted. In addition, it helps to explain the relative lack of interest in the history of the South – at least before the Albigensian Crusade – that has been shown by scholars, compared to the amount of work being done on the North. Of course, a very legitimate objection can be raised that modern historical method has long since outgrown the sort of excessive reliance on narrative sources that

---

[46] R. W. Southern, 'The Place of England in the Twelfth Century Renaissance', in his *Medieval Humanism and Other Studies* (Oxford, 1970), pp. 160–2.

[47] See G. M. Spiegel, *The Chronicle Tradition of Saint-Denis: A Survey* (Medieval Classics: Texts and Studies, 10; Brookline, Mass., 1978).

characterized the ways in which nineteenth- and early twentieth-century historians decided what was important about the Middle Ages and how what happened could be reconstructed. Much research into medieval society today does not need chronicle evidence: as we have seen, historians base much of their work on records such as charters, of which a large number survive from southern France, for example. Nevertheless the value of having access to detailed frameworks constructed in whole or large part from the sort of information provided by chroniclers extends beyond research into those particular fields that deal most directly with the sorts of issues that routinely engaged medieval historians – for example, the careers of secular and ecclesiastical leaders, the development of religious houses or orders, or political and military affairs. The types of history that are less event-centred, such as the study of social change, thought, and cultural patterns, can profitably draw on the precise framework. A recent study of the impact of chivalric values on the behaviour of lords and knights in England and northern France, for example, demonstrates the value of studying attitudes towards warfare as an abstraction through an analysis of specific instances of war which can be situated in their particular chronological and political contexts thanks to the rich historiographical record.[48]

The picture for southern France is not entirely bleak, for the area did produce some historical writers of importance. In the context of the present study, particular mention must be made of Geoffrey of Vigeois (d.1184), a chronicler close in space and time to the Rocamadour miracle collection. A monk of Saint-Martial, Limoges, and the prior of the small abbey of Vigeois in the southern Limousin, Geoffrey lived and worked in the region just to the north of Quercy.[49] He was a writer of wide interests who drew on a range of sources of information. His chronicle does not get the attention it deserves; despite the fact that a modern edition has been proposed by a number of scholars in recent decades, it is still only available in a seventeenth-century version.[50] Although concerned principally with events in the Limousin, Geoffrey's work is a capital source for political, ecclesiastical, military and dynastic affairs in southern France more generally. It is used to excellent effect, for example, by John Gillingham in his study of the efforts of the future King Richard I of England to consolidate his authority as duke of Aquitaine in the 1170s and 1180s; as Gillingham observes, once the information supplied by Geoffrey dries up, our ability to chart Richard's activities in an important part of the Angevin political world is substantially

[48] M. Strickland, *War and Chivalry: The Conduct and Perception of War in England and Normandy, 1066–1217* (Cambridge, 1996).

[49] See M. Aubrun, 'Le prieur Geoffroy de Vigeois et sa chronique', *Revue Mabillon*, 58 (1974), pp. 313–26.

[50] Geoffrey of Vigeois, 'Chronica', ed. P. Labbe, *Novae Bibliothecae Manuscriptorum Librorum*, 2 vols. (Paris, 1657), ii.279–329.

diminished.[51] Geoffrey was part of a distinct Limousin historiographical tradition which links him to the eleventh-century writer Adhemar of Chabannes and to the later chronicler Bernard Itier, and which Bisson differentiates from the output of what he terms the 'deep South'.[52] As we shall see, Rocamadour was closely linked to the ecclesiastical world of the Limousin. There is, therefore, a case for seeing it as an outlier of a monastic cultural zone which to some extent bucked the trend of southern French indifference to historiographical endeavour. On the other hand, Quercy itself did not produce its own Geoffrey of Vigeois. This means that the Rocamadour miracle collection is the most substantial twelfth-century narrative record of recent events that survives from that area. It dominates the Latin textual landscape much as, for example, the Conques miracles represent the principal narrative source for the eleventh-century Rouergue, the region to the east of Quercy. This fact alone makes the Rocamadour collection worthy of our attention.

The potential value of the Rocamadour miracles as a quasi-historiographical source further emerges from a consideration of various aspects of the literary culture of southern French Benedictine monasticism in the eleventh and twelfth centuries. A chronicler such as Geoffrey of Vigeois was in the nature of an exception to the general rule, but if we turn away from 'conventional' chronicle-writing to other ways in which the past was recorded by southern monks, we can detect broader trends which have interesting implications for how we might interpret the production of *miracula* and mobilize them as evidence. In an important study Amy Remensnyder has drawn attention to a vogue among southern monasteries for writing foundation legends that purported to describe how a monastic community first came into being and then established itself both as a holy place and as an institution.[53] The legends could take a number of literary forms: free-standing narratives, saints' Lives, *miracula* and charters were among the possibilities. And in non-textual terms the legends could also be expressed through architecture and art. In an application of what Remensnyder terms 'imaginative memory', many monasteries fashioned accounts of their origins which looked back to an authoritative founding figure such as a saint, Roman ruler or Frankish king. To take one example, in the twelfth century the monks of Mozac, in the Auvergne, produced a Life of one Calminius, a saintly aristocrat located in the distant Roman imperial past, as well as texts that emphasized the protective role later played by the first Carolingian king, Pippin the Short.[54] As accurate accounts of real people and events, of course, foundation

---

[51] J. Gillingham, *Richard the Lionheart*, 2nd edn (London, 1989), p. 104.
[52] Bisson, 'Unheroed Pasts', p. 281.
[53] A. G. Remensnyder, *Remembering Kings Past: Monastic Foundation Legends in Medieval Southern France* (Ithaca, 1995).
[54] *Ibid.*, pp. 60–1, 78, 90–1, 104–6, 137–41, 243–7, 306–8, 319–20.

stories such as these cannot stand up to close scrutiny, even though a number of them seem to contain traces of authentic historical memories. For example, the figure of Charlemagne that appears in a substantial number of legends owed more to how he was portrayed in *chansons de geste* from the late eleventh century onwards than to any attempt to retrieve his historical persona through texts written about him closer to his own time.[55] On the other hand, to regard the foundation stories as simply 'bad' history would be to miss the central point that they were creative exercises whose authors sought to project the ideals and concerns of the institutions in which they were writing back into an earlier age, in order to confer legitimacy and status on their present-day circumstances. In other words, the past was not a neutral quantity preserved for its own sake; it was, rather, a tool which could be used selectively and carefully in the fashioning of institutional identities, in much the same way that noble families might create genealogies for themselves in order to express their present-day feelings of prestige and status.[56]

This interest in recording versions of the past to address present needs is potentially relevant when we consider miracle collections written in the same southern French monastic milieu. It is worth noting that Rocamadour was itself one of the religious communities that participated in the process of legend-creation through its use of the figure of St Amator, who is considered more fully later in this Introduction.[57] Of course, there is an obvious and important distinction to be made: foundation legends were concerned with creating long-term connections between past and present. People and events set in distant eras were particularly potent sources of authority, and stories that had a long chronological reach were difficult to invalidate. Significantly, a strategy used by a number of monasteries, when faced with the foundation legend of a rival institution that threatened it in some way, was not to attempt to disprove the other monastery's story but to trump it by going back even further into the past with a story of their own.[58] On the other hand, most miracle collections dealt with events that were much closer in time to when they were written. Indeed, the authors of *miracula* often treated the topicality of their material as a strength; their wish was to validate stories by situating them within their own direct experience or that of witnesses in

---

[55] *Ibid.*, pp. 71–5, 146–9, 182–211.

[56] See L. Genicot, *Les généalogies* (Typologie des sources du moyen âge occidental, 15; Turnhout, 1975); G. Duby, 'French Genealogical Literature', in his *The Chivalrous Society*, trans. C. Postan (London, 1977), pp. 149–57; J. Dunbabin, 'Discovering a Past for the French Aristocracy', in *The Perception of the Past in Twelfth-Century Europe*, ed. P. Magdalino (London, 1992), pp. 1–14.

[57] See Remensnyder, *Remembering Kings Past*, pp. 97, 321.

[58] But for a celebrated instance of a monastery's hostile reaction to the challenging of its myths through an appeal to something more closely resembling our understanding of textual and historical criticism, see Peter Abelard, 'Historia Calamitatum', trans. B. Radice, *The Letters of Abelard and Heloise* (Harmondsworth, 1974), pp. 85–6.

whom they placed confidence.[59] As we shall see, topicality is a particularly pronounced feature of the Rocamadour miracles: most took place only a few months or years before the collection was written, and it is unlikely that any dated any further back than one generation. To this extent, then, foundation legends and miracle collections such as that from Rocamadour were rooted in very different understandings and applications of the past. But in broad terms there are interesting overlaps. The two approaches were not mutually exclusive: the experience of the monks at Rocamadour and other monasteries that created both types of material is proof of this. And both approaches were creative explorations of the ways in which the recording of past events could serve to communicate an institution's understanding of itself to a present-day audience and project an image of itself into the future. Just because recent happenings were in their nature more difficult to refashion and manipulate than stories of long ago, it should not be assumed that they had no potential in this respect. Part of this Introduction will therefore attempt to use the Rocamadour miracles to identify and explore questions that, it is hoped, can be applied to other examples of the genre. What do the Rocamadour stories tell us about the interests and priorities of the monastic community that produced them? Can the stories be linked to specific stages in the community's institutional development, or to a period of conflict, similar to some of the triggers which Remensnyder has identified behind the generation of monastic foundation myths? What do the miracles tell us about the identity of the monks, and about their understanding of their relationship with the outside world? Central to these questions is the issue of why the miracle collection was written. In order to address this fundamental problem, it is first necessary to examine the form and content of the text in order to establish what it is that we are dealing with.

---

[59] See P.-A. Sigal, 'Le travail des hagiographes aux XIe et XIIe siècles: Sources d'information et méthodes de redaction', *Francia*, 15 (1987), pp. 149–82.

2

The Miracles of Our Lady of Rocamadour:
Text and Content

Authorship, content and form

The miracles of Our Lady of Rocamadour, in Quercy, are associated with a place that is a well-known feature on today's tourist map. One of the most visited historical locations in France, the site is built onto and into the steep side of a gorge above the Alzou, a tributary of the Dordogne. The monastic compound and church of Our Lady occupied a ledge approximately halfway up the cliff face; substantially built up since the twelfth century, the place is a fascinating exercise in the ingenious use of very limited space to create a complex of ecclesiastical structures. Nowadays a thriving village lies further down the cliff near the valley floor, providing goods and services for the tourists; in a similar way, a settlement existed there by the time of the writing of the miracle stories, doubtless largely reliant on the economic benefits brought by pilgrims.

The miracle collection is much the most substantial textual survival from Rocamadour, whose archive was destroyed in a fire in the fifteenth century and suffered again in the Wars of Religion in the sixteenth.[1] The manuscripts that preserve the collection were made elsewhere, copies at least one remove from the original(s) written *in situ*.[2] The collection was created between 1172 and 1173 (we shall return to the question of dating in more detail later). We do not know the name of the author. On the basis of stylistic features, such as the recurrent (and sometimes very laboured) use of alliteration, it seems likely that there was a single author. On the other hand, a collaborative effort cannot be ruled out: Book III differs from the preceding parts in that it is characterized by a fuller, more sustained use of biblical quotation and in containing longer authorial insertions in the form of prayers, invocations and meditations embedded within the narratives. In addition, as we shall see later, Book III was most probably written in 1173 whereas the earlier parts date from 1172. There was probably a hiatus in the writing process in the interim; the number of pilgrims arriving at Rocamadour with miracle stories to relate would have fallen away during the winter months, and often the work of monastic scriptoria was suspended or wound down when changes in

---

[1] J. Rocacher, *Rocamadour et son pèlerinage: étude historique et archéologique*, 2 vols. (Toulouse, 1979), i.19.
[2] See Rocacher, pp. 24–6.

the temperature and length of daylight made writing more difficult. So it is possible that a second writer in 1173 picked up a text put down by a colleague the previous autumn. But whether one or many people were directly involved in the composition of the text, we can be certain that the author or authors belonged to the monastic community of the Benedictine priory on the site. Rocamadour was a dependency of the abbey of Tulle, which was situated 55 km to the north in the Bas Limousin. A number of indications attest to the monastic quality of the text. The work is that of an insider, and the number of prayers and invocations in the text, as well as scriptural quotations and allusions, suggests someone well versed in the sort of liturgical, devotional and classical learning to be expected of a twelfth-century Benedictine.

It is not a grave problem that we can only locate the author(s) of the text within a particular monastic community rather than as one or more identifiable individuals, for it is from the point of view of the collectivity of monks at Rocamadour that we should approach the miracles as a literary creation. It is extremely unlikely that the collection was in the nature of a private initiative sustained by an individual's particular interests and devotional enthusiasms. The monastic community at Rocamadour was not large – possibly no more than a dozen or so brethren. Clear evidence of this is provided by the restricted space within the twelfth-century church of Saint-Michel which was built above and to one side of the Marian church, and which would seem to have been reserved for the monks' own use.[3] A literary undertaking as substantial as the miracle collection must have been something that all the monks knew about, and it is likely that it represented a communal decision in which the mother house at Tulle was also involved. It is also worth noting that the writing of the miracles had implications beyond the use that the particular author could make of his time alongside his routine liturgical and administrative duties. The gathering of material for possible inclusion in the collection would have had an important impact on the manner in which the monks organized the movement of pilgrims within their site, observed their actions, interrogated those who were claiming to have experienced a miracle, and made preliminary records for later working up. The whole nature of their institutional interaction with the outside world stood be to be affected. And the organizational effort required to make the collection possible must have been substantial: we have one direct clue in the preface to Book II, in which the author observes that the record-taking system broke down when the notary (the word indicates that this was not one of the monks but a paid outsider) who used to take down the details of those reporting miracles was off sick.

The collection comprises 126 stories.[4] It is divided into three books, each

[3] See Rocacher, *Rocamadour*, i.131ff.
[4] For discussions of the collection see R. Pernoud, ' "Le livre des miracles de Notre-Dame de Rocamadour": étude des manuscrits de 1172', *Le livre des miracles de Notre-Dame*

of which is introduced by a prologue and a list of the rubrics, or chapter headings, attached to each entry. Books I and II, containing 53 and 49 stories respectively, are very similar in overall length, quite possibly a reflection of their originally being written on gatherings of parchment of the same size. Book III contains only 24 stories, but the average length of each episode is greater – in part because of the larger amount of authorial insertion as noted above. It is possible that the original intention was to create a third book to match the length of the others, but it was in due course felt that there was not enough available material. In any event the final story in Book III, a long and detailed narrative dealing with an unusual incident and interwoven with a good deal of authorial meditation, reads as though it was meant to bring the collection to a close – at least for the time being.[5] Whether or not the collection was continued thereafter (we know that news of later miracle stories from Rocamadour was reaching a chronicler in Normandy in about 1180),[6] the body of material from the period 1172–73 was what was subsequently communicated to others for copying, and as such we may regard the text as we now have it as a completed piece of writing. Certainly, while each of the three books stands to some extent as a discrete composition, it is clear that they were conceived as parts of a whole. It was unusual for a collection of this length to be produced within the space of only about a year: many other examples of the genre were built up piecemeal over decades or even centuries. And there are signs that the author(s) thought in terms of a single enterprise. An obvious link is made, for example, in the choice of opening story in each book: all three deal with the perils of drowning. Moreover, the preface to Book I, which is the longest and most elaborate of the three introductory sequences, functions as a prologue to the collection as a whole because it addresses the broad issues of how the material had been selected and the nature of the Virgin's role at Rocamadour. The two later prefaces speak in terms of a continuation of work in progress.

As we shall see in due course, the collection contains descriptions of a wide variety of human experiences. But the unifying theme that applies to every episode is the idea of God intervening in the normal workings of the world, thanks to the intercessions of the Virgin Mary. Mary is the text's ever-present central character. The events that are described flow from the operation of her manifold qualities, among which particular emphasis is placed on her

---

de Rocamadour, ed. M. François (2e Colloque de Rocamadour; Rocamadour, 1973), pp. 9–23; R. W. Frank Jr., 'Pilgrimage and Sacral Power', *Journeys Toward God: Pilgrimage and Crusade*, ed. B. N. Sargent-Baur (Studies in Medieval Culture, 30; Kalamazoo, 1992), pp. 31–43; Rocacher, pp. 26–43.

[5] For the potential open-endedness of collections, see Sigal, 'Le travail des hagiographes', p. 174.

[6] Robert of Torigny, *Chronica*, ed. R. Howlett (Rolls Series, 82:4; London, 1889), pp. 292–4.

compassion, mercy and solicitude towards those who enter into a relationship with her through going on a pilgrimage, the act of prayer or making a vow. A notable feature of the stories is the wide range of titles and invocations that are applied to Mary: she is the door to heaven, the mediator between God and humankind, the saviour of all through her Son, the ivory tower, the star of the sea, the fount of mercy and the medicine of mortal men, among many others.[7] The dominant attributes asserted through the stories are her authority as Lady and Queen, her relationship with Christ as Mother, and the uniqueness of her status as Virgin. These three aspects of Mary's saintly identity form the basis of her ability to intervene on behalf of her devotees. The miracle collection is, fundamentally, an extended eulogy celebrating and giving thanks for that ability.

In broad terms, therefore, the Rocamadour miracles are one expression of the heightened attention to the Blessed Virgin Mary that was a feature of twelfth-century religious thought and popular devotion. Not that Mary was little venerated before then: there was an active cult, for example, in pre-Conquest England.[8] But there is little doubt that the twelfth century witnessed a remarkable upsurge in interest in her. The reasons for this are complex, and it is impossible to pin them down to a single series of related causes.[9] To some extent increased attention to Mary both as 'historical' figure (there is, in fact, very little in the way of detail about her in the New Testament) and as saint exercising her patronage flowed from the growing sensitivity to the humanity of Christ, his suffering and mercy, which was an important strand of twelfth-century religiosity. In part also, the faithful were drawn to Mary as the representation of merciful compassion because changes in the Church's penitential disciplines were encouraging the view that penance in itself could not wash away the effects of one's sins: rather, it was necessary to throw oneself on the mercy of the Lord, and by extension it made sense to appeal to his Mother, who was believed to have a unique ability to encourage her Son to exercise forgiveness. A further stimulus to the cult of the Virgin was that it spread in tandem with the organizational centralization and the growth of new religious orders which were expressions of the ideals of eleventh- and twelfth-century reformers. For example, the Cistercians, an order that placed great emphasis on administrative system

---

[7] See Rocacher, *Rocamadour*, i.55, 69–70.

[8] See M. Clayton, *The Cult of the Virgin Mary in Anglo-Saxon England* (Cambridge Studies in Anglo-Saxon England, 2; Cambridge, 1990).

[9] The literature on the cult of the Virgin in the Middle Ages is vast. A useful starting point is H. Graef, *Mary: A History of Doctrine and Devotion*, rev. edn (London, 1985). A stimulating but controversial study is M. Warner, *Alone of All Her Sex: The Myth and Cult of the Virgin Mary* (London, 1976). See the useful remarks of R. W. Southern, *The Making of the Middle Ages* (London, 1953), pp. 227–9, 234–43. See also P. S. Gold, *The Lady and the Virgin: Image, Attitude, and Experience in Twelfth-Century France* (Chicago, 1985), esp. pp. 43–75, 148–9.

and consistency, were noted for their devotion to the cult of Mary. Universal saints fitted particularly well within a Church trying to establish and impose a more clearly unified identity.

On the other hand, it is important to note that the Virgin Mary who emerges through the Rocamadour miracle stories is not simply the property of the Church in its entirety. Although her universal appeal is made implicit throughout, both in terms of the social range of the devotees mentioned – men and women, rich and poor, young and old, townspeople and country dwellers – and in the geographical distribution of those who feature in the collection, this is not the whole story. There is also a very strong and immediate connection between the saint and one particular place: she is presented as 'Our Lady *of* Rocamadour' or given a similar title in virtually all of the stories. In this respect the collection differs from another type of text that was beginning to come into vogue in the twelfth century: collections of Marian miracles, known as *Mariales*, which were not linked to particular cult centres, and in which the incidents were described in ahistorical, decontextualized terms. (This is so even though some of the raw material for stories in *Mariales* was adapted from site-specific collections, the Rocamadour miracles included.)[10] In other words, the emphasis in our text on the connection between the Virgin and Rocamadour has important implications: it means that the author's material is meant to be located in real time and space, however hazy the precise details might actually be in many of the stories. This in turn has implications for the ways in which we are able to approach the collection as source material for ideas and events beyond the immediate context of what the particular author saw as his principal focus.

If Mary is the animating force behind the collection of stories as a whole, and if her special connection to Rocamadour supplies the constant point of reference that unites all the disparate material in the text, how does this affect the structure and content of the work? A first reading of the collection can give the impression of a loosely arranged anthology of discrete entries. There seems to be little of the sense of system brought, for example, to the closely contemporary miracle collection of St Thomas Becket at Canterbury, the authors of which used chronological sequence or grouping of stories by type of miracle as the organizational principles for much of their material.[11] It seems likely that the relative lack of organization in the Rocamadour text was the result of the speed with which a large amount of material was collated. The miracle collection as we now have it is sometimes described as the culmination of a long-term effort involving the gathering of stories over a number of decades – from the 1140s if not earlier.[12] But this view is misleading. While there is indeed evidence to suggest that some of the

[10] Ward, *Miracles and the Medieval Mind*, pp. 149–50, 155–65.
[11] For the organizational schemes deployed by authors of *miracula*, see Sigal, 'Le travail des hagiographes', pp. 177–82.
[12] Albe, pp. 63–9; Sigal, *L'homme et le miracle*, p. 205.

material did go back several decades, it would appear that the majority of stories were reported to the monks only a short time before the writing of the collection was begun or even while it was in progress. In other words, the monks had not been sitting on most of the material for long, and the collection's reliance on very recent events would have made it difficult to impose a single, rigid system of organization on the entire work.

It is therefore unsurprising that when one does detect authorial devices used to break down the random sequencing of the stories, these devices are miscellaneous, and each governs no more than a small portion of the whole text. One technique used by the writer(s) was to arrange, in small groups of two or three, stories that had an obvious connection in terms of subject matter. For example, pairs of consecutive stories deal with mothers and children in peril,[13] injuries to knights' faces[14] and cures of blindness.[15] Another organizational strategy was to group stories in which a thematic linkage could easily be inferred: thus three stories in Book II (cc. 25–7) deal with different ways in which Rocamadour's status as a sacred space was violated and ultimately protected. Two back-to-back miracles, also in Book II, have in common references to *confratres* of Rocamadour.[16] And a run of three stories in Book I share an emphasis upon the importance of vows.[17] The linkages can also flow from the literary self-awareness of the author: two stories are brought together by his wish to apply rather recherché classical terms (*Gallia comata, Gallia braccata*) when differentiating between parts of France. At other points the hook on which to hang a sequence of different episodes is provided by the reminiscences of the writer's informant.[18]

The most complex technique – or at least the one that permitted the author to sustain a connecting thread through more than two or three stories – involved a form of serial association, in which a feature of one story is picked up in the next, which in turn provides a possibly very different link to what follows it. The most intricate example of this stringing together of stories occurs, significantly, early in the text. The fifth story in Book I describes how an excommunicate is first punished by an affliction for his presumption in entering the church at Rocamadour, and then cured. The following story is linked to this by a rare use of chronological bridging: 'not long afterwards' a pilgrim is punished for stealing money by losing the use of his tongue, but is then healed. A further connection between the two episodes is their shared emphasis upon the beneficial effect of confessing one's sins, which in both instances triggers the cure. Similarly the seventh story in Book I turns on the value of acknowledging one's faults, although

---

[13] I.7–8.
[14] I.29–30.
[15] II.18–19.
[16] II.28–9; cf. I.33–4 which share references to the church's *custos*.
[17] I.14–16.
[18] II.22–3; II.31–2 (and see also II.33).

here the slant is different: a knight whose wife is driven by his teasing to attempt suicide throws himself on Our Lady's mercy while asserting that he is not in fact guilty of the adultery that his wife suspected. The story after this is linked because it describes how another knight's wife escaped from mortal peril – this time in the very different circumstance of being trapped under a fallen building. The ninth story in turn picks up the thread by returning to the theme of danger involving buildings, describing how a house was saved from a conflagration. Fire then becomes the link to the tenth story, in which a man unjustly condemned to death by burning is miraculously protected from the flames. He later escapes from imprisonment, which provides the theme carried over into the next story, in which someone escapes from a cruel form of confinement. The two stories after this then deal with escapes from other dangerous situations – falling down a cliff, drowning and hanging.[19] This is the most complex of the chains created by the author. It suggests that some care was taken over the selection and ordering of the material, especially early on in the composition, but also that as a methodology it was not enough to shape the collection as a whole and could not do the work of the sort of *a priori* organizational schema that is absent from the text.

Historical veracity

One obvious question that presents itself on a reading of the Rocamadour miracles amd similar texts is the extent to which the episodes that they describe actually happened in any meaningful sense. And if there is some basis in fact, is it possible to retrieve this, given the way in which the information is preserved and presented? The problem is, of course, that once one eliminates the miraculous as a causal principle – and even if as a matter of personal belief one considers that miracles can indeed happen, that is quite a different proposition from accepting the author's say-so in the particular instances in the collection – then one is left with a very uneven body of raw material. Clearly some of the incidents can be put down to the operation of chance: for instance, one building can be left undamaged in a fire that destroys many others; if a pet bird flies off, it might happen to find its owner later; some knights would indeed have recovered from the wounds they received. Clearly, too, there is a pronounced element of self-selection at work in terms of who reported their experiences to the monks: for every person who survived a storm at sea or a fall from a tree there would have been many others who perished. With regard to the most common type of miracle in the collection (as in most other examples of the genre) – the cure of illness or injury – there are various explanatory possibilities. In the first place, the terminology that *miracula* applied to illness, such as 'blind', 'possessed',

---

[19] For shorter sequences built on similar principles, see I.48–53; II.8–11; II.31–3; II.39–42.

'deaf' or 'crippled', amounts to a collection of open-ended and vague categories which could subsume a very wide range of the sorts of conditions that would be identifiable to modern medical science. The result of this is that what in fact constituted a 'cure' must have varied considerably from case to case. Moreover, cures need not have amounted to a complete and permanent reversal of a given condition: some must have been partial improvements, the relief of just some of the symptoms of a disease, or temporary remissions of the effects of chronic illness. The authors of miracle stories seldom had a 'follow-up' mechanism to check the long-term health of someone believed to have been cured by a saint's intercession. In the case of those who believed they had been cured *en route* to or from a shrine, changes of routine and diet while on pilgrimage, and the psychological reinforcement of the formal, public act of making a vow before departure, would have encouraged in many desperate and sick people a predisposition to read any change in their condition as tantamount to a cure.[20]

Yet the more one pursues these sorts of explanatory approaches – valid as they are – the more one appreciates that there is a very fine line between explaining a given miracle and simply explaining it away. In addition, an unavoidable side-effect of this technique is to 'score' individual episodes on a scale of how explicable or far-fetched their particular details appear: a potentially straightforward case that can be rationalized as, say, misdiagnosis or the operation of chance will score high on the credibility scale, the case of someone immersed in water for several hours or hanging from a gibbet for days necessarily very low. The temptation then is to introduce the variable of exaggeration to compensate: the more bizarre and inexplicable an episode, the greater must be the distortion of what really happened that has been inserted by the informant, the writer or both. But the problem here is that this introduces a complicating and subjective element that cannot be checked against any independent evidence. Just because a story seems to be readily explicable in terms of modern ways of solving problems, does it necessarily follow that it is any less a distortion of what happened than a patently exaggerated and unrealistic episode? To compound the problem, it is clear that the plausibility scale that one can end up constructing does not readily match the criteria that the authors of *miracula* themselves applied when judging their material: what to them could appear particularly unusual and worthy of comment might be quite easy to explain in our modern terms, whereas some of their commonplaces defy easy explanation. In short, then, any attempt to rationalize the episodes found in miracle collections soon runs up against insurmountable problems, and the results are at best patchy.

A way round this problem is to remember that miracles, as presented to us by their authors, do not represent random instances of rare or odd

[20] For a useful discussion of what could constitute 'cures' in these circumstances see Finucane, *Miracles and Pilgrims*, pp. 69–82, 103–9.

happenings, but attempts on the part of medieval men and women to create ordered and comprehensible explanations of various of their experiences.[21] The point to stress here is that the act of placing a miraculous interpretation on an event did not have to preclude other ways of explaining what had happened. Resorting to the idea of the miraculous was not some knee-jerk reaction but a considered choice. For example, Book III includes the story of a city wall, that around Mende in southern France, which fell on some attacking mercenaries, driving the survivors back and delivering the inhabitants from a dreadful fate.[22] Part of the interest of this story is that we have independent evidence, very close in time to the miracle story, that the bishop of Mende ordered the building of city walls precisely because of the threat of attack from mercenary bands. A rationalist explanation of what happened might therefore lead to the speculation that the walls fell down because they had been built hastily. Alternatively, perhaps the mercenaries were attempting to mine the wall and just got their calculations wrong. We cannot tell. But those in Mende who lived through the crisis were perfectly capable of understanding the collapse of the wall in these sorts of practical terms – and perhaps they did. Not every falling wall, after all, was *ipso facto* a clear sign of miraculous intervention in the workings of the world. Yet the people of Mende chose to apply a miraculous explanation to their experience because this spoke to the longer-term background of their anxiety about mercenary bands, and it vindicated their sense of liberation and asserted the communal identity that had been heightened by the siege. This was neatly symbolized by their offering of a model of the whole city as an *ex voto*.

It follows from an example such as this that we should treat the majority of miracle stories as the end-product of genuine attempts to formulate explanations of real experiences. This is not to say that all stories would have been informed by the same degree of honest reporting. Cult centres were alive to the possibility of being deceived by fraudulent claims by people who intended to exploit the celebrity achieved by involvement in a miracle for monetary gain. It is also fair to suppose that claiming to have experienced a miracle was a route open to people seeking attention for various psychological reasons. On the other hand, the possibility of fraud and deceit existed precisely because there was an environment in which real, or at least uncontested, episodes were experienced, communicated, recorded and propagated as instances of the operation of saintly power. The possible presence of the miraculous in everyday life – however rare in practice – was a shared cultural reference point accessible to people from different backgrounds operating in a variety of circumstances.

This means that the Rocamadour miracles can be seen to some extent as evidence for the ideas and perceptions of both the faithful and the monks,

---

[21] For a different view see Signori, 'Miracle Kitchen', esp. p. 302.
[22] III.4; 'Chronicon breve de gestis Aldeberti', c. 2, p. 126.

who ultimately controlled what was included in the collection and how it was expressed. It is significant that many of the episodes mentioned in the collection took place well away from Rocamadour – sometimes many hundreds of miles.[23] In other words, the stories as we now have them were not created out of a mass of unformed factual data that was presented to the monks in a neutral way and only then given its miraculous loading when the writing up took place. Apart from the minority of cases in which the author directly observed what happened and was thus able to impose his own interpretation at source, each story originated in a decision on the part of the person or persons affected by the key events to introduce the element of the miraculous soon after the experience. Some stories suggest that this could in fact be virtually simultaneous.[24] This interpretative potential was not limited to people with a particular reason to be familiar with *miracula* as a literary form. Most of the people who feature in the collection would have been illiterates, after all. But an awareness of comparable paradigms – perhaps based on hearing about the miracles of a saint or reinforced by the experience of pilgrimage – would no doubt have aided this process. The references in the Rocamadour stories to people having heard of the celebrity of the cult centre suggest that underlying the spread of information about which pilgrimage sites were 'in' was a more fundamental flow of ideas about what could be hoped for from invocation of saintly patronage – in crude terms, what saints might actually be expected to do. Present experiences would then be slotted into explanatory frameworks constructed from the lessons of past stories, and the miraculous as an interpretative mode would thus reproduce itself, in the process generating new material for future generations in turn to recall.

In this context, it is significant that the act of recounting the miracle – usually by the beneficiary, more rarely by a third party – is routinely part of the concluding sequence in the stories. It forms part of a common pattern that also includes arrival at Rocamadour, the giving of thanks, the showing of physical evidence such as scars where appropriate, and in many cases the making of an offering. These were the actions that cumulatively turned one pilgrim among possibly many into something qualitatively distinct – a source for a miracle story. The Rocamadour stories do not go into detail about what the act of recounting a miracle actually involved; the terse construction *miraculum retulit* ('he/she told the miracle') or a similar phrase is the norm.[25] But the interesting point is that the act of recounting events should be included at all, and in the process made part of the wider experience itself. After all, the detail is in most cases redundant. How else would the monks

---

[23] See J. Juillet, 'Lieux et chemins', *Le livre des miracles de Notre-Dame de Rocamadour*, ed. M. François (2e Colloque de Rocamadour; Rocamadour, 1973), pp. 25–43. For a distribution map see Sigal, *L'homme et le miracle*, p. 204.

[24] See e.g. I.4; I.13; I.20; II.20; II.43.

[25] E.g. I.2; I.4; I.12; I.18; I.27; I.42; I.43; I.47; II.2; II.6; II.14; II.28; II.38; II.45; III.2; III.4; III.13.

have known what had happened? In addition, there are clues – reinforced by information in other collections – that something substantially more than a single, possibly one-to-one and private, recitation of events was expected.[26] At some stage the pilgrim might be expected to recount his or her experiences in front of a group of other pilgrims and, probably, monks.[27] In addition, the presence of a notary whose role was to record the pilgrim's details[28] suggests that the pilgrim was expected to discuss his story with one or more monks beforehand in order to fashion his narrative into the 'official' version which could be noted for later writing up. The notary, as an outsider, would not have been allowed ultimate editorial control. The significance of all this is that it would not only have had a bearing on the ways in which the monks, as recipients of information, went about gathering, sifting, restructuring and recording what they heard; the pilgrim with a story to tell would also have been aware that this was no casual procedure. He or she would be drawn into the giving of a performance – sometimes literally, as is revealed by references to the showing of scars or use of visual aids – that would change his or her status and self-perception.

The bringing of *ex voto* offerings and objects which served to reinforce stories reveals that incoming pilgrims often anticipated participating in this process; in other words, the expectation of assuming the role of narrator was an integral part of the whole devotional impulse that drew them to Rocamadour.[29] It follows that there would have been plenty of opportunity to reflect on, tell and retell the miraculous episode – and in the process to refashion it in ways which reinforced their personal investment in what they believed had happened – well before it reached the ears of the monks at their journey's end. The importance attached to physical objects that 'contained' the events is significant in this context. The offering of chains by escaped prisoners, for instance, was not simply in the nature of providing physical evidence – after all, what might have happened in the dark and isolation of a dungeon could not be corroborated – but also a symbol of the pilgrim's investment in the interpretation of events that he intended to publicize. *Ex votos* and offerings can be seen as the concretizations of *a priori* choices about how to explain and structure experiences that could then be presented at Rocamadour as givens. It is significant that the objects given served to communicate the notion of active interpretation. At the most straightforward level, this was achieved iconographically: a model of a

---

[26] See Sigal, 'Le travail des hagiographes', p. 169.

[27] See esp. the performative aspect in I.38.

[28] See II., prologue.

[29] For *ex votos* see A.-M. Bautier, 'Typologie des ex-voto mentionnés dans des textes antérieures à 1200', in *La piété populaire au moyen âge* (Actes du 99e Congrès Nationale des Sociétés Savantes, Besançon, 1974; Paris, 1977), pp. 237–82; P.-A. Sigal, 'L'ex-voto au Moyen-Age dans les régions du Nord-Ouest de la Méditerranée (XIIe–XVe siècles)', *Provence historique*, 33 (1983), pp. 13–31; idem, *L'homme et le miracle*, pp. 86–101.

city or of a body part transfixed by an arrow drew attention to the crux of the narrative that explained it. But this could also emerge less directly in terms of the material used. Silver models, for example, reinforced the truth of the associated story because of their cost. And in the case of the most usual material, wax, its attraction did not simply lie in the fact that it was a relatively affordable and durable substance that was a familiar presence in churches, which got through very large numbers of candles. It was also a material that had associations as a means of validation through its use in the seals of documents. In a sense, therefore, a wax offering 'sealed' the authenticity of the narrative to which it was attached. Overall, then, it may be concluded that the 'realness' of the events contained in a story resided in the minds of those who reported them; this is a historical factor more important than the ultimately unanswerable question of how much a given story actually reflected an objectively observable reality.

The importance attached to the act of recounting the miracle and the offering of symbolic representations which served to validate the version of events being provided is reflected in the nature of the stories. For the most part they involve a single miraculous episode in which the experiences of a central individual, recounted in chronological order with little retrospection or anticipation, form the basis of the narrative structure. But there are several ways in which the author was able to depart from this straightforward model, with the result that the figure of 126 stories does not translate into the same number of beneficiaries/victims, nor into the same number of events that were interpreted in miraculous terms. For example, more than one person could be directly involved in the miraculous process: a number of stories involve Our Lady aiding groups, from as small as a handful of pilgrims to the inhabitants of an entire city. In addition, a significant number of stories are focused on one person's problems but also have a collective dimension; this is the case, for example, in those stories that deal with the illnesses of children and young people, in which family and friends share in the benefits of the miraculous resolution of the individual's crisis. Interestingly, in the case of children, it is sometimes the parents who function as the principal actors in the narrative once the child's condition has been introduced at the start. They would have had the main role as narrators of what happened, and that status translates into the manner in which their story unfolds. There are also examples in the collection of narratives in which more than one miraculous intervention is evident, and instances of a miraculous episode having different consequences for different parties, as when a would-be thief is punished and the intended victim saved. Overall, then, the miraculous is presented as something more than a change effected in discrete individuals in ways that affect only their immediate circumstances. It has the potential to have social consequences and to shape exchanges between different people and groups. Much of the value of the material as a source for contemporary ideas and behaviour flows from this.

The subject matter of the collection is broadly similar to many other examples of the genre from the period. About 70% of the stories deal with the cure or relief of illness, injury or mental disorder. Other types of story include: protection from dangers, both natural and man-made; divine vengeance visited on those threatening pilgrims or failing to show due respect to the cult of Our Lady and Rocamadour's status; and the freeing of captives, the incidence of which suggests that this aspect was understood to be one of the distinctive features of the cult, but without it dominating the site's reputation as was the case at, for example, the shrine at Saint-Léonard, Noblat, in the Limousin. It has been observed that the proportion of vengeance miracles is low compared to other collections from southern France;[30] Mary's exercise of mercy is the predominant motif. Nonetheless, a number of miracles reveal that the cult was engaged with issues of violence, a theme that is discussed below.

---

[30] See P.-A. Sigal, 'Un aspect du culte des saints: Le châtiment divin aux XIe et XIIe siècles d'après la littérature hagiographique du Midi de la France', in *La religion populaire en Languedoc du XIIIe à la moitie du XIVe siècle* (Cahiers de Fanjeaux, 11; Toulouse, 1976), pp. 39–59.

3

Dating and Purpose

Problems

One of the greatest challenges presented by the Rocamadour miracle collection lies in the fact that when the author addressed the issue of why it was being written, he did so in ways which avoided any sense of chronological specificity. Two elements of the preface to Book I, in which the most complete statement of authorial purpose was made, suggest that the absence of an overt link between when the collection was being made and why it was being written was the consequence of deliberate choices about what to emphasize. In the first place, the author presents the stories that he is recording as simply the latest instances in a long and continuous process; the only significant difference between what is finding its way into the collection and the 'infinity' of examples from before 'our times' is the practical point that he is limiting himself – so he says – to what he has seen himself or learned from reliable sources. To focus upon recent events is, then, an editorial strategy designed to cope with a potentially enormous amount of material; the author states that he is preparing a 'pick' (*flos*) of the Virgin's miracles. Of course, this idea of making a choice selection from a large body of material is a rhetorical device to be found in many miracle collections.[1] But the inference to be drawn from the Rocamadour author's use of this motif is that in his formulation the chronological setting of the text was simply an incidental consequence of his act of writing – his opening words are in fact 'Scripturus miracula', 'As I begin to write the miracles' – and not a reflection of any developments in the cult or the wider world that he wanted to stress.

Secondly, the author's emphasis in his justification of the writing of the text suggests that he was much more interested in issues of space than of time in relation to his church and its reputation as a site of the miraculous. Rocamadour, he argues, is the centre of a cult that is characterized by so many signs and miracles because it has been singled out by the Virgin Mary; it is this act of choice which has given the place its particular status among the churches of the world. Furthermore, Rocamadour's pre-eminence – and by extension the significance of the Virgin's special attachment to it – is all the more noteworthy in that the church itself is located in an awkward site surrounded by difficult terrain. From this it

[1] See Sigal, 'Le travail des hagiographes', pp. 151–7.

can be seen that the author construed his act of writing as a way of celebrating the importance of the relationship between place and holy power: the 'where' of the stories, in the sense of the seat of the saintly power that they describe, lends them a distinctive identity and importance to which the 'when' of their composition would seem to add little, and from which it might even detract.

It would be misleading to see the author of the miracles as being evasive or obtuse in his preference for the two emphases that we have identified. It is easy to imagine a monk in his position, someone who was not simply observing the cult of the Virgin being played out around him but also taking an active part in it himself, projecting his immediate experiences back into an indefinite past. There must have been plenty of clues in the church of Rocamadour to encourage such a view in the shape of ex votos and offerings commemorating past miracles, the details of which might no longer be easily retrieved. In addition, there were sound reasons for stressing the closeness of Rocamadour's claimed relationship with Mary. In the first place, Rocamadour was not a Marian shrine in the strict sense that it did not claim possession of relics linked to the Virgin.[2] In this it differed from a number of other Marian centres such as Chartres, Laon and Soissons, the twelfth-century miracle collections from which reveal that the objects they housed with claimed associations with the Virgin – for example, some of her hair, her slipper, a sponge and a shift – were far more than adornments of the cults.[3] On the contrary, these relics acted as important focal points of devotion and were used to help to legitimate and publicize the link between saint and place. They consequently had a substantial influence on how the relationships between the faithful and the cult 'impresarios' were formed and expressed. Secondly, while the monks of Rocamadour no doubt had a vested interest in emphasizing the wildness and remoteness of their surroundings in order to translate this into a sense of wonder at the Virgin's election of their church, this strategy would have served to draw repeated attention to the fact that Rocamadour was not a high-status church when viewed as part of the Church's institutional structures. It was a priory dependent on an abbey that was a substantial distance away. Many other Marian centres, in contrast, were cathedrals, major abbeys, or important establishments staffed

---

[2] An object that may have acted in lieu of a reliquary as a devotional focus was the celebrated wooden statue of Virgin and Child from Rocamadour, which still survives. It is unclear, however, whether this existed by the time of the writing of the miracle collection, and it probably dates from the final decades of the twelfth century: see I. H. Forsyth, *The Throne of Wisdom: Wood Sculptures of the Madonna in Romanesque France* (Princeton, 1972), pp. 144, 185, fig. 143; D. Freedberg, *The Power of Images: Studies in the History and Theory of Response* (Chicago, 1989), pp. 27–8; Rocacher, *Rocamadour et son pèlerinage*, i.93–7. In any event, if it did predate the miracles, the text makes no mention of it. Rocacher (*ibid.*, p. 95) is incorrect in his belief that the story in I.34 makes reference to the statue.

[3] Ward, *Miracles and the Medieval Mind*, pp. 134–45, 153–5.

by canons. Some were located in important population centres, and had long histories which entrenched them in durable networks of political power and social influence. Their economic, juridical and institutional status could both reflect and reinforce the prestige that they gained from association with the cult of the Virgin. This was not so obviously available to the monks of Rocamadour. A strategy of emphasizing the church's prominence and celebrity despite its being what and where it was thus made good sense.

It is also important to note that the terms of the preface to the Rocamadour miracles place the author firmly within a well-established hagiographical tradition. For many of those who composed and compiled *miracula*, it was not seen as necessary to expatiate on the particular set of circumstances that triggered their production. The fact that what were believed to be miracles were taking place could be presented as a self-evident justification for the commemorative act of creating a permanent written record. Nonetheless, it would be misleading to take the authors' perspectives at face value when analyzing what they say about their work. Otherwise we might be misled into expecting that miracle collections were a more commonplace feature of the written culture of pilgrimage churches than was in fact the case. It is useful to remember, firstly, that not all pilgrimage centres were known for miracle-working or drew on the miraculous in creating their appeal. To take an extreme but useful example, the status of Jerusalem as a goal for European pilgrims rested on its links to Christ – the Holy Sepulchre was the holiest site of all – and on the fact that pilgrimage there was widely regarded as a penitential exercise of particular merit.[4] But it was not noted principally as a place to which the faithful travelled in the hope of receiving cures or some other miraculous relief. Indeed many went in the hope of dying and being buried there. Of course, Jerusalem's unique status and the length of the journey to it make it untypical of medieval cult centres generally. But it serves as a useful reminder that pilgrimage was not always driven by the main needs and impulses that emerge from a reading of miracle stories.[5]

---

[4] See B. Hamilton, 'Rebuilding Zion: The Holy Places of Jerusalem in the Twelfth Century', *Renaissance and Renewal in Christian History*, ed. D. Baker (Studies in Church History, 14; Oxford, 1977), pp. 105–16; *idem*, 'The Impact of Crusader Jerusalem on Western Christendom', *Catholic Historical Review*, 80 (1994), pp. 695–713; A. Grabois, *Le pèlerin occidental en Terre Sainte au Moyen Âge* (Bibliothèque du Moyen Âge, 13; Brussels, 1998).

[5] For a useful survey of the different forms of pilgrimage, see. P.-A. Sigal, 'Les différents types de pèlerinage au Moyen Age', *Wallfahrt kennt keine Grenzen*, ed. L. Kriss-Rettenbeck and G. Möhler (Munich and Zurich, 1984), pp. 76–86. See also C. Vogel, 'Le pèlerinage pénitentiel', *Pellegrinaggi e culto dei Santi in Europa fino alla Ia Crociata* (Convegni del Centro di Studi sulla Spiritualità Medievale, 4; Todi, 1963), pp. 37–94, esp. pp. 39–40, 52–68, 90. For overviews of pilgrimage in the Middle Ages see E.-R. Labande, 'Recherches sur les pèlerins dans l'Europe des XIe et XIIe siècles', *Cahiers de civilisation médiévale*, 1 (1958), pp. 159–69, 339–47; *idem*, '"Ad limina": le pèlerin

Just as significantly, the miraculous was seldom a constant factor in the drawing power of even those pilgrimage centres which were noted for it at some stages in their history. Whether one locates the principal impulse for building up the reputation of a miracle-working saint and his or her cult in the interests of the clergy who controlled the cult sites, or in the enthusiasms and needs of outsiders drawn to them, both of these factors were necessarily subject to change over anything more than the short term. Many cult centres were, in miraculous terms, quiescent or even dormant for long periods. In some cases *miracula* throw a spotlight on a cult for just a few weeks or months.[6] And even in those instances where a longer chronological frame is present, miracle collections might represent nothing more than episodic slices in the life of the cult they celebrated and of the institutions that created them. A text such as the Miracles of St Benedict from Fleury, which covers the period between the later ninth century and the first decades of the twelfth, is unusual in its wide range, and even in this instance one is not presented with an even record of Benedict's miraculous works. It is a chronologically 'lumpy' text shaped by the distribution in time and the different interests of the various authors who contributed to it.[7]

A further point to note is that while miracle collections could serve many useful functions such as providing material for readings and preaching, they were not in themselves fundamental elements of the liturgical or para-liturgical celebration of a cult.[8] Saints' Lives, to which an account of post-mortem miracles might or might not be added, were of more immediate value than free-standing miracle collections.[9] Put another way, the absence of *miracula* was not a basic impediment to the workings of a religious community based around a cult centre, either in its internal operations or in its dealings with the pilgrims who visited it. It follows from this that there must be a geographical as well as a chronological dimension to the distribution

médiéval au terme de sa démarche', *Mélanges offerts à René Crozet*, ed. P. Gallais and Y.-J. Riou, 1 vol. in 2 (Poitiers, 1966), i.283–91; J. Sumption, *Pilgrimage: An Image of Mediaeval Religion* (London, 1975); R. A. Fletcher, *Saint James's Catapult: The Life and Times of Diego Gelmírez of Santiago de Compostela* (Oxford, 1984), pp. 78–101; D. Webb, *Pilgrims and Pilgrimage in the Medieval West* (London, 1999).

[6] For an informative mid-twelfth-century example see Sigal, 'Maladie, pèlerinage et guérison', pp. 1522–39.

[7] *Les Miracles de saint Benoît*, ed. E. de Certain (Paris, 1858). See A. Vidier, *L'historiographie à Saint-Benoît-sur-Loire et les Miracles de saint Benoît* (Paris, 1965); D. W. Rollason, 'The Miracles of Saint Benedict: A Window on Early Medieval France', *Studies in Medieval History Presented to R. H. C. Davis*, ed. H. Mayr-Harting and R. I. Moore (London, 1985), pp. 73–90; T. Head, *Hagiography and the Cult of the Saints: The Diocese of Orléans, 800–1200* (Cambridge, 1990).

[8] In the case of the Rocamadour miracles the clearest indication that at least some of them were intended for public reading is the presence of concluding doxologies in a minority of the stories: see I.31; I.35; I.41; I.50; I.53; II.15; II.20; II.34; II.43; II.49; III.10; III.24. Note the uneven distribution of this form of ending.

[9] See de Gaiffier, 'L'hagiographie et son public', pp. 136–48.

of miracle collections. Of course, many collections that once existed are now lost, with the result that we have what is at best a representative sample. And it is useful to remember that the rate of attrition with respect to this sort of material has been high: for the most part, miracle stories that were linked very precisely to a given site did not have much currency beyond the institutions that produced them, and consequently it would have been relatively rare for multiple copies to be made and dispersed, which would have increased the chances of survival. The Rocamadour miracles, it is worth remembering, survive because their Marian theme made them attractive to copyists and compilers in northern France despite the absence of a direct link between their institutions and Rocamadour itself. On the other hand, the miracle collections that do survive are sufficiently numerous and varied in length and form to demonstrate that *miracula* were not the automatic, or even frequent, accompaniment of a cult. They were one particular response to the experiences that surrounded the functioning of a pilgrimage centre. Some cult centres did not produce miracle collections. Others felt the need for them differently at different times.

Four comparable texts

It follows from this argument that it is a useful exercise to explore the factors that may have triggered the writing of miracle collections. Four examples help to demonstrate the potential value of this approach. It should be emphasized that the four are to some extent untypical of collections generally, in that we are unusually well informed about the circumstances in which the miracles were recorded or the roles of the authors in the process of creating the written record. On the other hand, the chosen examples are valuable because they offer important points of comparison with the Rocamadour stories: two collections, those from Laon and Soissons, relate to Marian cult centres that were popular in the twelfth century; the third, from Conques, is of value because although it predates the Rocamadour material by more than a century it comes from a neighbouring region in south-central France and shares with it a number of noteworthy features such as its length and a pronounced interest in the experiences of members of the aristocratic elites; and the fourth, from Canterbury, is very close in time to the Rocamadour collection. The lessons to be drawn from these four samples do not add up to a comprehensive picture of why *miracula* were produced. But they may be approached as significant illustrations that cumulatively reveal that a variety of reasons could lie behind collections. Moreover, each example demonstrates the importance of specific factors operating in individual cases.

The Laon miracle collection was the result of a remarkable sequence of events. The process that led to the writing of the miracles began with a period

of grave crisis and exceptional disruption: the burning of the cathedral of
Our Lady in 1112 as the result of urban unrest in Laon, and the violent death
of the bishop, Gauldricus.[10] To speed the rebuilding of the cathedral, the new
bishop, Bartholomew, sent out two fund-raising tours, one around parts of
northern France between June and September 1112, the other across the
southernmost counties of England between March and September 1113.[11]
The urgency behind the tours was clear; significantly, the author who later
described them was unabashed in stating that England was chosen for the
second trip because it had a reputation for wealth and the sort of settled
conditions that could allow outsiders with valuable property to operate
safely.[12] On both tours the focus of the money-raising effort was the feretory,
or portable reliquary, which contained some of the Virgin's relics from the
cathedral. The feretory served as the devotional draw which the party of
canons and their lay assistants used to stimulate interest among the
inhabitants of the areas through which they travelled.[13] The excitement
created by the movement of important relics resulted in various miracles
being claimed, both cures and other benefits for those who were attracted to
the feretory, as well as miracles of protection which eased the party's
progress.[14] This happened with sufficient regularity and publicity for it to
become an obvious framework by means of which those involved could
structure, condense and lend narrative coherence to their many different
experiences when they reported back to Laon. Writing close to these events,
in 1115, Guibert of Nogent reveals that those who had been on the tours
(the two parties were not identical but their composition overlapped) were
already using the miracles that they had experienced or witnessed as the main
hook on which to hang the memory of their efforts.[15] The potential was
clearly present, then, for the miraculous to be used as a structural and
thematic device in any written commemoration of events that the cathedral
community at Laon might choose to produce.

In the event, a full written account of the tours did not appear until
about thirty years later. Its author was Herman, who may have been a
canon from Laon or, more probably, the man of that name who was abbot of

---

[10] 'De miraculis S. Mariae Laudunensis libri tres', I.1, 3, *PL* 156.963–5, 967–8. See also
Guibert of Nogent, *Autobiographie*, III.7–9, ed. and trans. E.-R. Labande (Les
classiques de l'histoire de France au moyen âge, 34; Paris, 1981), pp. 316–56; English
translation: *Self and Society in Medieval France*, trans. J. F. Benton (New York, 1970;
repr. Toronto, 1984), pp. 165–82.

[11] Ward, *Miracles and the Medieval Mind*, pp. 134–41. See also J. S. P. Tatlock, 'The
English Journey of the Canons of Laon', *Speculum*, 8 (1933), pp. 454–85.

[12] 'De miraculis S. Mariae Laudunensis', II.1, col. 973.

[13] See *ibid.*, II.2, col. 975; Ward, *Miracles and the Medieval Mind*, pp. 135, 137–8.

[14] For the use of tours more generally see P.-A. Sigal, 'Les voyages de reliques aux
onzième et douzième siècles', in *Voyage, quête, pèlerinage dans la littérature et la
civilisation médiévales* (Sénéfiance, 2; Aix-en-Provence, 1976), pp. 73–104.

[15] *Autobiographie*, III.12–13, pp. 378–92; trans. *Self and Society*, pp. 191–7.

Saint-Martin, Tournai.[16] The reason for the long gap is not immediately obvious. But it is likely that a version of events was finally produced because the need was felt to create a clear, permanent record before the tours passed from living memory, and to bring some order and consistency to whatever earlier written evidence existed. The fact that Book II of the *De miraculis S. Mariae Laudunensis*, which deals with the English tour, differs from the preceding account of the 1112 journey in being voiced in the first person plural suggests that some written accounts had been produced earlier but did not amount to a satisfactorily comprehensive and internally consistent description of the two tours seen as a pair. More specifically, Herman observes that he was writing at the request of Bishop Bartholomew, for whom he had produced hagiographical works in the past.[17] This suggests that the miracle narrative was seen as part of a broader commemorative process. Bartholomew could claim to have done much to restore the fortunes of his cathedral and diocese over the course of a long and very full pontificate.[18] But the tours of 1112–13 had a valuable and special role as markers of the dire situation which he had faced right at the start of his episcopate. In this connection, it is significant that the first tour was organized only a matter of weeks after the fire that had damaged the cathedral, and very soon after Bartholomew's election; it could therefore be presented as a decisive first stage in the process of renewal. Moreover, the commemorative emphasis further emerges from the fact that Book III, which was probably written a few years after the first two,[19] focuses on the defining event that the tours had helped to make possible, the consecration of the now partly rebuilt cathedral in September 1114. It then extends its range to take in other significant events and processes such as Bishop Bartholomew's support for Norbert of Xanten and his new Premonstratensian order (for which this text is an important early source).[20] Themes of reform and renewal evident over many years in a variety of contexts are thus portrayed as the extension of the early momentum and sense of purpose generated by the tours.

In this way the Laon miracles represent part of the resolution of a crisis and an attempt to order the memory of past events in ways that spoke chiefly to the interests of the bishop and cathedral community. The miracles from the nunnery of Our Lady of Soissons were similarly rooted in crisis, but in this instance the dynamic was significantly different: a religious institution's response to the needs of outsiders is what prompted and initially shaped the

[16] For the question of authorship see G. Niemeyer, 'Die Miracula S. Mariae Laudunensis des Abtes Hermann von Tournai: Verfasser und Entstehungszeit', *Deutsches Archiv für Erforschung des Mittelalters*, 27 (1971), pp. 136–63.

[17] 'De miraculis S. Mariae Laudunensis', cols. 961–2.

[18] It is noteworthy that a detailed account of Bartholomew's family history and connections appears early in the text: *ibid.*, I.2, cols. 965–7.

[19] See Niemeyer, 'Die Miracula', pp. 163–74.

[20] 'De miraculis S. Mariae Laudunensis', III, cols. 987–1018; Niemeyer, 'Die Miracula', p. 136.

written record, which then mutated into forms closer to the Laon experience. In 1128 the region around Soissons was beset by an outbreak of ergotism, a highly unpleasant disease caused by the consumption of mouldy rye. Often known as the *ignis sacer*, the holy fire, it both produced grave physical and psychological effects in the individual sufferer and regularly triggered bursts of communal religious fervour which sought an outlet in a saint's cult. The significance of the disease as the initiating force behind the miracle collection is revealed by the fact that the author, Hugh Farsit, devoted his opening chapter to a full and well-informed description of its physical and social effects.[21] The trigger for the sequence of miracles was the cure of a young girl who had been looked after by the abbess of Soissons, Matilda, and her nuns. News of this spread, and the number of claimed cures mounted rapidly. Hugh states that 103 cases were observed within a fortnight.[22]

As with the Laon collection there was a significant interval between the first events described in the miracles and the production of the surviving written record (which dates from no earlier than December 1143).[23] Again, the reasons for this are not immediately apparent, but a number of significant factors suggest themselves. In the first place, Hugh Farsit was a canon in a nearby church who claimed to have had first-hand experience of the events of 1128. It is useful to remember that miracle collections were not spontaneous creations; they depended on the availability, enthusiasm and literary competence of writers, either within the religious community concerned or interested outsiders such as Hugh. Second, there is an institutional and commemorative purpose evident in the fact that Hugh states that he committed the miracles to writing soon after the death of Abbess Matilda in 1143; her role in the first, trigger, miracle is emphasized by Hugh, and by extension the events that unfolded thereafter could be seen to have flowed on one level from her initiative. In this way the miracles could function as a memorial to a respected leader. Third, it is significant that even though the miracles have a clear initial focus in the 1128 ergotism outbreak, Hugh in fact devotes only a small portion of his text to specific incidents related to the epidemic. His oddly precise figure of 103 cures is possibly invented, but it seems to have been intended to convey the impression that it was based on a secure oral or written memory. This permitted the author to draw attention to just a few illustrative samples before developing the narrative in other directions. Indications of what is to come are provided by the two chapters that immediately follow the description of the first cure: one recounts the sighting of a large star which drove mist and fog away from the church of Our Lady; the next tells the story of how someone venerating Soissons' Marian relic, a slipper, became so carried away that she tried to bite into it.[24]

[21] 'Libellus de miraculis B. Mariae Virginis in urbe Suessionensi', c. 1, *PL* 179.1777–8.
[22] *Ibid.*, c. 3, cols. 1779–80.
[23] See Ward, *Miracles and the Medieval Mind*, pp. 142–5.
[24] 'Libellus de miraculis B. Mariae', cc. 4–5, col. 1780; see also c. 9, col. 1783.

Already, then, the opening device of the ergotism outbreak is giving way to a statement of the community's status as sacred space and home of a great holy object. Thereafter Hugh's narrative quickly extends from cures of the 'judgement fire' to take in other miracle types similar to those in many other collections: for example, cures of deafness, facial disfigurement, muteness, blindness, paralysis, demonic possession, labour pains, inflammation and epilepsy.[25] Also the collection's chronological range is extended; one of the later stories is located during Pope Innocent II's visit to Soissons in 1131.[26] And it attempts to convey a sense of change and development in the outward face of the cult of Our Lady; as Hugh puts it, the rumour (*fama*) of the miracles spread 'amongst the people',[27] the inference being that the shrine's appeal outgrew in both chronological and spatial terms the initial connection to the *ignis sacer*, the incidence of which was irregular and unpredictable and therefore not a secure basis for the long-term promotion of a wonder-working saint.

The third case study, from Conques, provides an example of an unusually overt and complex intrusion of the person of the author into the written record of miracles that he was creating. The author of what became the first two of the four books of the miracles of St Faith was Bernard, a *scholasticus* - master of the cathedral school – from Angers, far to the north of Conques.[28] The simple fact that we know his name places him in a minority of *miracula* authors. But his case is even more exceptional. Usually we are informed of the identity of authors from outside the religious community concerned because they were well-known writers – sometimes with a particular specialism in hagiographical composition – who were commissioned to rework old material or to create new texts celebrating a saint.[29] In Bernard's case, however, his relationship with the monks of Conques was, at least on the surface, more fortuitous and flexible. As he informs us, he was moved by the existence of a small chapel dedicated to St Faith near Chartres to seek out the centre of the saint's cult.[30] Arriving at Conques, probably in the summer of 1013, he began to collect and record the miracle stories that were the subject of local oral tradition. Over the course of this and two further visits – the final one was in 1020 – he assembled material on about forty miracles. Originally devised as three books, they were subsequently run together to form two. Two further books were composed by one or more monks at Conques in the second quarter of the eleventh century.[31]

---

[25] *Ibid.*, cc. 7, 10–11, 13–17, 19–24, cols. 1781–2, 1784–95.

[26] *Ibid.*, c. 22, cols. 1792–3.

[27] *Ibid.*, c. 18, col. 1790.

[28] For the miracles see *Liber Miraculorum Sancte Fidis*; trans. *The Book of Sainte Foy*.

[29] See Sigal, 'Le travail des hagiographes', pp. 171–2.

[30] *Liber Miraculorum Sancte Fidis*, I, preface, pp. 73–4; *Book of Sainte Foy*, pp. 39–40.

[31] See Sigal, 'Le travail des hagiographes', pp. 174–5; *Liber Miraculorum Sancte Fidis*, pp. 58–68; *Book of Sainte Foy*, p. 25.

The particular interest of Bernard's text is that in it the *miracula* are interwoven with his own reflections on the circumstances in which he was writing, the manner in which his relationship with the monks at Conques evolved, and his personal reactions to the cult of St Faith. For example, in a celebrated passage Bernard describes how on his first trip south he and his companion Bernier were shocked by the apparently idolatrous nature of the statue reliquary of St Gerald at the monastery of Aurillac, the point being that Conques possessed a similar object representing St Faith (which, in a somewhat altered form, still survives).[32] Once he had arrived at Conques, Bernard adds, he was persuaded by the dean of the abbey that the statue of St Faith was a fitting object of veneration and a suitable housing for the saint's relics; what he had initially seen as an illicit superstition which offended his learned sensibilities became the occasion of reverent awe. It is possible to see Bernard's acceptance of the statue reliquary as a metaphor for the manner in which he entered into a relationship with the Conques monks and their cult which helped to validate his authorship of their miracles. Combining the roles of devotee and outside observer, and carefully negotiating the tensions between the two positions, he could project himself as an ideal vehicle to propagate Faith's celebrity further afield. Bernard's many reminiscences and authorial asides can be seen as rooted in this self-perception.

Bernard's authorial self-awareness has meant that he has attracted a good deal of scholarly attention, and deservedly so.[33] But there is a danger of underestimating the role of the monastic community at Conques in the process that led to the writing of the miracles. Bernard was willing to cast himself as the bringer of northern French literary sophistication and educational attainment to a part of the Midi that he portrayed as something of a cultural backwater. But a number of factors suggest that this was at best an over-simplification of how his relationship with Conques developed, and that we should not picture the monks as essentially passive parties gratefully receiving an outsider's unexpected bounty. In the first place, the fact that a monk at Conques was able to take up the task of recording miracles within about a decade of Bernard's last visit, and do so in a style not unlike that of his predecessor, suggests that members of the monastery were not as educationally deficient as Bernard liked his readers to believe. Second, Bernard himself provides a number of clues that the monks recognized the potential created by a northern stranger touting his literary credentials. He informs us that as early as the first of his visits he was accommodated near the abbey; he was steered towards people who had miracles to relate; and at

---

[32] *Liber Miraculorum Sancte Fidis*, I.13, pp. 112–14; *Book of Sainte Foy*, pp. 77–9.

[33] See B. Stock, *The Implications of Literacy: Written Language and Models of Interpretation in the Eleventh and Twelfth Centuries* (Princeton, 1983), pp. 64–71; A. G. Remensnyder, 'Un problème de cultures ou de culture? La statue-reliquaire et les *joca* de sainte Foy de Conques dans le *Liber miraculorum* de Bernard d'Angers', *Cahiers de civilisation médiévale*, 33 (1990), pp. 351–79.

one point he makes the telling admission that the monks were eager for him to see a girl who had just regained her sight in the abbey church because 'they knew that I longed to witness a new miracle'.[34] Bernard reveals that he discussed with one monk the merits of composing part of his narrative in verse.[35] And he states that during his third visit he was put under pressure by the monks to compose a further book of miracles despite his reservations that the best material had already been used up.[36]

In addition, it would be wrong to imagine the relationship between Bernard and the monks of Conques in terms of a literary *grand homme* moving among an appreciative public, even though Bernard would seem to have cast himself in this role. Central to what Bernard saw as his status with the monks was his ability to present himself as a leading light of the learned elites of the northern French Church, an image centred on his claimed acquaintance with the greatest figure in that circle, Bishop Fulbert of Chartres (1004–28).[37] Significantly the introduction to the miracles takes the form of a dedicatory letter addressed to Fulbert. Bernard also concludes Book I with a letter to the monks of Conques which amongst other things – Bernard delivers himself, for example, of a short disquisition on the correct Latin form of 'Faith' to rub in his greater learning – stresses that he had shown earlier drafts of his work to Bishop Hubert of Angers and Bishop Walter of Rennes.[38] It is clear that Bernard was a practised name-dropper. It is most probably the case that he moved on the periphery of the learned circles to which he was staking a claim; the people whom he says helped him most in improving his text were actually lesser lights. Here was a man with a reputation to make who seized on the Conques material as a vehicle to demonstrate his talents. It is tempting to believe that the statement that his interest in the cult of Saint Faith was prompted by a chapel was simply a device to cloak the reasons behind his choice of subject matter: he had done his homework, and this cult, with its remoteness and rumours of unusual happenings, seemed a prime target.

But the fact that Bernard's account of the miracles of St Faith survives is not evidence that the monks at Conques were duped by their visitor's claims to importance. In fact, it suggests quite the reverse. It is noteworthy that the manuscript tradition of the miracle collection flows back to Conques, not Bernard.[39] Although later copyists could, and sometimes did, excise those passages in which Bernard's personal agenda was most overt, the earliest examples of the surviving manuscript tradition reveal that Conques continued to preserve the full record – Bernard's authorial insertions

---

[34] *Liber Miraculorum Sancte Fidis*, I.9, p. 104; *Book of Sainte Foy*, p. 70.

[35] *Liber Miraculorum Sancte Fidis*, I.7, p. 98; *Book of Sainte Foy*, p. 63.

[36] *Liber Miraculorum Sancte Fidis*, II.7, pp. 168–9; *Book of Sainte Foy*, p. 130.

[37] *Liber Miraculorum Sancte Fidis*, I, preface, pp. 73–6; *Book of Sainte Foy*, pp. 39–41.

[38] *Liber Miraculorum Sancte Fidis*, I.34, pp. 144–7; *Book of Sainte Foy*, pp. 108–11.

[39] See *Liber Miraculorum Sancte Fidis*, pp. 3–12, 15–49.

included – for many decades after he had passed from the scene. That is to say, his experience was appropriated by the monastic community and subsumed within its collective memory.

Why was this? Part of the reason why Bernard's efforts were first encouraged and then perpetuated at Conques is that they sat perfectly with wider developments at the abbey in the eleventh century. This was a period of remarkable growth, both in terms of resources and prestige, the key to which was an intensified emphasis on the cult of St Faith as the foremost defining element of the monastery's institutional identity and of the manner in which it projected itself onto the outside world. The significance of this emerges if one examines the evolution of the monastery's charters between the ninth and early eleventh centuries. One can plot a progressive narrowing and sharpening of communal identity as articulated in the clauses in the charters that described the monastery: whereas Faith starts out at the end of the list of saints to whom the abbey was dedicated – once her relics had arrived there in about 866[40] – Conques was being described simply as 'the church of the Holy Saviour and St Faith' by the time that Bernard arrived there.[41] It is also significant that it is from the early decades of the eleventh century that the charter evidence reveals a marked growth in the grant of properties to the abbey in areas more widely dispersed than its initial concentration of resources in its immediate locality.[42] This points to a growing network of lay benefaction stimulated by Conques's association with Faith. Under Abbot Odolric (1031–65) the abbey church was rebuilt, in part to accommodate increasing pilgrim numbers. And further written commemorations of Faith's power and fame were composed: prose and verse accounts of the translation of her relics from Agen in the ninth century;[43] a vernacular verse rendering of her Passion, which is a remarkably early example of literary composition in Occitan;[44] and additions of further

---

[40] See P. J. Geary, *Furta Sacra: Thefts of Relics in the Central Middle Ages*, rev. edn (Princeton, 1990), pp. 58–63, 138–41.

[41] See e.g. *Cartulaire de l'abbaye de Conques en Rouergue*, ed. G. Desjardins (Paris, 1879), nos. 181 (c.1019), 209 (c.1019), 263–5 (996 × 1031), 286 (c.1010), 325 (c.1007), 388 (c.1012), 394 (c.1019), 408 (c.1012). A charter of 1004 refers to the 'monastery of St Faith at Conques': *ibid.*, no. 395. Typical of the earlier formulation is the construction in *ibid.*, no. 343 (903), which locates the abbey by reference to the *pagus* of the Rouergue, the nearby River Dordou and the monastery's foundation in honour of Christ, the Virgin Mary, St Peter, St Vincent and, finally, St Faith.

[42] E.g. *ibid.*, nos. 65 (997 × 1030), 136 (997 × 1031), 286 (c.1010), 326 (1003), 387 (996 × 1030), 395 (1004).

[43] *AASS* Oct. 3, pp. 290–99; *Book of Sainte Foy*, pp. 26, 263–74. For translations generally see M. Heinzelmann, *Translationsberichte und andere Quellen des Reliquienkultes* (Typologie des sources du moyen âge occidental, 33; Turnhout, 1979).

[44] *La Chanson de Sainte Foy*, ed. E. Hoepffner, trans. P. Alfaric, 2 vols. (Publications de la Faculté des Lettres de l'Université de Strasbourg, 32–3; Paris, 1926); *Book of Sainte Foy*, pp. 26–7, 275–84.

miracula to complement Bernard's text.[45] From all this activity it can be seen that the miraculous record at Conques became part of a strategy of expansion and communication rooted in the monastery's needs.

Our fourth example – the miracle collection made at the shrine of St Thomas Becket at Canterbury – serves as a useful case study because of the abruptness and notoriety of the events that brought the cult into being. Whereas the experience of Conques was one of the gradual evolution of a cultic identity, into which the particular and unanticipated circumstances of Bernard's arrival on the scene were integrated, the brutality and shock of Becket's murder in his cathedral on 29 December 1170 forced the monastic community of Christ Church, Canterbury, to effect sudden and profound changes in how it conceived its institutional identity and the manner in which it interacted with the outside world. The miracles that were committed to writing in the years immediately after Becket's death may be seen as part of the process of reacting to, and attempting to control, enforced change.

The creation of the written miracle record at Canterbury was a result of two convergent processes. First, there was the momentum generated by popular pressure to regard Thomas as a martyr and miracle-worker. Very soon after the murder itself local people were drawn to the scene of his killing, and the belief soon developed that the archbishop's blood had curative properties when smeared or soaked into a cloth.[46] As news of the murder spread, the cult snowballed. By the spring of 1171, when access was made possible to the crypt in which Becket's body lay, crowds of pilgrims were visiting the cathedral, many in search of cures or reporting miracles that they accredited to the saint. The ritual reconciliation of the cathedral in December 1171, which restored it to its proper function as a liturgical space and thus permitted an integrated pattern of monastic and popular worship, further encouraged pilgrim numbers.[47] Becket's cult was not self-limiting either in terms of specialization in certain types of miracle or by appealing to only some segments of society. Its maximal appeal created the conditions for a remarkable growth of popularity, one indication of which is the number of pilgrims who came to Canterbury from abroad.[48] On one level, then, the needs and aspirations of the pilgrims – or at least those who had experience of or wanted Becket's miraculous assistance – were the basic precondition that made the miracle collection possible.

But a second factor, the willingness of the monks of Christ Church to modulate their response to outside pressures in certain ways, was also necessary before the collection could be created. It is useful to remember

[45] *Liber Miraculorum Sancte Fidis*, III–IV, pp. 65–8 (for authorship), 181–269; *Book of Sainte Foy*, pp. 142–221.
[46] Finucane, *Miracles and Pilgrims*, p. 122; F. Barlow, *Thomas Becket* (London, 1986), pp. 265–6; Ward, *Miracles and the Medieval Mind*, pp. 101–3.
[47] Finucane, *Miracles and Pilgrims*, pp. 122–3; Barlow, *Thomas Becket*, pp. 264, 266–7.
[48] Ward, *Miracles and the Medieval Mind*, pp. 97–8.

that the enthusiasm of the cathedral community for a cult that had exploded into being in the heart of its institutional world would not have been a foregone conclusion. Any decision to support it had political as well as devotional implications. Becket had been a controversial figure, scarcely a model of sanctity during his career, and he was disliked by many within the English Church. More specifically, his relations with Christ Church had not always been easy; and he must have seemed a remote figure to the monks, having spent six years in an exile that ended only a few weeks before his death. Outside pressures were also at work: the de Broc family, implacable opponents of Becket and a powerful presence in the area around Canterbury, were in a position to intimidate the monks for some months after the archbishop's murder.[49] And there was also the reaction of King Henry II to consider. Only gradually, then, in the weeks and months after the murder did the monks arrive at some consensus about how they should react to events. Central to this process was the decision to make a record of Becket's miracles.

The record was at first made the responsibility of Benedict, one of the monks at Christ Church, who probably began to collect material at the time of the opening of the crypt in April 1171.[50] Benedict informs us that he was in part moved to take on this task because of visions that he had experienced. But a communal as well as an individual initiative is revealed by his statement that he took up his pen 'because the brothers so wished and instructed'.[51] Benedict kept up his work until 1177, when he left Canterbury to become abbot of Peterborough. But as early as 1172 he had been joined by another monk, William.[52] Working in parallel rather than as direct collaborators – their material overlaps on many occasions[53] – they together created a collection of about 700 *miracula*, much the largest of its kind to survive. The two monks placed themselves in the thick of the action, taking up position by the crypt to observe and interview pilgrims and to take notes for later working up. The result of their efforts is a remarkable (and still largely untapped) resource.

The question therefore poses itself: why go to so much trouble, especially in light of the fact that Benedict and William were clearly obliged to sift

---

[49] See Barlow, *Thomas Becket*, pp. 264–5, 267.

[50] Finucane, *Miracles and Pilgrims*, p. 125; Ward, *Miracles and the Medieval Mind*, pp. 89–90.

[51] 'Miracula sancti Thomae Cantuariensis', I, prologue, ed. J. C. Robertson, *Materials for the History of Thomas Becket, Archbishop of Canterbury*, vol. 2 (Rolls Series, 67:2; London, 1876), p. 26.

[52] William of Canterbury, 'Miracula gloriosi martyris Thomae, Cantuariensis archiepiscopi', I, prologue, ed. J. C. Robertson, *Materials for the History of Thomas Becket, Archbishop of Canterbury*, vol. 1 (Rolls Series, 67:1; London, 1875), p. 138; Barlow, *Thomas Becket*, p. 267.

[53] For a useful list of the parallels between the two collections, see E. A. Abbott, *St. Thomas of Canterbury: His Death and Miracles*, 2 vols. (London, 1898), ii.76–273.

through very much more data than actually made it into their written versions? One possible stimulus, in the first years of the cult, was the prospect of Becket's formal recognition as a saint. But the importance of this factor should not be exaggerated. Canonization procedures in this period were not subject to the systemization and bureaucratization that were to become evident from the thirteenth century onwards. The miracle collection was thus not a forerunner of the dossiers that were compiled in later centuries in support of a canonization claim.[54] Significantly, the two legates whom Pope Alexander III sent to make inquiries about the emerging cult in 1172 would seem to have reported back on the basis of whatever oral testimony they could gather rather than any scrutiny of the written miracle record as it then existed.[55] And although Pope Alexander was impressed by the stories of miracles attributed to Becket, this was not an element of the claim to sanctity that he chose to emphasize when he wrote to the monks of Christ Church in March 1173 to announce the canonization.[56] Moreover, the collection was kept going for several years after papal confirmation of the cult had been obtained. It had a momentum independent of the niceties of Becket's official saintly status.

The implication of this is that the collection was chiefly driven by forces at work within the community at Christ Church. Part of the rationale was to generate material that could be shared with other churches and individual ecclesiastics in spreading the celebrity of Becket's cult. There is evidence for copies of the miracles being sent out (Henry II himself was given a copy of William's collection), and for preachers drawing on stories to publicize the cult.[57] But a collection of about 700 stories would seem an unwieldy and unnecessarily elaborate response if propagation had been the sole, or main, aim. Similarly, the quantity of material must soon have outstripped what was useful for formal readings at Christ Church or as a pool of *exempla* to draw on in instructing the laity. Consequently, the reasoning behind the collection would seem to have been as much emotive as functionalist. An important clue in this regard is provided by Benedict's account of the opening of the crypt in the spring of 1171, which had the important effect of enabling the monks to direct and control the pilgrimage crowds and to create an environment in which people reporting miracles could be observed and interrogated in something approaching a systematic way. Benedict observes that witnessing the excitement caused by the crypt's opening and the miracles taking place had a beneficial, healing effect on the monks, restoring a sense of community that had been fractured by the shock of the murder and the

---

[54] But see Barlow, *Thomas Becket*, p. 268.
[55] *Ibid.*, pp. 268–9.
[56] *English Historical Documents: Volume II, 1042–1189*, ed. D. C. Douglas and G. W. Greenaway, 2nd edn (London, 1981), no. 157, p. 827. See Barlow, *Thomas Becket*, p. 269.
[57] Ward, *Miracles and the Medieval Mind*, p. 93.

uncertainties of its aftermath: 'Then for the first time our spirit was greatly revived, and as if awakening from a deep sleep we became consoled to some extent.'[58] As an element of the formal, institutional response to the cult, the miracle collection became part of the process of communal renewal. It is perhaps significant that, on an individual level, both Benedict and William may have had ghosts to exorcise. Both men had been present in the cathedral at the time of Becket's slaying but had scarcely emerged with credit. Benedict had probably been hiding out of harm's way; William had tried to stand firm alongside the archbishop but had fled as soon as the first blow was struck.[59] As with the individual, so with the collective: the miracle stories were testament to the ability of good to emerge from bad and to the power of communal regeneration.

The four examples that we have considered illustrate the variety of circumstances that informed the writing of *miracula*. This is in itself a crucial point. But there are also two important common denominators that unite them. Each required the input of the faithful, whose search for miraculous assistance or interest in interpreting experiences as miraculous episodes generated the raw material that could be noted, sifted and written up. And each flowed from a specific decision or evolving strategy on the part of a religious community to celebrate the power and fame of a saint by means of a particular form of written commemoration. As was noted earlier, the first of these two factors has received more scholarly attention than the second, not least because there are relatively few opportunities in the surviving sources to open a window on the ideas and behaviours of 'ordinary' people in this period, whereas we do have many other points of entry – many of them characterized by greater literary sophistication and intellectual depth – into the thought-worlds of the literate elites. But the second element, the input of the religious institution, must be taken into consideration: *miracula* were not written as disinterested exercises.

In this connection it is worth remembering that even in those situations in which miracles were believed to be happening with sufficient regularity to be treated as a significant manifestation of a cult's operations, other commemorative strategies were available to the churches concerned. For example, we should not underestimate the ability of oral traditions to survive within religious communities, which were, after all, predicated on the ideals of institutional continuity and the long-term stability of individual members within the communal setting.[60] In addition, the memory of miraculous events could be fixed in artistic or architectural representations, as well as in choices about how much outsiders could contribute to the visual setting in a church. At St-Léonard, Noblat, for instance, the many chains left by pilgrims who claimed miraculous escapes from imprisonment were given a

[58] 'Miracula sancti Thomae Cantuariensis', II.6, pp. 60–1; cf. I, prologue, pp. 22–4.
[59] Barlow, *Thomas Becket*, pp. 4, 245–6.
[60] See Sigal, 'Le travail des hagiographes', pp. 152–4, 158–64.

prominent place by being displayed on specially erected poles.[61] A further strategy was to deploy some of a church's resources in order to support some of those who claimed to have benefited from a miracle. It was not uncommon for some pilgrims in this position, especially the poor and the young or the old with no domestic ties to return to, to stay on at a shrine and live off alms or enter into the service of the religious community. Bernard of Angers met one such living witness surviving on the fringes of the institutional organization at Conques; it was partly through him that Bernard learned of a miraculous event that had happened thirty years before, one that he chose to emphasize by making it the opening story of his collection.[62]

These sorts of commemorative methods had the great merits of flexibility and the capacity to mutate in accordance with the community's changing needs and perspectives. Oral traditions could develop as they were passed from one generation of shrine custodians to the next, and in the process receive new inflections. Visual representations could be subjected to reinterpretation. *Ex votos* such as chains could be replaced by more recent examples. And new beneficiaries could supply stories to replace those passing from living memory. In stark contrast, the act of writing miracle stories was potentially very limiting. Even if overt chronological precision was not made a priority (the Rocamadour collection is a case in point), the recording of details such as names, places and circumstantial material, as well as decisions about how to preface and sequence the different stories, served to make the written versions of events relatively more permanent and inflexible. Moreover, the establishment of a written record represented a choice to privilege one moment in a cult's existence. If the record were not kept up beyond the short term – and most were not – then what would be bequeathed to later generations was a fixed and increasingly distant point of reference which might not readily relate to developments in their own cultic experience. Thus the decision to produce a miracle collection was not a random impulse. Our four examples demonstrate that specific circumstances, resulting in particular sets of needs on the part of the various cult centres, must be examined closely in any analysis of what prompted recourse to the composition of *miracula* as a literary exercise. With this in mind, we can now turn to the Rocamadour collection in order to investigate possible reasons for its creation.

[61] *Le guide du pèlerin de Saint-Jacques de Compostelle*, c. 8, ed. and trans. J. Vielliard, 5th edn (Paris, 1997), p. 54; English translation: *The Pilgrim's Guide to Santiago de Compostela*, trans. W. Melczer (New York, 1993), p. 106. The liberation of prisoners was the predominant theme of the *miracula* written about St Leonard: see M. G. Bull, *Knightly Piety and the Lay Response to the First Crusade: The Limousin and Gascony, c.970–c.1130* (Oxford, 1993), pp. 240–8; C. Cheirézy, 'Hagiographie et société: L'exemple de saint Léonard de Noblat', *Annales du Midi*, 107 (1995), pp. 427–31.

[62] *Liber Miraculorum Sancte Fidis*, I.1, pp. 78–86; *Book of Sainte Foy*, pp. 43–51.

Chronological clues in the text

This investigation needs to be conducted in two stages. First we need to consider the evidence for when the collection was written and for the chronological relationship between the material it contains and the time of writing. This will allow us to examine aspects of the author's access to his material and the editorial strategies that he brought to bear on it. This in turn will enable us to proceed to the second stage of the inquiry: an exploration of some of the possible conditions that made the monks of Rocamadour want to invest resources and manpower in the creation of a long miracle collection.

The stories contain only one overt reference to when they were written. In Book II c. 15 the author concludes his account by giving the year of the events he has just described, 1166, and then adding 'We, however, are writing this in the sixth year after the aforementioned reckoning of time.' The abrupt insertion of this sort of detail mid-text is puzzling. There is only one other occasion in which the year of the Incarnation is supplied: 1169 is given (incorrectly, in fact) as the date of an earthquake in the Middle East, and here no interval between event and writing is specified.[63] Two reasons suggest themselves for why the date 1166 should have impressed itself on the writer's mind. It was the first year of a conflict between the count of Toulouse and the king of Aragon which we shall see formed the background to a number of stories in the collection and had a notable impact on much of the Midi. And, more significantly in the context of the immediate interests of the monastic community at Rocamadour, it was the year in which the monks there discovered a buried body which they identified as that of St Amator, an episode that will be discussed more fully later. Although suggestive, however, neither of these factors provides a compelling reason for why 1166 should have been singled out and flagged in a manner intended to draw particular attention both to it and to the time of writing.

Perhaps the answer should be sought in the nature of the story to which the dating construction is appended. This account is one of the longest in the collection, especially if one measures length against the amount of space devoted to the description of action as opposed to authorial insertions such as prayers and invocations. The story is also one of the most complex in terms of narrative structure. Whereas most of the accounts in the collection revolve around a single miraculous episode, or a closely linked pairing such as when someone is punished for a transgression and then cured of the punitive affliction, the central figure of this story passes through a series of mishaps. As the rubric to the story states, she suffered 'many scourges'.

[63] II.20. For the earthquake, see H. E. Mayer, 'Das syrische Erdbeben von 1170: Ein unedierter Brief Königs Amalrichs von Jerusalem', *Deutsches Archiv für Erforschung des Mittelalters*, 45 (1989), pp. 474–84.

The narrative unfolds as follows. The Rouergue, the region to the east of Quercy, was infested by a plague of fierce wolves, which would snatch young children from their mothers' grasp and devour them. One Stephana of *Tienere*, who had lost a young brother to the wolves – we are given the graphic detail that the mother was left clutching one severed arm – was attacked and horribly mauled by two wolves before being dragged into a nearby forest. The woman then ordered the wolves to desist, and they suddenly broke off, defending her against other predators arriving on the scene. Discovered by a search party the following day, Stephana was carried back to her village. But her terrible wounds began to putrefy, and she became so repulsive a sight, even to her own family, that one night she was taken to a remote village and abandoned. Here she so horrified those who looked at her that she was shunned. Strapped to a donkey, she was taken far off to be abandoned once more. The woman then fell off the donkey into a river, but the Virgin saved her from drowning. Discovered on the river bank, she was allowed to recover in the barn of a noble who was moved by her plight. Gradually her condition improved a little. Having fixed her hopes on the Virgin, whose merits are lauded by the author, Stephana in time rejected the medical help that she was being given and indicated that she wanted to be carried to Rocamadour. There she prayed for a long time near the altar and was eventually cured, though precisely what the change in her condition was which merited this description is not made clear.

This story is worth describing in some detail because it has a number of interesting features. Some of the elements – the tenacious hope placed in the Virgin in the face of great adversity, the praise of the Virgin, the rejection of earthly medicine, and the devotional and contritional behaviour at the church immediately prior to the cure – are themes that can be found in many other stories. But others are more unusual, pointing to a careful interweaving of biblical and folkloric motifs to fashion a narrative with a particularly overt didactic message. It has been plausibly suggested that this story had its origins in material that was used in preaching to pilgrims.[64] The account is unusual in opening with a series of scriptural quotations that emphasize the Lord's mercy, especially towards the humble, and lead into the observation that the Lord can afflict the just in order to test their love or to deflect them from evil. The detailed description of Stephana's trials and tribulations then begins as an extended illustration of that assertion. Moralizing commentary reappears, again with biblical support, at the point at which the woman is cast out by her neighbours. Similarly, there is a clear evocation of the Good Samaritan in the actions of the compassionate nobleman. In addition to the biblical resonances the story displays numerous features that suggest that it was constructed with oral delivery in mind, drawing on the familiar, the folkloric and the visually vivid: the role of the wolves in the story as a source of communal danger; the significance attached

---

[64] Rocacher, p. 299.

to the forest, and the manner in which the boundary between settled and wild space is broken down; the woman's ability to communicate with beasts; the importance attached to the social bonds that should have tied the victim to her family and neighbourhood; the significance of movement as a narrative device; and the rustic setting. Of course, all the stories in this collection were to a greater or lesser extent capable of forming the basis of religious instruction for the laity; but the difference in this instance is that this didactic aspect seems to have been worked through with particular thoroughness and embedded in all parts of the narrative.[65] This would suggest that the process had taken place before the version that we now have was composed. It is possible that an earlier written version of this story existed, to which the date 1166 was attached. Or the author of the miracle collection may have been drawing on oral memory. In either event, the peculiarities of this story are evidence that the systematic compilation of material for the collection as a whole, and by extension the decision to create the collection in the first place, should be dated after 1166. There is a clear sense of distance between what happened and the written account: 1166 represented a time far enough back for our author to locate it in 'quadam tempestate', which, given the content of the story, we might almost translate as 'once upon a time'.

The suggestion that it was not until some time after 1166 that the miracle collection was conceived is significant because its terminal dates are sometimes given as 1148–1172,[66] as if to imply that we have material more or less evenly distributed over about a quarter of a century. This would lead to the conclusion that the monks at Rocamadour were placing a sustained emphasis on the miraculous over a long period, and by extension that the collection embodied an evolving tradition maintained over many years. In fact, a close investigation of the identifiable people and events mentioned in the miracles points to a pronounced weighting towards very recent occurrences. A good way to demonstrate this is to begin with an examination of those stories close in time to the events they describe, and then compare them with miracles that are set in the more distant past.

Only a minority of stories contain clear clues about dating, but they are sufficiently numerous and evenly distributed throughout the collection to be very suggestive. Taking the miracles book by book, the clearest instances are as follows:

Book I

c. 15: The Count Robert of Meulan who is the central figure in a story of an arm injured in a riding accident is almost certainly Robert III (1166–1207). The last Robert before him, his grandfather, died in 1118.

---

[65] Cf. I.5; I.13; I.35.
[66] Sigal, *L'homme et le miracle*, p. 205; cf. Signori, 'Miracle Kitchen', p. 281, suggesting c.1160–72.

c. 36: The Gaston of Béarn whose death opens the story is Viscount Gaston V, who died in 1170. The judicial proceedings described – Gaston's widow is unjustly condemned in the court of King Sancho of Navarre for aborting the child that she was carrying at the time of her husband's death – must have taken place in that year or 1171.

c. 45: This story is set against the background of King Henry II of England's expedition to Ireland, which took place between October 1171 and April 1172. It is implied that the two central figures, Hugh of Gondeville and Robert fitz Robert, left the expedition early, but they may not in fact have sailed from Ireland much before the king, for there is evidence that Hugh was one of those whom Henry appointed to maintain royal interests as his own stay in Ireland was drawing to a close.[67] It is therefore unlikely that the two men could have reached Rocamadour to recount their experiences before the late spring of 1172. And they probably did so in the summer of that year.

c. 46: This story concerns a trial by combat arranged to decide a dispute brought before the bishop-elect of Verdun, Arnulf. Arnulf of Chiny's predecessor as bishop, Richard of Durbuy, died in 1171.[68] A letter of Pope Alexander III dated 23 January 1172 refers to Arnulf as 'electus virdunensis'.[69] It is therefore likely that the beneficiary of the miracle reported his experience to the monks at Rocamadour in the later part of 1171 or, more probably, the spring months of 1172. Thereafter the use of 'electus' would have been inappropriate once Arnulf had been consecrated.

Book II

c. 1: This story centres on a journey by sea, from Venice, made by Abbot Alexander of Cîteaux, Abbot John of Beaulieu and Abbot Itier of Toussaint de Châlons with the intention of visiting the pope. This is almost certainly to be identified with an embassy on behalf of Emperor Frederick Barbarossa to Pope Alexander which was undertaken by Abbot Alexander and Abbot Pons of Clairvaux in the early weeks of 1169.[70] The detail of the departure from Venice – not a stage in the routine itinerary between Germany and central Italy – is significant, because there is evidence that the party were nervous of

---

[67] For Hugh's role in the Irish expedition see Gerald of Wales, *Expugnatio Hibernica: The Conquest of Ireland*, ed. and trans. A. B. Scott and F. X. Martin (Dublin, 1978), pp. 104–5 and n. 194 at p. 318.

[68] M. Parisse, *Noblesse et chevalerie en Lorraine médiévale: Les familles nobles du XIe au XIIIe siècle* (Nancy, 1982), pp. 242, 254.

[69] 'Epistolae et privilegia', no. 849, *PL* 200.768.

[70] See W. Holtzmann, 'Quellen und Forschungen zur Geschichte Friedrich Barbarossas', *Neues Archiv der Gesellschaft für ältere deutsche Geschichtskunde*, 48 (1930), pp. 400–409; M. Preiss, *Die politische Tätigkeit und Stellung der Cisterzienser im Schisma von 1159–1177* (Historische Studien, 248; Berlin, 1934), pp. 118–22.

taking a more westerly route through northern Italy because of the threat posed by the anti-imperial forces of Milan and its allies.[71]

c. 2: This story is set against the background of 'the expedition of William, marquis of Montferrat, against the Milanese'. This is William V 'the Old', whose dates are 1135–90. As a close supporter of Frederick Barbarossa and a powerful noble whose lands occupied a strategically important area where the western Lombard plain meets the Alps, it is likely that William was regularly engaged in hostilities at some level against Milan, the dominant anti-imperial city in Lombardy, especially after the formation of the Lombard League in 1167. But the word *expeditio* points to a substantial, concerted military effort with strategic goals. In this connection it is noteworthy that a closely contemporary Lombard source singles out the year 1172 in the context of conflict involving William: '1172. Monday 19 June. A hundred knights from Piacenza and those from Milan, Alessandria, Asti, Vercelli, and Novara fought a battle against the marquis of Montferrat near his castle of *Montembellum*, and forced him and his men to turn in shameful flight from the field and flee more than six miles.'[72] The fact that our story implies a reverse for the marquis – the central figure is captured by the Milanese – suggests that it is set against the background of this 1172 conflict.

c. 20: This story is dated 1169 by the author. It centres on the effects of an earthquake in the Middle East. The scale of the disaster implied in the narrative makes it very unlikely that what is being described is an otherwise unrecorded event in 1169, but rather the earthquake that took place on 29 June 1170. This was a momentous disaster noted by a substantial number of Latin, eastern Christian and Muslim writers.[73]

Book III

c. 1: The story is located 'at the time of the war between the king of Aragon and Raymond, the count of Toulouse'. These two antagonists, Alfonso II (1162–96) and Raymond V (1148–94), headed families with a long history of rivalry that had regularly grown into armed conflict. But it is likely that the *terminus a quo* for the events described is not the beginning of Alfonso's reign but a heightening of the disputes between the two families in 1166/67, after Raymond married Douce, the widow of Ramon Berenguer of Provence, who

---

[71] Otto of Freising and Rahewin, *Gesta Friderici I. Imperatoris*, ed. G. Waitz and B. de Simson (MGH Scriptores rerum Germanicarum in usum scholarum, 46; Hanover and Leipzig, 1912), p. 351.

[72] 'Annales Placentini Guelfi a. 1012–1235', *MGH SS* 18.413; L. Usseglio, *I marchesi di Monferrato in Italia ed in Oriente durante i secoli xii e xiii*, 2 vols. (Biblioteca della Società Storica Subalpina, C ns 6; Casale Monferrato, 1926), i.368.

[73] Mayer, 'Das syrische Erdbeben', p. 474 n. 2.

belonged to a cadet line of the count-kings of Barcelona–Aragon. The issue of when the story could have been written is more problematic, for the phrase 'tempore belli regis Arragonensis et raimundi Tolosani comitis' suggests that the author was looking back at a process that he considered had come to an end by the time that he was writing. In other words, this chronological marker should be interpreted as *the* recent war between the two men, as opposed to a reading of *bellum* as 'one period of warfare [amongst others]'. This is supported by the fact that the same formula is used later in Book III, in c. 17. The evidence for how this war was conducted is meagre. The one event about which we are well informed and which most probably constituted the formal ending of hostilities is a meeting between Henry II of England and Count Raymond, which Alfonso attended, at Limoges in February 1173.[74] It is likely that the main business of this conference, the resolution of the dispute between Raymond and Henry over Toulouse, was bound up with a peace (in the event temporary) between Raymond and Alfonso, whom Henry supported.

c. 4: This story contains an intriguing chronological clue when read in conjunction with a text from Mende which is close in time to the Rocamadour miracle collection. The miracle is set against a siege of Mende by a force of Brabançon and Basque mercenaries; after inflicting great hardship on the defenders, the attackers are miraculously repulsed when the Virgin causes part of the city walls to collapse on top of some of them. A text, written around 1170, which commemorates the deeds of Bishop Aldebert III of Mende (1151–87) reports that he had become alarmed at Mende's vulnerability to the frequent predations of mercenaries because the city was situated in an open site (*campestris*); he therefore ordered the building of defensive walls and ditches.[75] This story therefore ties in with very recent developments in the urban life of Mende and is likely to be based on events that took place very soon – a matter of two or three years at the most – before the writing of the collection.

In contrast to these recent events,[76] a number of stories are located in a more distant past. The date that is sometimes proposed as the *terminus a quo*, 1148, rests on an interpretation of two stories. First, the account of a man's escape from a fall down a cliff in Book I is set in the valley of Maurienne 'in

---

[74] See R. Benjamin, 'A Forty Years War: Toulouse and the Plantagenets, 1156–96', *Historical Research*, 61 (1988), pp. 274–5.

[75] 'Chronicon breve de gestis Aldeberti', c. 2, p. 126.

[76] See also the clues that the events described were recent in I.1 (set in 'our times'), I.6 (set 'not long after' the events in the undated I.5, but referring to the large crowds which fill the church), I.24 (a man who suffered from the holy fire is believed to be 'still' afflicted), II.18 (the beneficiary speaks to the author), II.24 (the unusual details suggest that the author was an eye-witness), II.38 (set during the abbacy of Stephen of Cluny, 1161–73), II.45 (the beneficiary speaks to the author).

the land of Count Amelius' (*in terra comitis Amelii*).[77] Albe supposed this name to be a corruption of 'Amedei', in which case the reference would be to Count Amadeus III of Savoy, who died in 1148 while on the Second Crusade.[78] This would seem to be a reasonable suggestion given the geographical information provided by the author. But it does not automatically follow either that the events took place before 1148 or that the account was written that early. The fact that the knight who features in the story is not named would suggest, however, that this was an episode that was made known to the monks at Rocamadour some time before the writing of the miracle collection, by which time memories of the full details were fading.[79]

The second story is more securely datable. It relates how a companion of Abbot Reynald of Cîteaux (1133–50) was taken ill by a fever at Obazine but recovered against expectation. This incident is almost certainly to be linked to the abbot's visit to Obazine in 1148, or possibly 1149, to finalize the arrangements for the abbey's affiliation into the Cistercian order, as had been decided by the Cistercian general chapter in 1147. To this extent, then, this is the clearest evidence for a story in the Rocamadour collection set a generation or more in the past. But two important qualifications must be made. In the first place, the story makes no mention of Rocamadour: the ill man prays to the Virgin, but she is not specifically linked to that place. The companion of a Cistercian abbot would not have needed Rocamadour to put him in mind of the Virgin's patronage; and Obazine had its own Marian dedication. Secondly, the informant for this story was Manfred of Escorailles, dean of Mauriac (d.1175), who we can assume was in close contact with the monks at Rocamadour around the time that the collection was being composed because he was the source for the preceding story;[80] in addition we know that he in fact retired to Rocamadour at about the same time.[81] In other words, if one distinguishes between the date of the actual episode and when it probably became known at Rocamadour, it is clear that this story is not at all evidence for the notion that the collection gradually evolved over about 25 years. On the contrary, it reinforces the idea that the recording of the miracles was planned and executed within a short time frame. Overall, we can say that a small proportion of our author's material dated from far back – either stories remembered by other institutions and individuals, or part of

---

[77] I.12.

[78] Albe, p. 120 n. 55.

[79] Cf. II.4, which may be set no later than 1162 because it refers to one of the counts of Montbéliard, who died out in the male line in that year. Note, however, the absence of the count's name, the sort of detail that our author would have included had he known it.

[80] II.22.

[81] *Chronique de Saint-Pierre-le-Vif de Sens, dite de Clarius*, ed. and trans. R.-H. Bautier and M. Gilles (Sources d'histoire médiévale, 3; Paris, 1979), p. 214.

Rocamadour's own collective memory, in some instances shaped by the presence of old *ex votos* in the church.[82] But for the most part, the material gathered was new: this is evidence for a creative effort which probably did not come into being until very soon before the actual writing of the collection started in 1172.

Possible reasons behind the writing of the collection

The picture that emerges of the dating of the collection and of the material within it leads into an investigation of the circumstances that brought it into being. It is worth repeating that there is no direct statement to this effect in the text, and we are further hampered by a lack of evidence about the internal workings of the monastic community at Rocamadour. In these circumstances a useful approach is to examine various hypotheses concerning what might have had a bearing on the background against which the author of the miracles was operating. The possible influences differ in their scope – some bear on the immediate interests of Rocamadour's monks, others relate to broader religious and political trends affecting the Midi generally – but they have in common the notion that the composition of the *miracula* should be seen as a reaction to pressures that were acting on the monastic community from outside.

A useful first line of inquiry is to ask whether the miracles bore any relation to the issue of Rocamadour's institutional status. This was problematic because control of the church had been disputed between the abbeys of Tulle and Marcilhac (in eastern Quercy) since at least the beginning of the twelfth century.[83] According to a late twelfth-century version of events written from the Marcilhac perspective, the original church at Rocamadour had been served by a monk of that abbey who lived near Gramat. When he grew ill and tired of his responsibilities, he asked the monks of a nearby priory belonging to Tulle (possibly Blanat) to assume responsibility for the church.[84] Whatever the truth of this story, it is clear that by the early twelfth century at the latest Tulle regarded Rocamadour as its own; the church is listed in a bull of 1105 in which Pope Paschal II confirmed the abbey's possessions.[85] The Marcilhac version of events states that when Bishop William III of Cahors asked Tulle in 1112, or shortly after, to reach a

---

[82] Note the absence of names and some other normally routine details from those stories with the more fantastic or fanciful plots: I.7 (an unnamed wife's attempted suicide), I.13 (a man hangs unharmed for three days), I.17 (an unnamed knight has his teeth grow back).

[83] For the course of the dispute see E. Rupin, *Roc-Amadour: étude historique et archéologique* (Paris, 1904), pp. 87–93, 96–100.

[84] *Ibid.*, p. 88 n. 2; *Tulle*, p. 655.

[85] *Tulle*, no. 3.

settlement with their opponents, to whom the bishop had adjudged control of the church, the abbey resisted. A party from Tulle arrived at Rocamadour, stripped the church down and left nothing but the chains that pilgrims had deposited there in the past.[86] In this they were supported by the brother of Abbot Ebles, Viscount Raymond of Turenne (d. c.1125). If this account does have a basis in fact, the events described possibly took place around the time (1114) that Tulle obtained a second bull from Paschal II confirming its possessions.[87] The dispute smouldered on thereafter, with Tulle retaining effective control of Rocamadour. A formal resolution was only reached when Pope Celestine III ruled in Tulle's favour in 1193.[88]

The miracles, then, were written against the background of institutional rivalry between two monasteries which bore directly on the identity and status of the monks at Rocamadour. To this extent any activity on their part that went beyond the norms of monastic routine – including the manner in which they dealt with pilgrims and the writing of the miracles – was most likely informed by sensitivity to this issue. Beyond this, however, it is difficult to establish a direct connection. Certainly, it is reasonable to suppose that Tulle was involved in the decision to create the miracle collection: it is unlikely that a priory that was within quite easy reach of its mother house would have undertaken a work of this type and length as an independent initiative. And it is probable that there were considerations of human and material resources that required Tulle's support. Thus it must have been to Tulle's purpose to project the image of a renowned and successful pilgrimage centre flourishing under its supervision. But it would be unwise to go beyond this because we do not have evidence for the precise state of play in the dispute with Marcilhac at the time that the collection was made. If the Tulle position was particularly threatened in the early 1170s, this has left no trace. If anything, the Marcilhac version of events, which was probably written shortly before the settlement of 1193, suggests that it acknowledged that Tulle's control of Rocamadour had become secure *de facto* by the middle of the century at the latest.[89] Also, it is noteworthy that the connection between Tulle and Rocamadour, though present, is not a theme that is emphasized in the miracles: Abbot Gerald of Tulle appears almost literally in passing, bringing news of a miracle that took place in Spain on his return from a pilgrimage to Santiago de Compostela.[90] Similarly, while there are indications that Rocamadour's community perceived itself as a southerly outlier of ecclesiastical networks centred on the Limousin, and most likely the priory was largely staffed by monks from that orbit, this too is not emphasized. If, as

---

[86] *Tulle*, p. 655.
[87] *Tulle*, no. 601.
[88] *Ibid.*, nos. 623–4; Rupin, *Roc-Amadour*, pp. 96–9. The case was revisited by Innocent III in 1212: Rupin, *Roc-Amadour*, p. 100.
[89] *Tulle*, pp. 655–7.
[90] I.36.

Jean Rocacher has argued, Tulle's control of Rocamadour amounted to an expression of a 'politique expansioniste du Limousin',[91] then the miracle collection is at most a very muted victory celebration. The international emphasis of the stories means that they could have been nothing more than an oblique appeal to the devotional loyalties of those who lived in the particular parts of eastern Quercy where the interests and territorial power of Tulle and Marcilhac most heavily overlapped.[92]

A second line of inquiry is suggested by the doctrinal orthodoxy and devotional intensity that inform the miracle collection. Were the stories conceived as assertions of correct Catholic belief and as lessons in some of the ways in which the faithful should translate that belief into appropriate behaviour in the face of the growth of dualist heresy in southern France from around the middle of the twelfth century? In broad terms there is much to support this hypothesis. Both as one example among many of a cult centre, and more specifically as a consequence of its Marian identity, Rocamadour could be seen to represent a range of fundamental doctrinal positions and practices that clearly differentiated between Catholic and Cathar belief-systems – for example, notions concerning the relationship between the material world and the spiritual domain as reflected in the idea of saintly intervention and intercession, the human and divine nature of Christ, and the authority of the institutions of the Church in people's lives. In addition, the basic idea of a threat posed by heretics – even if their ideas were not clearly understood – must have been very present to southern French ecclesiastics by the early 1170s: a well-publicized debate between Cathar leaders and orthodox clergy had been staged at Lombers, near Albi, in 1165; in 1167 the developing Cathar community in the south had taken the important step of organizing itself into bishoprics; and only a few years after the Rocamadour miracles were composed, the Third Lateran Council of 1179 was to treat heresy as a grave danger.[93] With the benefit of hindsight we know that Catharism did not affect all parts of the Midi equally, its influence being most concentrated to the south and south-west of Rocamadour in the areas centred on Albi, Toulouse and Carcassonne. But this would not have been obvious to observers in the early decades of the heresy's growth. And from the particular perspective of Rocamadour's regional location, it is perhaps significant that there were indications of the spread of Catharism into the neighbouring Agenais by the late 1160s.[94] To this extent, then, it is reasonable to conclude that the author of the miracles was aware that he was producing material that was predicated on basic ways of thinking and behaving that were being more vigorously contested than they had ever been before, at least in western Europe.

[91] *Rocamadour et son pèlerinage*, i.36.
[92] For references to local people, see I.2; I.6; I.33; I.39; I.41; II.27.
[93] M. D. Lambert, *The Cathars* (Oxford, 1998), pp. 41–2, 45–8, 83.
[94] *Ibid.*, pp. 69–73.

On the other hand, there is no obviously direct link between this possible background and the writing of the collection. No story deals directly with heresy, and the one possible exception is unlikely to be about a Cathar. Book II c. 40 describes how a knight from the Toulousain lost his mind (*amens et sui non compos*) and started to blaspheme against Christ the Saviour and his Mother, claiming that he had renounced God and sworn allegiance in a written instrument to the devil. His family and friends vowed a wax model equal to his weight to Our Lady of Rocamadour, and he regained his senses. The location fits a possible heretical context, as do hints in the story that the knight remained more rational than losing one's mind might imply, subscribing to some formal belief-system rather than simply denigrating orthodox Christianity. But this is a slender basis on which to build any suggestion that what was being described was a Cathar reverting to orthodoxy. If this were so, it would represent a use of coded language and metaphor that is not paralleled elsewhere in the collection. In the absence of direct engagements with the issues raised by heresy, it is safest to conclude that the miracles were written in the spirit of asserting and vindicating orthodoxy, as must have been the case with any sustained treatment of Catholic belief written in the Midi in this period, but that they were not primarily conceived as a response to Catharism.

A third hypothesis flows from Rocamadour's status as an institution affecting its immediate social, economic and religious environment. Here the central factor to consider is the success of the monastery of Obazine, 42 km to the north in the southern Limousin, in establishing a tight network of properties close to Rocamadour and in the process creating a relationship with the priory that was unmatched by any other monastic foundation in the region. In order to explore the ramifications of this, it is useful to sketch in outline how Obazine was able to impose its presence in Rocamadour's neighbourhood. In many respects the emergence of Obazine conforms to a pattern that is familiar from the history of reformed monasticism in the twelfth century. It had an influential founder-figure in the shape of Stephen of Vielzot, whose Life describes him searching for an opportunity to practise his vision of asceticism and contemplation; a group of followers built up around him; institutional structures emerged as the community grew; and relationships were forged with the wider world in the form of support given by ecclesiastical and secular leaders.[95] In 1142 the monastery of Obazine was consecrated by the bishop of Limoges, with Stephen as its abbot. In 1147–48 it was absorbed into the Cistercian order. The abbey attracted the support of the major kindreds in the Bas Limousin, most notably the viscounts of Comborn, Ventadour and Turenne, as well as many lesser families. A

---

[95] *Vie de Saint Etienne*, I.2–14, II.1–3, pp. 44–66, 94–100; B. Barrière, *L'abbaye cistercienne d'Obazine en Bas-Limousin: Les origines – le patrimoine* (Tulle, 1977), pp. 44–69.

substantial part of Obazine's appeal to the local aristocracy was the provision made for women in the nearby nunnery at Coyroux, the building of which began as early as c.1140.[96] The female community there would seem, in fact, to have outgrown the number of monks at Obazine, an indication that its development was a central element of Stephen's programme. Significantly a substantial number of grants of property and rights to Obazine were linked to women entering Coyroux. And women would seem to have been important figures in the networks of related noble kindreds which gave Stephen's foundations their support.[97]

The most important expression of the support of high-status families was, of course, the transfer of resources to the monks in the form of landed property rights. It is here that we can begin to see the impact that Obazine made on Rocamadour. As Bernadette Barrière's researches into Obazine's properties have demonstrated, there was a remarkable, and sustained, growth in its acquisitions during the abbacies of Stephen and his two immediate successors Gerald I (1159–1164) and Robert (1164–1188).[98] Already during Stephen's period of rule the main pattern of resource distribution was becoming clear. Thereafter the priority was not so much to gain new holdings but to round off existing ones. To this end large sums were spent in making counter-gifts to or making purchases from those willing to transfer their rights in units of agricultural exploitation – *villae* and *bordariae* – in which Obazine already had an interest. In addition to the sums of money expended there were also substantial hidden costs for the monks in that it was quite common for the surrendering of rights or the confirmation of earlier grants to be bound up with a lay person's entry into the monastic life. To this extent Obazine's experience of expansion followed by consolidation is typical of many monastic foundations in this period. But the point to note is that in this specific instance the process resulted in the creation of two distinct and compact clusters of landed resources, which is an indication that although decisions about the timing and location of grants of property were substantially a matter for lay benefactors rather than the recipient monks, the abbey had clear policies about where to concentrate its efforts. Benefaction was not a one-way process: the monks could make careful decisions about which families and localities to target, and the weight of documentation in the abbey's cartulary reveals that this is precisely what happened.

As is to be expected, one of the clusters of property was situated in the vicinity of Obazine itself.[99] This constituted the core resource which enabled Obazine, Coyroux and offshoot communities in the Bas Limousin to function. But a mapping of the abbey's acquisitions also reveals that there

[96] *Vie de Saint Etienne*, II.3, pp. 98–100. See Barrière, *L'abbaye cistercienne*, pp. 91–108.
[97] Barrière, *L'abbaye cistercienne*, pp. 125–9.
[98] *Ibid.*, pp. 109–82.
[99] See map in Barrière, *L'abbaye cistercienne*, facing p. 182.

was a second cluster, located to the south in Haut Quercy and separated from the zone around Obazine by a belt of territory in the southern Limousin.[100] Various reasons for this discontinuous pattern can be suggested. The intermediate area had a long-established pattern of monastic settlement thanks to the Benedictine abbeys of Uzerche, Tulle, Vigeois and Beaulieu. Their presence would have limited the scope for a newer foundation to develop a network of properties. The part of Haut Quercy around Rocamadour, on the other hand, was significantly freer of potentially competing monastic interests. It is also possible that the monks of Obazine were mindful of Cistercian legislation against locating granges – centres of agricultural production – at inconvenient distances from the abbey they served. The cluster in Haut Quercy balanced various needs: it was close enough to Obazine to offer it substantial economic benefits, but also sufficiently distant to be worth developing as a discrete network.

Rocamadour was situated in the very heart of this southern cluster. It was very common, of course, for different churches to create property networks that brought them into close proximity with others, and in broad terms there was nothing exceptional in the idea of one religious community emerging as the dominant landed presence in another's immediate vicinity. But in the case of Rocamadour the extent and nature of that presence is nonetheless noteworthy. Three granges – Les Alys, Couzon and La Dame – had developed very close to the priory by the 1160s; a fourth, at Bonnecoste, appeared around the time that the miracle collection was being written. Of these, Les Alys, 2 km to the north-west of Rocamadour on the far side of the Alzou, was the centre of the complex. An interesting indication of the importance of the granges is Barrière's calculation that of the approximately 53,5000s. spent by Obazine under Abbot Robert on the acquisition and rounding off of properties, nearly 21,000s. went towards the cluster near Rocamadour.[101] In other words, the miracles were composed at a time when a vigorous policy of expansion and investment on the part of another monastic community was in full force right on the priory's doorstep.

What were the implications for Rocamadour? It is reasonable to suppose that Obazine's concentration of effort in the area was partly a response to the needs and opportunities created by pilgrimage traffic, and in this way stimulated economic activity of benefit to both communities. There is an interesting irony in the fact that the roughness and remoteness of the terrain around Rocamadour, which we have seen was interpreted by the author of the miracles as a sign of the Virgin's favour, was from another perspective the point of entry for Obazine's presence in the area. Moreover, by the 1170s that presence must have been negating the idea of an undeveloped wilderness. In any event, the notion of a wilderness was to some extent a construct as well as

[100] *Ibid.*, pp. 167–71, 176–9 and map facing p. 172.
[101] *Ibid.*, p. 179.

an expression of observable reality: it was Obazine's practice to acquire existing units of agricultural exploitation as well as to create new ones from unworked land. This can be observed in the documents preserved in the abbey's cartulary, many of which detail the grant of *villae* and *bordariae* that were already functioning. This means that Obazine's economic contribution to the area around Rocamadour operated on two levels: more agricultural activity was made possible; and the greater integration of resources within a single organizational framework, as opposed to their dispersal among a multiplicity of parties, would have encouraged a more efficient generation of surplus for sale. In so far as the meagre charter evidence on Rocamadour's part can reveal, it would seem that the priory did not have a substantial landed presence in its locality. Much of its income would have been in the form of cash from pilgrims. It therefore stood to benefit enormously from the economic growth taking place around it.

Nor was Rocamadour in a position to be threatened by Obazine in terms of its monastic identity. It would be a mistake to set the relationship between the two monasteries in the context of antipathy and rivalry between the traditional and reformed expressions of the religious life that they represented. In recent years scholars have been moving away from the once popular view that the old and the new in twelfth-century monasticism were cast as opponents.[102] The notion of conflict reads too much, for example, into the more confrontational rhetoric to be found in the polemical debates between some Cluniacs and Cistercians, whereas there is a great deal of evidence for mutual respect and co-operation. The corollary of this is that it is unrealistic to imagine that the typical reaction of older monasticism when confronted with newer orders was one of resentment and a sense of being passed over. Specifically in the context of Rocamadour's experience, it is important to note that relationships between different monastic institutions were not only governed by perceptions of type and order; overlapping these broad categories were more complex ties created by a host of factors such as unions of confraternity, regional allegiance and political sympathy, friendship networks, and family connections. A number of suggestive links between Rocamadour and Obazine can be detected. Stephen of Vielzot came from an area on the borders of the Auvergne and the Limousin in which one of the prominent aristocratic kindreds were the lords of Escorailles.[103] Members of this family are found associated with Stephen at various junctures as followers and benefactors, and it is possible that Stephen himself was related to them in some way. The Escorailles family also looms large in the history of Rocamadour's mother-house at Tulle: a Gerald of Escorailles became abbot

---

[102] See G. Constable, *The Reformation of the Twelfth Century* (Cambridge, 1996) for an excellent discussion of the nature of reform in this period and its implications for the exponents of older-style monasticism.

[103] *Vie de Saint Etienne*, I.1, p. 42; Barrière, *L'abbaye cistercienne*, pp. 44–5, 161–2.

in 1152, and this man or someone closely related to him was abbot at the time of the writing of the miracles.[104] The bishop of Cahors in the second half of the twelfth century was a member of the family, as was Manfred, the dean of Mauriac, whose reminiscences were one of the sources for the miracle collection and who spent his final years in virtual retirement at Rocama-dour.[105] With these links in mind, it is unsurprising that the little direct evidence we have for links between Rocamadour/Tulle and Obazine points towards an uncontentious relationship.[106]

Indeed, it is the closeness of the relationship with Obazine which might help to explain the creation of the miracle collection. The miracles were not a defiant assertion of old-style monastic worth in the face of reformist pressures. But they do implicitly differentiate between the experiences of Rocamadour and Obazine in a fundamental way in their emphasis upon the widely dispersed, international quality of the pilgrimage centre's appeal. In contrast to a number of miracle collections that draw particular attention to the dynamic between church and local population, the Rocamadour material has, for a text of its length, notably little to say about the people, and particularly the arms-bearing classes, of Haut Quercy.[107] The one reference to a member of the local aristocracy is not positive: the story of some hunting dogs allowed to wander too close to the church is critical of their owner and draws attention to Rocamadour's detachment from its immediate environ-ment as a special holy space.[108] In stark contrast the cartulary of Obazine reveals that a large number of noble and knightly families around Rocama-dour, often those linked to the vicomital houses of Turenne and Comborn which supported the monastery, were active as benefactors and supporters: for example, the viscounts of Brassac and the lords of Belcastel, Miers, Curemonte and Saint-Michel.[109] The paucity of equivalent charter material for Rocamadour makes it impossible to state how far these sorts of families were also active in support of that church, but it is extremely unlikely that a pattern of local patronage was established on the scale of that enjoyed by Obazine. The miracles may therefore be seen as a statement of Rocamadour's distance from the local networks of the Obazine type. Both economically and

[104] It is usually supposed that the abbot in 1172 was Gerald of Escorailles, whose dates are traditionally given as 1152–88. Geoffrey of Vigeois, however, suggests that the Abbot Gerald of Escorailles elected in 1152 ruled for only eight years: 'Chronica', c. 53, p. 307. On the other hand the Abbot Gerald attested in the 1170s was the *germanus* of Manfred of Escorailles: *Chronique de Saint-Pierre-le-Vif,* pp. 216–18 (a letter of 1175). See also Geoffrey of Vigeois, 'Chronica', c. 68, p. 320.

[105] *Chronique de Saint-Pierre-le-Vif,* p. 214; Dufour, *Les évêques,* p. 65. See II.22–3.

[106] Barrière, *L'abbaye cistercienne,* pp. 40, 171–2, 177. See *Cartulaire de l'abbaye cistercienne d'Obazine (XIIe–XIIIe siècle),* ed. B. Barrière (Clermont-Ferrand, 1989), nos. 129, 478, 562, 661.

[107] For references to local people see I.2; I.6; I.33; I.39; I.41.

[108] II.25.

[109] Barrière, *L'abbaye cistercienne,* pp. 34–5, 116–24.

in terms of its constituency of actual and potential devotees, Rocamadour was placing itself on a different level, permitting it to assert its identity and find a *modus vivendi* with its vigorous, popular neighbour.

This can only be a hypothesis, but it is suggestive because it takes into account what may have been the experiences and perceptions of the author of the miracles and his fellow-monks in terms of changes in the community's circumstances close in time and space to the act of writing. The same consideration also applies to a fourth possible factor, which similarly turns on the manner in which Rocamadour might have reacted to local change by shaping the image of itself that it projected onto the wider world. Here the starting point is an entry in the closely contemporary chronicle written by Robert of Torigny, the abbot of Mont-Saint-Michel in Normandy:

> Henry king of the English went on pilgrimage to Rocamadour, which occupies a site in Quercy which is surrounded by mountains and is horribly remote. Some people say that the Blessed Amator was the servant of the Blessed Mary and sometime steward and tutor of the Lord. When the most gentle Mother of the Lord was assumed into the heavenly mansions, this Amator acted on her instructions and crossed to Gaul, spending a long life as a hermit in the aforementioned place. When he died he was buried in the entrance to an oratory dedicated to the Blessed Mary. And the site was for a long time little regarded, except that people used to say that the Blessed Amator's body was lying there, even though his exact location was unknown. In the year of the Incarnation 1166, a woman who lived in those parts was nearing the end of her life and ordered her household – perhaps through divine inspiration – to have her body buried in the entrance to the oratory. A hole was therefore dug in the ground, whereupon the body of the Blessed Amator was discovered intact. It was placed in the church next to the altar, where it is shown in its entirety to pilgrims. And in this place there occur many miracles, and ones hitherto unheard-of, through the Blessed Mary.[110]

Why Robert should have been interested in events at Rocamadour is not immediately clear, but the fact that he knew of Henry II's pilgrimage there in 1170, and the inclusion later in his text of a miracle story set at Rocamadour and datable to c.1180, reveal that he had some degree of close and sustained contact, no doubt facilitated by the movement of informants between parts of Henry's dominions.[111] Robert's interest may have been stimulated by the fact that he was abbot of a celebrated pilgrimage church with affinities to Rocamadour. In particular, there is evidence for a cult of St Michael at Rocamadour which was probably linked to the regular association between that saint and rocky, precipitous sites such as Mont-Saint-Michel itself and

[110] Robert of Torigny, *Chronica*, p. 248.
[111] See *ibid.*, pp. 292–4.

Monte Gargano in Italy.[112] Robert's account of what happened in 1166 may therefore be treated as based on solid information reaching him through secure channels. Certain imprecisions in the story as Robert relates it – the absence of a name for the woman and his qualifying 'some people say' – suggest that he was not working from a written version. But the story resembles many other narratives fashioned by religious communities about the discovery of relics. It is therefore reasonable to trace its origins back to the monks of Rocamadour. In other words, Robert's account would seem to be a reflection of an effort to publicize the discovery of St Amator's body and by extension Rocamadour itself.

It is easy to be cynical about religious communities' claimed discoveries of relics, and to treat them as staged, manipulated events. But this view is simplistic. Manipulation there certainly was, but it is important to establish its exact forms. In the first place, chance discoveries of bodies must have been made quite often in the sort of circumstances that Robert describes. Also it is important to note that larger churches and the areas around them must often have resembled building sites: programmes of enlargement or new construction could involve years, if not decades, of work, and in the process it must have been quite common to excavate traces of past generations' use of the site. The site of Rocamadour itself was beginning to be developed in the third quarter of the twelfth century. So it is perfectly possible that the discovery of the remains identified as those of Amator was indeed a chance event. But what was done with the find in such circumstances is what matters. Each claim for a discovered saint in this period represented a specific strategy on the part of a religious institution to interweave an interpretation of the object (the remains) and the circumstances of its discovery in order to create a precise explanatory narrative. For every skeleton interpreted as belonging to a saint there must have been many others that were not privileged in this way by their discoverers. In other words, the equation made between unearthed remains and Amator the saint amounted to a deliberate policy on Rocamadour's part to modify its self-identity and the way in which outsiders perceived it, courtesy of the publicity attached to the find.

This is significant because although most of the miracles in the Rocamadour collection involve incidents that took place elsewhere and were then reported to the monks – in the process drawing attention to the international character of the pilgrimage's appeal, as we have seen – a significant minority of cases are located at Rocamadour itself in circumstances that allowed the author to say something of the devotional environment within which the miracles occurred. This type of miracle story – typically involving cures 'on site' – is sufficiently common to suggest that it was not included simply because the writer was at hand to observe the events

[112] Rocacher, *Rocamadour et son pèlerinage*, i.131–51.

for himself, but rather represents a deliberate authorial strategy intended to nuance the principal emphasis on geographical dispersal by including material demonstrating what it was at and about Rocamadour that connected pilgrims and the miraculous.[113] In this connection, Robert of Torigny's statement that the monks translated St Amator's body in order to aid access to it by pilgrims is very significant when set against the complete absence of any mention of this saint in the miracle stories, even in those cases in which a miraculous cure took place within the church and thus only yards from where Amator's tomb was situated. This could be explained by the fact that *miracula* sometimes focus on one saint to the exclusion of others venerated in the same location; and of course there was no way in which to elevate Amator to a status matching the Virgin herself. Nevertheless the omission of any reference, in a lengthy text devoted to the theme of saintly intervention, to a saint with Marian connections and one discovered in that very place only a few years earlier must be seen as deliberate.

Thus the question why this should be so presents itself. It is possible that a choice was made about how Rocamadour could further its reputation, particularly in the context of attracting pilgrims travelling to or from Santiago de Compostela.[114] Major Marian centres were quite few along the pilgrimage roads in southern and central France – Le Puy being an obvious exception – and clearly an emphasis upon Rocamadour's associations with Our Lady would resonate far more than a hitherto little-known saint such as Amator. Not that cult centres on the pilgrimage routes needed universal saints in order to flourish: there were many that were rooted in their own regions. But the more region-specific cults that punctuated the pilgrim's journey – for example St Martial at Limoges and St Eutropius at Saintes – tended to be of long standing, which meant that they were established features of the devotional landscape geared to attracting outsiders as well as their own local populations. It would have been difficult to promote the cult of St Amator in similar terms.

Amator's absence from the miracle stories may also point to debate within the monasteries of Rocamadour and Tulle about the validity of the identification between the discovered remains and the saint, and their misgivings about the appropriateness of developing a cult around him. If so, the miracles would represent a revision of the publicity efforts that can be detected through Robert of Torigny. This can only be a suggestion. But whether Rocamadour's concern with Amator was about how to maximize the church's reputation or a more fundamental problem with the appropriateness of the cult, it is clear that the miracle stories amount to a detailed

[113] See I.5–6; I.21–2; I.26; I.33; I.34; I.36; I.38; II.5; II.10; II.16; II.24; II.26–7; II.36.
[114] For Rocamadour's place within the complex of routes to Compostela, see L. Vázquez de Parga, J. M. Lacarra and J. Uría Ríu, *Las peregrinaciones a Santiago de Compostela*, 3 vols. (Madrid, 1948–49), ii.66. A number of the Rocamadour stories reveal an awareness of the importance of the Compostela pilgrimage: I.4; I.24; I.36; II.44.

effort to 'Marianize', or perhaps 're-Marianize', Rocamadour's identity, viewed in terms of both the monks' self-perception and the church's renown in the outside world. This helps to explain the abrupt disjunction in the concluding part of Robert of Torigny's account, in which he jumps from describing Amator's translation to the statement that today Mary performs many miracles at that place. Amator may have helped to put Rocamadour on the cultic map; it was unambiguously the case that Mary would be the one to keep it there. In addition, it is worth remembering that Rocamadour did not claim any relics of the Virgin to bolster its status. A cult such as that of St Amator squarely based on the discovery of relics could have drawn attention to this and blurred the signals being sent out about the church's place in the devotional landscape.

This conclusion is supported by the subsequent history of Amator's cult, which suggests that the assertion of Rocamadour's Marian identity did limit its development. By the later Middle Ages a number of legends were in circulation offering differing versions of who Amator was and how he came to be buried at Rocamadour; the details were sometimes at variance with Robert of Torigny's statements about the saint.[115] For the earliest extant full Life we have to look to a fourteenth-century Italian manuscript copy of a text that was probably written earlier, possibly in the Limousin.[116] Even allowing for the likelihood that much material has been lost – for example, in the fire that destroyed the church's archive in the fifteenth century – it does not appear likely that the cult of Amator generated a substantial body of texts. The mutability of ideas about Amator's identity suggests that this was a low-profile cult which was kept alive at Rocamadour but little more. By way of a postscript, it may be noted that the cult did not find its way into the breviary of the diocese of Cahors – in other words become part of the formal liturgical cycle of its own region – until the mid-nineteenth century. It was Mary whose cult swamped all others and whose association with Rocamadour remained predominant.

The contemporary political and military context

In examining the background to the writing of the Rocamadour miracle collection, it is useful to consider one further factor: the experience of violence in general and of warfare in particular. Although it would be an exaggeration to regard this as the main stimulus behind the *miracula*, it certainly had a significant influence on how the material was selected, presented and con-textualized. A substantial number of the stories address this aspect of contemporary life in various ways, and collectively they amount to the

[115] See Rupin, *Roc-Amadour*, pp. 9–72; B. Bulles, 'Saint Amadour: Formation et évolution de sa légende (XIIe–XXe siècle)', *Annales du Midi*, 107 (1995), pp. 437–55.
[116] See E. Albe, 'La vie et les miracles de S. Amator', *Analecta Bollandiana*, 28 (1909), pp. 57–90.

most prominent formulation of the Virgin's – and Rocamadour's – projection onto the lives of people in the outside world beyond the contexts of her cures of the sick and lame and her protection of those threatened by natural forces. Indeed, the incidence of stories involving violence in some form – be it knightly combat, theft of property, or assault on the person – suggests that they feature in the collection, not as a neutral reflection of the fact that twelfth-century Europe was often a troubled and dangerous place, but rather because they were included to express a belief on the part of the monks at Rocamadour that their cult was engaged in a dynamic relationship with some of the problems created by violence, and by extension was able to offer various solutions to those problems.

This interest in violence is evident on one level in the large number of stories that feature lords or knights – in other words, those social groups that not only made it their business to specialize in fighting in functional terms but also exploited military language and imagery, alongside that rooted in ideas of family and property, as a central facet of how they construed their own identity and communicated it to other social groups.[117] So, even though a number of the Rocamadour stories describe members of the arms-bearing aristocracy (or those who can be safely assumed to belong to that type) in situations in which their military activities and knightly image are not immediately relevant – for example, coping with illness or domestic crisis[118] – their status as fighters would have been present to the reader or listener as an automatic function of who these men were and the social roles that were bound up with their position.

What significance, then, attaches to the large number of adult, male aristocrats to be found in the stories? Their predominance should not be read as a sign that the author of the collection wanted to exclude either women and children or men from other social levels. There is ample evidence that pilgrims from these categories went to Rocamadour and, more to the point, were in a position to be given a sympathetic hearing if they had a miraculous incident to describe.[119] Moreover, the frequency of arms-bearers in the stories must to a large extent be a simple function of their greater wealth and mobility, and their relative freedom from the sorts of domestic, agricultural or occupational ties that could have inhibited members of other groups. There is thus an element of self-selection in a text that so clearly stresses the

---

[117] Cf. Signori, 'Miracle Kitchen', pp. 286–7. For good treatments of the aristocracy and its image see M. H. Keen, *Chivalry* (New Haven, 1984); D. Crouch, *The Image of Aristocracy in Britain, 1000–1300* (London, 1992); P. Coss, *The Knight in Medieval England 1000–1400* (Stroud, 1993); J. A. Green, *The Aristocracy of Norman England* (Cambridge, 1997); J. Flori, *Chevaliers et chevalerie au Moyen Age* (Paris, 1998); C. B. Bouchard, *Strong of Body, Brave and Noble: Chivalry and Society in Medieval France* (Ithaca, 1998).

[118] E.g. I.7; I.8; I.9; I.12; I.48; I.52; II.6; II.7; II.24; II.40; III.2; III.3; III.9; III.11; III.14.

[119] E.g. I.3; I.16; I.20; I.21; I.22; I.23; I.26; I.28; I.33; I.39; I.43; I.44; II.5; II.9; II.11; II.14; II.19; II.21; II.29; II.36; III.19; III.20; III.21.

wide geographical distribution of Mary's devotees. It is useful to note that, by contrast, miracle collections which focus more tightly on the local or regional impact of their saint's cult often give greater prominence to women and to lower-status individuals. In other words, it would be mistaken to read the miracles as evidence that the cult of the Virgin at Rocamadour privileged high-status males solely as a matter of calculated policy on the part of the monks there.

That said, however, it is clear that the cult did not function as simply some form of passive indicator of the sorts of people who chose to present themselves at Rocamadour as pilgrims. The miracle stories themselves represent an active exercise in defining and communicating what the Virgin offered her followers, and in the process they preserved choices about the types of people whom the monks wanted to feel included as actual or potential devotees, and about the problems for which they could realistically entertain hopes of a solution. In other words, the Rocamadour miracles – no more than any other example of the genre – are not an encyclopaedic survey either of all the groups that comprised medieval society or of the totality of problems that people faced in the many different aspects of their lives. *Miracula* were exercises in selectivity. To this extent, then, the prominence accorded members of the aristocracy in the Rocamadour material – more pronounced than that evident, for example, in the closely contemporary Becket miracles, and comparable to that found in the Conques stories of the previous century – is evidence for an awareness on the part of the monks that their cult was attractive to men of that class in ways that permitted a dialogue to take place between them.

The stories reveal an interest in the impact of violence on both individuals and groups. The significance of this may be explored by considering Rocamadour's position in relation to areas where conflict was either taking place or at least latent. Not all the instances of violence in the miracles can be reduced to clear geographical and political patterns, of course. The story of a predatory lord who threatens a pilgrim in the northern marches of Poitou, for instance, describes events that could potentially have been played out in any part of Europe, or at least in those places where castellans were not wholly disciplined by the laws and policing of rulers. Here the identity of the lord and his location amount to incidental information: his 'Poitevinness' is not at issue, nor is he held up as untypical of men of his status.[120] Similarly, other stories relate events that were so far removed from Rocamadour's social and political environment that they amount to representative types – the sorts of happenings that could take place somewhere 'out there' as particular expressions of conditions that were more or less endemic. But by no means can all the incidences of violence in the stories be treated as randomly distributed flash-points that just happened to be made known to

[120] I.24.

the Rocamadour monks. Behind many of them there lies an interpretative framework that points to their being seen as parts of larger patterns, one that was shaped by an understanding of Rocamadour's regional situation. For it was an important consequence of Rocamadour's location that it was situated in an area in which the effects of various conflicts overlapped. This becomes clear if the different conflicts concerned are examined in turn.

The first conflict to note, and the one that bore most on Rocamadour's immediate locality, was that born of the rivalry between Count Raymond V of Toulouse and Henry II, king of England. As duke of Aquitaine through his wife, Eleanor, Henry was the heir to claims to Toulouse that dated back to the end of the eleventh century; Eleanor's grandfather William IX (1086–1126) had intermittently been in possession of the city and parts of its surrounding county, though never for long enough to make Aquitanian control secure. In 1159 Henry launched what was most probably the largest and most ambitious campaign of his career against Toulouse.[121] The scale of the effort, a feature noted by many contemporary observers, is an indication that his interest in that part of the Midi was not in the nature of an addendum in relation to his plans for the heartlands of the 'Angevin Empire' to the west and north. On the contrary, the conquest of Toulouse represented an important element of his territorial policy in the early, expansionist years of his reign. We know with the benefit of hindsight that Toulouse was to remain resistant to absorption into the Aquitanian polity, and that Henry's ambitions were to be realized more fully elsewhere in France as well as in the British Isles. But the eventual, and never complete, marginalization of central southern France as an element within the Angevin orbit was by no means a foregone conclusion in 1159, nor would it have so appeared for many years thereafter – certainly not by the time that the Rocamadour miracles were composed.

As is well known, Henry II was unsuccessful in his efforts to take Toulouse, in part because Count Raymond was able to draw Louis VII of France into the conflict; the king's rare foray into the deep south of his kingdom meant that Henry was confronted with the prospect of allowing the dispute to grow into an unwanted war with his overlord.[122] But whereas scholarly attention is usually paid to Henry's failure outside Toulouse – the first substantial setback in his career – it should not be forgotten that the 1159 campaign did result in some important territorial gains in Quercy, the north-western sector of the area traditionally claimed by the counts of Toulouse. However much control of Quercy, including Cahors itself, was in the nature of a consolation prize in the short term, its value as a forward position from which to launch any subsequent attacks on the Toulousain would have been readily apparent to Henry. The significance that the king attached to his gains

---

[121] See Warren, *Henry II*, pp. 82–7.
[122] Warren, *Henry II*, pp. 86–7; Y. Sassier, *Louis VII* (Paris, 1991), pp. 282–6.

in this area is revealed by the fact that he gave responsibility for consolidating and extending his power there to two major figures, his constable Henry of Essex and his chancellor Thomas Becket, still then a loyal servant of his royal master. It is interesting to note that the Life of Becket by William fitz Stephen, written at a time when views on the relationship between Henry and his chancellor were profoundly coloured by the momentous nature of subsequent events, describes in some detail the vigour with which Becket set about his task of imposing Angevin control in the region: an indication both of the ambitious nature of this policy and of the energy with which it was prosecuted.[123]

How might this have affected Rocamadour? William is imprecise about which parts of Quercy were most directly in the front line; if anything, the inference to be drawn from his account of Becket's attention to strategic castles is that the brunt of the military conflict was borne by the southern parts of the county, closest to Toulouse, rather than the more northerly region in which Rocamadour was situated. But even if this were the case, it would be a mistake to imagine a situation in which Haut Quercy – the north – passed smoothly and securely into the Angevin political orbit. For one thing, this area had been on the rough fringes of princely power – a liminal zone between Aquitaine and Toulouse – for a long time before 1159.[124] One indication of this was the extensive power built up there by the most aggressive and prominent local dynasty, the viscounts of Turenne. Geoffrey of Vigeois treated this family as part of the network of interrelated aristocratic kindreds whose members feature at many points in his chronicle.[125] From this perspective, then, Turenne becomes the southernmost element of a political world centred on the Limousin and thus, by extension, a part of the larger Aquitanian space (albeit an often troublesome and rebellious part). But this perspective may distort our view to some extent. There is little reason to cast the viscounts of Turenne as rigidly pro-Aquitanian in their orientation, or as potentially reliable coadjutors of Angevin power.[126] If anything, the growth of direct Angevin intrusion into their region must have been a source of alarm, and would help to explain their involvement in some of the coalitions of lords directed against Henry II

---

[123] William fitz Stephen, 'Vita sancti Thomae, Cantuariensis archiepiscopi et martyris', c. 22, ed. J. C. Robertson, *Materials for the History of Thomas Becket, Archbishop of Canterbury*, vol. 3 (Rolls Series 67:3; London, 1877), p. 34; cf. Herbert of Bosham, 'Vita sancti Thomae, archiepiscopi et martyris', II.11, *ibid.*, pp. 175–6. See also Barlow, *Thomas Becket*, pp. 57–8.

[124] See J. Boussard, *Le gouvernement d'Henri II Plantagenêt* (Paris, 1956), pp. 143–4. For Quercy in this period see J. Lartigaut, 'Nouvelles sociétés et nouvaux espaces (milieu Xe siècle–fin XIIe siècle)', *Histoire du Quercy*, ed. J. Lartigaut (Toulouse, 1993), pp. 91–106.

[125] 'Chronica', cc. 23, 51, 53, 68, pp. 290, 306, 307, 320.

[126] See *Gesta regis Henrici secundi*, ed. W. Stubbs, 2 vols. (Rolls Series, 49; London, 1867), i.115

and later his son Richard. In other words, it is best to see Henry's intervention in Quercy as a destabilizing factor in a region that had over previous decades developed power structures suited to the relative absence of assertive overlordship and to the area's uncertain, but hitherto less contested, status. Significantly, when describing Henry's journey to Rocamadour in 1170, Robert of Torigny includes the significant detail that he took with him a large armed following because he was afraid of his enemies, whose lands he was nearing.[127] And an account of a pilgrimage made there by the count of Flanders at around the same time similarly hints at the problem of dangerous conditions.[128] If not in a full-blown war zone, Rocamadour must nonetheless have found itself starkly confronted by the disruptive effects of princely power-politics at around the time that the miracles were being recorded.

In addition to the disorder and uncertainty created by the Angevin expansion into Quercy, it is also important to consider another, related, conflict: that which pitched the counts of Toulouse against the counts of Barcelona.[129] Viewed in the simple terms of the territories in which and over which this conflict was played out, Rocamadour was not itself immediately touched in the way that it was vulnerable to the effects of Angevin–Toulousain rivalry. But it is worth noting that the monks' perspectives would not only have been shaped by events in their own locality; they were also influenced by information reaching them from further afield. In this context it is significant that, although the distribution of the provenance of pilgrims in the miracle collection suggests that information networks reached out in all directions and over a variety of distances, there is a substantial weighting of material originating to the east and south-east of Rocamadour. This is to be expected because of the importance of the pilgrimage routes to Santiago de Compostela as arteries of communication, and the benefits to Rocamadour of situating itself within that matrix. The effect is that what is, roughly speaking, Rocamadour's south-easterly quadrant, from southern Burgundy round through Provence, Languedoc and the eastern Pyrenees, and up to the Toulousain, was the single most important zone viewed in terms of where the monks believed their cult of Our Lady was making an impact. This is significant because it was precisely in this zone – or more accurately in multiple dispersed areas within it – that the conflict between Toulouse and Barcelona was played out.

This conflict receives relatively little scholarly attention compared to the other great contest for political mastery in twelfth-century France – that

---

[127] *Chronica*, p. 248.
[128] Lambert of Wattrelos, 'Annales Cameracenses', *MGH SS* 16.553–4.
[129] See C. Higounet, 'Un grand chapitre de l'histoire du XIIe siècle: La rivalité des maisons de Toulouse et de Barcelone pour la prépondérance méridionale', *Mélanges Louis Halphen* (Paris, 1951), pp. 313–22; R. Abadal i de Vinyals, 'A propos de la "domination" de la maison comtale barcelonaise sur le Midi français', *Annales du Midi*, 76 (1964), pp. 315–45.

between the Capetian kings and the Norman and Angevin kings of England in their capacity as powerful French feudatories. The reason for the relative neglect is largely to be found in a problem that was discussed above: the absence in the south of the historiographical traditions that, for the north, have left us the sort of material that often permits detailed and nuanced reconstructions of events. It may seem somewhat strange to bemoan this fact; after all, medieval history as an academic discipline has long since outgrown its nineteenth- and early twentieth-century reliance on narrative sources, and most medievalists do not study them routinely. But the study of wars – as opposed to warfare as a social and cultural presence independent of its particular manifestations at any given moment, explicable only with reference to long-term economic, political and ideological patterns – is an event-driven type of history. The lack of a substantial body of material that can meet this need for the south of France means that by extension the wider processes behind warfare there remain largely obscure. What is more, it is not simply a problem of a lack of raw data, for it is noteworthy that warfare was a theme that engaged many of the northern chroniclers and featured in their understandings of how political authority was expressed and contested. The result is that where the narrative evidence is abundant it permits an analysis not just of what can be learned on the basis of chronological precisions but also of the complex ways in which different levels of royal, aristocratic, ecclesiastical, feudal and familial interest interacted to start, sustain, control and resolve conflicts. This sort of layered analysis is more difficult with regard to the Midi, with the result that scholars are often driven to argue in terms of endemic and persistent conditions – for instance, political fragmentation, weak feudal ties, under-resourced princely power, competition for the fruits of economic growth – as in some sense givens that suffice to explain why warfare was widespread.[130] Doubtless, factors of this sort were very significant, but they could not have been the whole story to judge by analogy with other areas about which we are better informed.[131]

In order to gain a sense of what was at stake in the Midi, it is useful to look further north to the conflict between the Angevins and Capetians. Theirs was not a national war waged by internally cohesive and homogenous political units. Rather it was a struggle for economic and political resource – conceptualized in terms of a wide range of contestable quantities such as rights, landed property, courts, strongholds, status, honour, prestige and

---

[130] See A. Fliche, 'L'état toulousain', *Histoire des institutions françaises au moyen âge. I: Les institutions seigneuriales*, ed. F. Lot and R. Fawtier (Paris, 1957), pp. 74–84; W. L. Wakefield, *Heresy, Crusade and Inquisition in Southern France 1100–1250* (London, 1974), pp. 50–4; J. Sumption, *The Albigensian Crusade* (London, 1978), pp. 18–23; J. Given, *State and Society in Medieval Europe: Gwynedd and Languedoc under Outside Rule* (Ithaca, 1990), pp. 19–25.

[131] For an excellent recent study of the Midi, which reveals the value of literary materials as historical evidence, see. L. M. Paterson, *The World of the Troubadours: Medieval Occitan Society, c.1100–c.1300* (Cambridge, 1993).

dynastic success. This struggle was shaped by the actions of assertive and rich rulers whose resources and authority made them the focal points of disputes that could draw in a host of other rivalries and interests. Strong rulership, or at least rulership that aspired to strength, did not exist to catalyze conflicts that would otherwise not have happened – to release violent forces somehow present in medieval society – but it had the potential to accentuate other conflicts that clustered around, and fed off, it. For example, the rebellion of 1173–74, which came very close to overwhelming Henry II, amounted to a loose coalition – its looseness is what saved the king – of aristocratic interests pursuing different agendas but linked by a shared resistance to Angevin power. Similarly, Geoffrey of Vigeois has much to say about how lords in and around the Limousin fought each other, but he also recognized that support for or opposition to supra-regional figures such as Henry II or Richard could activate collective responses that, in the process, enlarged the scope and impact of the resulting warfare.[132] It is well known that the greatest military leader of the later twelfth century, Richard the Lionheart, died from wounds suffered while besieging a minor castle in the Limousin rather than in direct conflict with his highest-status foes such as Saladin or Philip Augustus of France. But the rebellious vassal in that castle was part of a network of aristocratic alliance which by degrees reached up to bear on Richard's larger struggle for power against the French king.[133] In short, warfare was made more prevalent and potentially more damaging by the presence of dynamic, or aspirant, rulership, which aggregated different levels of disputes into a more destructive whole.

This matters in the context of events in the Midi because, as was noted earlier, a chronological indicator used more than once by the compiler of the Rocamadour miracles was 'the war' between Count Raymond V of Toulouse and Alfonso II, king of Aragon and count of Barcelona. In reality what we know of this war reveals that it was a matter of different layers of territorial, familial and economic disputes – sometimes no more than localized vendettas running in parallel – interweaving at different points, in much the same way that the conflicts between the Angevins and Capetians were far more complex than a feud between two prominent dynasties. But the use of the phrase 'bellum regis Arragonensis et Raimundi Tolosani comitis'[134] suggests that a contemporary observer, fairly close to the action without being directly affected by it, was attempting to construct a framework to draw together different parts of the information reaching him, and in the process was alive to a pattern based on the notion of a pan-regional conflict

---

[132] See e.g. 'Chronica', cc. 45, 47, 51, 68, 69, 70, pp. 301, 304, 306, 320, 323–4.
[133] See J. Gillingham, 'The Unromantic Death of Richard I', *Speculum*, 54 (1979), pp. 18–41.
[134] III.1; III.17.

in which two principals, the counts of Toulouse and Barcelona, acted as central reference points to explain much of the violence taking place.

This patterning and ordering was made particularly possible because of an important feature of 'the war': it could be located within a long-term frame of reference, in that the rivalry between the comital houses of Toulouse and Barcelona stretched back into the eleventh century; and in the shorter term it referred to a specific spell of hostilities that had broken out in 1166–67. That is to say, the general – in the sense of an awareness of how the political scene in the south was affected by the long-standing dispute – and the specific – the particular incidents caused by the very current spate of hostilities – could reinforce one another. Furthermore, the war could be understood as an encapsulation of much that was happening in the Midi because it was geographically dispersed across the area from north of the eastern Pyrenees and the Toulousain to Provence and up into the southern parts of the Massif. Here comparisons with the conflicts between the Capetians and their Norman/Angevin rivals are once again instructive. As was the case with the northern power-contest, the counts of Barcelona and Toulouse had a core territorial dispute where their areas of authority abutted; this was not always the sole or main area of contention, but it served as a permanent reminder of the potential for competition. Without stretching the point too far, it may be said that the region north and north-east of the eastern Pyrenees, comprising Foix, Narbonne, Béziers, Carcassonne, Agde and extending as far east as Montpellier, stood in relation to the contest between Toulouse and Barcelona as the Vexin did in terms of the rivalry between the Capetian kings and the dukes of Normandy: a contested liminal zone, control of which at any point amounted to a symbol of which side was then in the ascendant. This core area was where the eleventh-century counts of Barcelona had first demonstrated their interest in extending their authority to the north of the Pyrenees, and their twelfth-century successors maintained and extended networks of lordship and patronage there.[135] But in addition to this there were other disputed territories in Provence, Gévaudan, Millau, Carlat and the Rouergue, in which the house of Barcelona had acquired interests in 1112 through the marriage of Count Ramon Berenguer III to Douce, the heiress of Count Gerbert of Provence.[136] These areas were among the bones of contention in the war registered by the Rocamadour miracle stories. When the cousin of Alfonso II of Aragon–Barcelona, Ramon Berenguer of Provence, died in 1166 without a male heir, the king intervened to thwart the ambitions of Raymond V of Toulouse, which

---

[135] Abadal i de Vinyals, 'A propos de la "domination"', pp. 320–34.

[136] Higounet 'Un grand chapitre', p. 316; J.-P. Poly, *La Provence et la société féodale 879–1166: Contribution à l'étude des structures dites féodales dans le Midi* (Paris, 1976), pp. 318–19.

were built on his marriage to Ramon Berenguer's heiress. This threw into confusion a settlement that had been reached back in 1125 whereby Provence had been divided between the two dynasties.[137] And the result was a renewal of conflict.

In short, then, the Rocamadour miracles were written at a time when the effects of warfare were to be observed with particular clarity in many parts of the Midi. The author seems to have engaged with this in two ways. First, there are suggestions in the text that he adopted the strategy of taking sides, for there are some hints that he regarded Raymond of Toulouse as the aggressor and sympathized with those opposed to him.[138] But this is not a theme that is consistently developed. Of greater importance is the manner in which the author approached the effects of warfare thanks to the opportunities that his material offered him to pronounce on how it was conducted. Of particular interest in this context are the references in the text to the activities of mercenaries, a recurrent motif which encapsulates the author's ideas about warfare more generally.

Who were the mercenaries?[139] They are a rather elusive group. Their activities are mentioned in a large number of narrative sources, but chroniclers were virtually unanimously hostile in their views. This means that our information comes to us deeply coloured by moralizing rhetoric that can tend towards hyperbole and over-simplification. In discussing twelfth-century mercenaries, Matthew Strickland has made the valuable point that contemporary verdicts on these men closely resemble the views expressed by an earlier generation of writers about the Vikings.[140] And it is also noteworthy that much of the rhetoric of condemnation turned against mercenaries – for example, allegations of the desecration of churches, the spoliation and destruction of agricultural resources, and aggression directed towards clergy, monks, nuns, women and children – is very redolent of the language used by the proponents of the Peace and Truce of God movements in the late tenth and eleventh centuries.[141] It was very easy, therefore, for

---

[137] J. Dunbabin, *France in the Making 843–1180* (Oxford, 1985), p. 300; T. N. Bisson, *The Medieval Crown of Aragon: A Short History* (Oxford, 1986), p 37.

[138] See III.17.

[139] See P. Contamine, *War in the Middle Ages*, trans. M. Jones (Oxford, 1984), pp. 243–7; J. France, *Western Warfare in the Age of the Crusades 1000–1300* (London, 1999), pp. 60–2, 68–75; Paterson, *World of the Troubadours*, pp. 42–4, 57–61. The best treatment of twelfth-century mercenaries remains H. Grundmann, 'Rotten und Brabanzonen: Söldner-Heere im 12. Jahrhundert', *Deutsches Archiv für Erforschung des Mittelalters*, 5 (1942), pp. 419–92. See also J. Boussard, 'Les mercenaires au XIIe siècle: Henri Plantagenêt et les origines de l'armée de metier', *Bibliothèque de l'Ecole des chartes*, 106 (1945–46), pp. 189–224.

[140] Strickland, *War and Chivalry*, pp. 291–301.

[141] See e.g. 'Epistolarum regis Ludovici VII et aliorum ad eum volumen', *RHGF* 16.130–1 (nos. 398–400); Ralph Diceto, *Opera Historica*, ed. W. Stubbs, 2 vols. (Rolls Series, 68; London, 1876), i.407; Walter Map, *De Nugis Curialium*, I. 30, ed. and trans. M. R. James, rev. C. N. L. Brooke and R. A. B. Mynors (Oxford, 1983), p. 118; *Gesta regis*

contemporary observers to treat mercenaries as conforming to preset models of misrule, misdirected violence and social upheaval. They were almost a cliché waiting to happen: a group of people whose alienness allowed commentators to engage in full-blooded condemnation uncompromised by the sorts of ambiguity and qualification that surrounded the violence generated by those elements more integrated into the social and political fabric.

Various aspects of who the mercenaries were, and what they did, help to throw light on how they could be viewed in these terms by monastic and clerical observers, including the author of the Rocamadour miracles. It should be borne in mind that our evidence for them is largely weighted towards their activities in Aquitaine, northern France and England, as well as in the context of the German emperor's campaigns in Italy; but it is reasonable to assume that lessons to be learned from these places can also be applied to their operations in the areas contested by the counts of Toulouse and Barcelona. The vividness of the rhetoric used against them is misleading in that they appear so beyond the bounds of normal social order that it might be assumed that it was in the interests of all secular leaders to deal with them swiftly and conclusively. But this was not always the case in practice because they could prove effective instruments of princely might.[142] Henry II, for example, made regular use of their services, as did both his son Richard and Philip Augustus of France. Rulers were also prepared to go to extreme lengths to find the money to pay for mercenaries.[143] In other words, they were a symptom of assertive rulership, allied to conditions of economic growth, which put cash – by fair means or foul – into the hands of their paymasters. It follows that their roles and status could be more ambiguous than the black-and-white disapproval of the chroniclers might at first sight reveal; and this ambiguity would have served to prolong and complicate the effects that they had on others.

So, to return to the question of who the mercenaries were, perception and reality cannot be wholly detached. At the simple level of being soldiers serving for reward, they were in the same broad category as any paid personnel, for example stipendiary knights who operated within a lord's military household. But it is noteworthy that observers sometimes made a clear distinction between them and *stipendarii*.[144] Mercenaries were typically

---

Henrici secundi, i.297; *Decrees of the Ecumenical Councils*, ed. N. P. Tanner (London, 1990): Lateran III c. 27.

[142] For a revealing contemporary statement of the value to rulers of using paid troops, see *Dialogus de Scaccario*, ed. and trans. C. Johnson, rev. F. E. L. Carter and D. E. Greenway (Oxford, 1983), p. 52.

[143] For indications of the costs involved and rulers' willingness to meet them, see William of Newburgh, *Historia Rerum Anglicarum*, II.27, ed. R. Howlett (Rolls Series 82:1; London, 1884), p. 172; Robert of Torigny, *Chronica*, p. 202; *Gesta regis Henrici secundi*, i.299; Geoffrey of Vigeois, 'Chronica', c. 67, p. 319.

[144] See S. D. B. Brown, 'Military Service and Monetary Reward in the Eleventh and

identified as foot soldiers, and it is clear that it was predominantly as such that they were deployed in military campaigns.[145] But it is reasonable to wonder whether this feature was exaggerated by observers because it helped to reinforce the idea that there was clear social, and thus moral, distance between them and the mounted aristocracy. There is evidence for the use of mounts by at least some within mercenary bands,[146] and it is likely that part of their recruitment was from the lower levels of chivalric society. Similarly, the regional labels that were often used to identify mercenaries, most notably 'Brabançons', extended beyond a statement of geographical origin (which in any case must usually have been an impressionistic generalization) to speak to their otherness; it is probably not a coincidence that people from the areas most commonly associated with mercenary bands – Brabant, Flanders, Germany, Basque Navarre and Gascony[147] – would have been associated with languages that were alien to Romance-speakers. It is perfectly possible that many mercenaries originated from regions in which dialects of northern French or Occitan were spoken, but the labels which stuck suited the sense of unfamiliarity and separation that observers wanted to stress.

The impact of the mercenaries was increased by their capacity for group cohesion and continuity. They were not roving gangs of footloose thugs – at least when they were in employment – but complex communities able to combine mobility with internal ordering. There is evidence for some form of hierarchy, at least to the extent that employers could deal with acknowledged leaders who must have been able to exercise authority over their followers, and also because they were able to conduct the sort of complicated and large-scale operations that would only have been possible if there had been effective chains of command. Clerics crop up associated with groups of routiers,[148] and there is evidence that some mercenary bands contained woman and children, which points to the existence of stable communities with internal economic and social structures. When describing a group of mercenaries that was defeated by a coalition of Limousin lords in 1177, Geoffrey of Vigeois makes the interesting observation that this was the same band that had served in Frederick Barbarossa's campaign against Rome: the

---

Twelfth Centuries', *History*, 74 (1989), pp. 20–38; cf. M. Chibnall, 'Mercenaries and the *Familia Regis* under Henry I', *History*, 62 (1977), pp. 15–23.

[145] See e.g. William of Newburgh, *Historia Rerum Anglicarum*, II.32, p. 181: Henry II's forces in 1174 comprise 'aliquanto equitato et una Brabantionum turma'.

[146] See e.g. William of Malmesbury, *Historia Novella*, ed. E. King, trans. K. Potter (Oxford, 1998), p. 32. See Grundmann, 'Rotten', pp. 486–7.

[147] For the various national or regional designations applied to mercenaries, see e.g. Robert of Torigny, *Chronica*, pp. 282, 461; *Decrees of the Ecumenical Councils*, Lateran III c. 27; *Chronicon universale anonymi Laudunensis*, ed. A. Cartellieri and W. Stechele (Leipzig and Paris, 1909), p. 37. See generally Grundmann, 'Rotten', pp. 424–36. In the Rocamadour stories the terms favoured are 'Basques' (I.51; III.4) and 'Brabançons' (III.4; III.15; III.17). See also I.5, which may refer to Gascon mercenaries.

[148] Grundmann, 'Rotten', pp. 485–6.

fact that this took place fully ten years earlier points to a significant level of group solidarity and direction.[149] The mercenary band attacked in 1177 had set itself up in the stronghold of Malemort (which is in fact not far from Rocamadour): this was possibly a form of 'holding base' in which rulers who might want to draw on their services could lodge them.[150] Overall, then, we can see that these sorts of groups were much more than a transient menace. Their impact could be sustained and grave.

The possible role of Rocamadour in articulating a response to this threat can be seen if one examines other contemporary reactions in various parts of southern France that also drew on the cult of the Virgin Mary. The most notable, and organizationally complex, manifestation of the impulse to respond took place in and around Le Puy in the early 1180s with the formation of a peace association to counter the threat posed by mercenaries.[151] The origins and early development of the association are not altogether clear: we have a number of chronicle accounts, but they do not agree at all points, and some of their verdicts were coloured by the knowledge that the group was eventually suppressed for directing its energies against local lords once the mercenary threat had been dealt with.[152] But a number of key elements emerge. In the first place, there was a broad social response to the appeal of the peace association. Its roots probably lay in the pressures faced by low-status people and their vulnerability at the hands of mercenaries: it was believed that a carpenter called Durand had experienced a vision instructing him to spread the message of peace. On the other hand, the association was made possible because of the backing that it received from the bishop of Le Puy and the local ecclesiastical and secular elites, who initially greeted the movement with enthusiasm. In other words, the momentum that the movement was able to generate flowed from the interaction between different groups and was channelled through the structures of the Church. Second, the Marian quality of the association is clearly evident at important points in its development. The belief was that Durand's vision had been of the Virgin, who had handed him a document or seal bearing a depiction of Mother and Child and the inscription 'Lamb of God, who takes away the sins of the world, give us peace'. In addition, whether the ecclesiastical authorities were genuinely taken by surprise by Durand's claimed experience or in fact used him from the start as a stooge, it is clear that the Marian emphasis was exploited fully in their efforts at publicity and organization: Durand was shown off by the bishop to the large crowds that gathered at Le Puy on the Feast of the Assumption in August

---

[149] 'Chronica', cc. 69–70, pp. 323–4; cf. Grundmann, 'Rotten', pp. 443–4, 458–60.
[150] I owe this suggestion to Dr John France.
[151] See *HGL* 6.106–9; G. Duby, *The Three Orders: Feudal Society Imagined*, trans. A. Goldhammer (Chicago, 1980), pp. 327–36.
[152] Robert of Torigny, *Chronica*, p. 309; Gervase of Canterbury, *Chronica*, i.300–302; Robert of Auxerre, 'Chronicon', *MGH SS* 26.247; *Chronicon universale*, pp. 37–40.

1183; and the sworn association that grew up used as its insignia a lead badge bearing an image of the Virgin, as well as the white cape that gave the group the name by which it was typically known – the *Capuciati*.

A further point to note is that the rationale and self-perception of the peace organization extended beyond dealing with the immediate problem of mercenaries operating in its region. Bound up with the practicalities of making itself an effective force – it raised funds, for example, by levying an entry-fee on recruits – was a programme of moral renewal which reflected many of the messages that the Church was trying to communicate to lay people. Recruitment to the group was described in the language of conversion, and was expressed by means of a solemn oath that created a permanent obligation. Mutual protection was one avowed aim, in order to create a united society of believers. There was an emphasis upon sexual restraint, ideally in the form of chastity and failing that within legitimate marriage. And regular attendance at Mass and processions at parish churches were central elements of their devotional agenda.[153] In short, the cult of Mary lay at the core of an ambitious programme of social and religious renewal, in which all elements of the Church and faithful could participate and which was made possible because of the manner in which mercenaries concentrated people's minds.[154]

The significance of the cult of Mary in formulating responses to mercenaries also emerges from an episode that was believed to have taken place in Berry in 1187. While lacking the broad social and political impact of the Le Puy association, it is nonetheless an interesting vignette which throws light on contemporary attitudes. More specifically in the context of lessons that can be applied to Rocamadour's experience, the earliest version of what happened was probably part of a large collection of Marian miracles – now lost – compiled at Déols in the twelfth century.[155] The background to the episode was war between Richard and Philip Augustus. Richard had occupied Châteauroux and stationed a garrison of mercenaries, some of whom occupied the nearby bourg of Déols, pillaging it and driving out the inhabitants. One night the inhabitants returned to beg the Virgin for assistance; the abbey church was closed, so they prayed under a statue of her that was situated over the north door. Mercenaries then set upon them, one of them throwing a stone at the statue. One of the Christ Child's arms fell to the ground, whereupon blood began to pour from the 'wound'. The offending soldier dropped dead. As news of the miracle spread, the monks gathered to sing hymns of praise, while Richard's troops were overcome by terror. An attempt was made to steal the bloody arm, but the monks managed to secure it for themselves, placing it on an improvised altar.

---

[153] Gervase of Canterbury, *Chronica*, i.301; *Chronicon universale*, p. 39.
[154] See Grundmann, 'Rotten', pp. 469–71.
[155] J. Hubert, 'Le miracle de Déols et la trêve conclue en 1187 entre les rois de France et d'Angleterre', *Bibliothèque de l'Ecole des chartes*, 96 (1935), pp. 285–300 (text edited at pp. 296–300).

Two nights later a large crowd gathered at the scene of the miracle, and the statue of the Virgin was observed moving her dress to bear her breast. Richard then arrived, declared his belief in the two miracles, requartered his mercenaries out of harm's way and placed the abbey under his protection.

It is impossible to know exactly what happened, of course. But it is clear that the story became quite well known beyond Berry: it was seized on by Rigord, in his panegyric of Philip Augustus, because it gave him ammunition to use against Richard;[156] and Gervase of Canterbury knew of the incident.[157] The narrative of events as constructed by the monks of Déols highlights themes that are similar to those evident over a more extended period in the experience of the Le Puy peace association. As at Le Puy, a popular reaction to the threat posed by mercenaries becomes associated with the responses of the Church's elites – here neatly symbolized by the monks gathering to chant as the news of the first miracle spread. Also, the role of Mary, linked to the person of her Son as a channel for popular and ecclesiastical responses, is manifest: in the case of Le Puy she is associated with the peace-bringing Lamb of God; here the link is reinforced by the operation of two miracles focused upon a single representation of Mother and Child. And finally, the resolution of the narrative consists of the acknowledgement, by the very man who was responsible for bringing the mercenaries to Déols, of the need to discipline his troops and to reaffirm, through his protection of the abbey and its goods, the proper function of princely authority. Similarly, the Le Puy association was reinforced by absorbing established structures of authority in the shape of co-operative secular leaders. A three-way alliance of people, religious centre and aristocracy, articulated through the cult of the Virgin, was set up as an ideal way to deal with the mercenaries and the disorder they brought; as long as this unity persisted – and within a few years it broke down at Le Puy, thereby condemning the *Capuciati* to destruction – the threat was manageable.

The events at Le Puy and Déols can shed light on Rocamadour's reaction to the same sort of mercenary threat a few year earlier when the miracle collection was being written. The central importance of the cult of Mary to the monks at Rocamadour would have enabled them to formulate their response and communicate it to others. In this context, it is important to note that the cult of Mary was not pacifist in its inspiration – pacifism was a position that very few in medieval society, including the Church, would have readily understood. It is sometimes supposed that the qualities attributed to Mary such as gentleness and mercy are an indication that she appealed in particular to the non-belligerent members of society, especially women, who sought in her an outlet for their resistance to the violence wreaked by

---

[156] *Oeuvres de Rigord et de Guillaume le Breton, historiens de Philippe-Auguste*, ed. H. F. Delaborde, 2 vols. (Paris, 1882), i.79–80.

[157] Gervase of Canterbury, *Chronica*, i.370.

aristocratic males and their subordinates. But this view is based on a grave misunderstanding both of medieval society's attitudes to violence as a moral quality and of the attraction of the Virgin as an object of veneration. It is perhaps not an exaggeration to say that more people in the Middle Ages were the victims of violence associated with the name of the Virgin Mary than was the case with any other saint. She was, for example, the principal patron of the Military Orders of the Temple and the Teutonic Knights, as well as one of the main saints venerated by the third major Order, the Hospitallers. And examples of knights invoking Mary in the prosecution of their conflicts are legion. Similarly, the Rocamadour miracles do not condemn violence in itself. When knights are described receiving wounds they are not censured for placing themselves in the sort of situations in which they are at risk; severe physical punishments are criticized specifically in those cases in which the victim has been unjustly condemned; even the violence of summary justice can be licit, as when a knight strings up a thief he meets on the road. In other words, violence could be validated in certain circumstances; and it was the aristocracy, the wielders of legitimate secular authority, who were its instruments. It follows that the cult of the Virgin at Rocamadour appealed in part to lords and knights, an important element of its 'constituency', because of messages it could send out about right order, social status and the appropriateness of violence informed by right intention – precisely the opposite of the qualities projected onto mercenaries, whose function was to be a cipher to bring these issues to the surface.

To return to the geopolitical situation in which Rocamadour found itself in the early 1170s, we can see that issues of political order and legitimate authority would have been pertinent to its experience as a cult centre. Rocamadour had become something of a symbol of Angevin claims over its region: Henry II went there on pilgrimage in 1159, the year in which he assumed control of Quercy;[158] and the connection was renewed shortly before the miracle collection was begun when Henry went there again in September 1170, possibly to give thanks for the cure of a recent illness.[159] To this extent, Rocamadour was in the 'front line' of political and military upheaval. Beyond this, moreover, its location on what was the newly extended margin of the Angevin world would have permitted it to take a detached but interested view of the even greater upheavals to the south and east, in the areas affected by the conflict between the counts of Barcelona and Toulouse. It was a beacon of light – the metaphor occurs more than once in the miracle stories – offering hope in troubled times. Of course, it is important to remember that most of the incidents described in the *miracula* did not demand this level

---

[158] *Cartulaire de l'abbaye d'Uzerche*, ed. J.-B. Champeval (Paris, 1901), no. 308.

[159] Robert of Torigny, *Chronica*, pp. 247, 248; *Gesta regis Henrici secundi*, i.6–7; E. Mason, ' "Rocamadour in Quercy above all Other Churches": The Healing of Henry II', *The Church and Healing*, ed. W. J. Shiels (Studies in Church History, 19; Oxford, 1982), pp. 39, 42–8.

of overt contextualization: people would be blind, paralysed or deaf irrespective of the political and military currents around them. Moreover, a substantial number of stories are located well away from the war zones of the Midi. But ideas of conflict and violence are sufficiently recurrent throughout the collection to suggest that they represent a significant inflection in the author's scheme. To this extent the author's engagement with and reactions to these issues of contemporary concern are what make the collection a quasi-historiographical text, participating in the discourse of chroniclers.

4

Conclusion

The miracle collection of Rocamadour is not a chronicle in disguise. It was written to conform to the requirements of a distinct literary genre, and the author realized the potential of his work within that context. This is important to stress because some examinations of the historiographical quality of *miracula*, and of hagiographical writings more generally, assess the material in terms of how closely it resembles a chronicle or similar form of narrative.[1] Thus, for example, the Miracles of St Benedict from Fleury 'pass' this test because its authors are supposed to have been principally interested in recounting the history of their abbey and their times, and simply used incidents of the miraculous to fashion the framework that structured their work. But it is clearly a mistake to judge a source type principally by comparison with a different genre. Such an approach can warp our understanding of what the author of a miracle collection was trying to accomplish; and it privileges the idea that somewhere 'out there' there is an objective reality, independent of the text, which can be rescued from the distortions and exaggerations of the literary medium in which it is imprisoned.[2]

On the other hand, it is clear that the author of the Rocamadour miracles believed that he was engaging with what he would have understood to have been perfectly real events and processes that were rooted in an understanding of the workings of the world that he would have seen as beyond debate. To this extent, the question of whether the stories are fact or fiction is inappropriate. The many references in the collection to people and events that are independently attested, and the fact that most of the events described had taken place in the very recent past, point to an author who cast himself as an observer of the contemporary scene. He did so because his vision of the cult he celebrated – and this was no doubt a communal policy on the part of

---

[1] See P.-A. Sigal, 'Histoire et hagiographie: Les "Miracula" aux XIe et XIIe siècles', *Annales de Bretagne et des pays de l'Ouest*, 87 (1980), pp. 237–57; cf. B. de Gaiffier, 'Hagiographie et historiographie: Quelques aspects du problème', in *La storiografia altomedievale*, 2 vols. (Settimane di studio del centro italiano di studi sull'alto medioevo, 17; Spoleto, 1970), i.139–66. See also F. Lotter, 'Methodisches zur Gewinnung historischer Erkenntnisse aus hagiographischen Quellen', *Historische Zeitschrift*, 229 (1979), pp. 298–356.

[2] For a stimulating critique see F. Lifshitz, 'Beyond Positivism and Genre: "Hagiographical" Texts as Historical Narrative', *Viator*, 25 (1994), pp. 95–113. See also the more general perspectives in G. M. Spiegel, 'History, Historicism, and the Social Logic of the Text in the Middle Ages', *Speculum*, 65 (1990), pp. 59–86.

his institution – emphasized the variety of places in which people had heard of Rocamadour. In their efforts to fashion and propagate a cult with such a far-flung base of support, the monks needed to be particularly sensitive to broad currents and contemporary affairs. This is why the miracle collection was able to register, for example, a recent earthquake that took place far away in the Middle East, the health problems faced by Henry II's forces in Ireland (which are also noted in the Becket miracles) and the threat posed by mercenaries drawn into the Midi by the many wars waged by the region's rulers. These sorts of events and trends are mostly retrievable through other sources: it is not as if our basic knowledge of these things hinges on the Rocamadour miracles. But the collection is evidence for something more valuable: the responses of one monastic community to the many pressures it observed around it. To this extent, then, the collection is similar to a chronicle, in the sense that it represents an attempt to explain and order the recent past for the benefit of future readers. What this means is that we must be careful not to exaggerate the 'constructedness' of the collection, or of other texts like it, to the point where it becomes evidence for nothing more than the ideas and perceptions of the author in isolation.[3] The monks of Rocamadour were engaged in a form of dialogue with people in the outside world, and the ideas of both parties do emerge from the text.

Ultimately, however, it was the needs of the monastic community at Rocamadour that brought the collection into being. For all the references to people from far-flung places, and despite the relative absence of information about the monastic community itself, the text is in one sense very inward looking. It is unlikely that the collection's primary purpose was to provide teaching material for use in the instruction of lay people. Clearly some of the stories suggest that they originated in orally transmitted tales that may have passed between monks and pilgrims. And no doubt some stories may have been incorporated into sermons. But we know very little about how the stories could actually have been communicated (in the vernacular) to lay people, when this could have happened, what sort of people might have listened, and how they reacted. Rather, the collection spoke more to the identity of the monks themselves: here was a communal resource, to be read and listened to by those with Latin within the institutional setting of their priory.

A corollary of this in-house reception of the text is the fact that it was probably triggered by pressures that were specifically felt by the monastic community. We have seen that the author of the collection did not expatiate on why he took up his pen, but that comparisons with other collections whose origins are more clearly identifiable suggest that the Rocamadour miracles were not some casual exercise. It should be remembered that the priory did not *need* this text: it had functioned for many years without a

---

[3] Cf. Signori, 'Miracle Kitchen', p. 302.

collection of miracles, and once made the collection was probably not kept up beyond the very short term. The pressure exerted by the territorial expansion of the abbey of Obazine would seem to have been one factor that prompted the creation of the text; the need to reassert the Marian identity of the church in the wake of the discovery of the body of St Amator was another. In both instances, what was at stake was the identity of the monastic community – an identity which could be clarified and reinvigorated through a celebration of the power of the Virgin Mary.

One problem that the Rocamadour miracle collection raises is that it appears, so to speak, virtually from nowhere. In other words, it dominates the evidence for the early history of Rocamadour as a pilgrimage centre, and yet it only covers a very brief period. How far back can we project the conditions it describes? As we have seen, the author wanted to convey the impression of a timeless, unchanging story of success. And it is possible that some more modern commentators, inspired by the revival of Rocamadour as a pilgrimage site from the mid-nineteenth century, have followed his cue in exaggerating the importance of the cult in the decades before the collection was written.[4] Granted that it is very difficult to know how one can meaningfully assess the success or renown of a cult centre in this period – we do not have statistics on pilgrim numbers, for example – a more cautious view would be that the miracle collection was not a celebration of a cult that had already achieved international celebrity, but of one that was in the process of trying to achieve just that. It is significant that independent evidence for the pilgrimage to Rocamadour begins to become available around the time of the collection: we have already noted Robert of Torigny's interest in the place around 1180, and it is at about the same time that references to it begin to appear in vernacular texts.[5] Interestingly, some of the earliest evidence for pilgrims to Rocamadour points to visits *en route* to or from somewhere else: Henry II in 1159 had just been campaigning in the Toulousain; in 1169 Gilbert Foliot, the bishop of London, visited Rocamadour on his way to Rome; and around 1170 Count Philip of Flanders was there on his way back from a pilgrimage to Saint-Gilles.[6] In addition the collection itself acknowledges the importance of through-traffic to or from Compostela, even as it tries to avoid implying that this might have relegated Rocamadour to a lesser position in pilgrims' minds. The sort of dispersed knowledge about Rocamadour that the collection mentions should not be dismissed too lightly; clearly people in many different places had indeed

---

[4] See esp. Rupin, *Roc-Amadour*, passim.

[5] *Les deux rédactions en vers du Moniage Guillaume: Chansons de geste du XIIe siècle*, II. ll. 6550–63, ed. W. Cloetta, 2 vols. (Paris, 1906–10), i.363–4; Garnier of Pont-Sainte-Maxence, *La Vie de Saint Thomas Becket*, ll. 5896–5900, ed. E. Walberg (Paris, 1964), pp. 181–2; English translation: J. Shirley, *Garnier's Becket* (London, 1975), p. 157.

[6] Ralph Diceto, *Opera Historica*, i.337; Lambert of Wattrelos, 'Annales Cameracenses', pp. 553–4.

heard of the cult. But it does not follow that it enjoyed the level of widespread renown that the author wanted to assert.

What, then, is the value of the miracle collection? Much recent research into *miracula* has been based on an aggregation of the many collections that survive from the central Middle Ages. The appeal of this methodology is manifest, for this period offers us very little information of the sort that can be collated, tabulated and subjected to statistical analysis – especially in the realm of what we can broadly term social history. So miracles seem too good an opportunity to miss. But one needs to be cautious about applying techniques that tend to work better when used on more modern sources and the more systematic types of data they can furnish. The preferable approach is to focus on the individual text, identifying questions that bear specifically on it. Why was it written, and what was its institutional setting? Is the dating of the text of possible significance? What prompted the decision to write it, and what sort of external influences can be detected? It is hoped that this introductory analysis and the translated text which follows provide some pointers which others can refine and improve upon when studying miracle collections such as this example from Rocamadour.

THE MIRACLES OF
OUR LADY OF ROCAMADOUR

The First Part

Prologue

Here begins the prologue of the miracles of Saint Mary of Rocamadour

As I begin to write the miracles of Mary, the Blessed Mother of God and perpetual Virgin of Rocamadour, I call upon the Paraclete, the Holy Ghost, for assistance. I do so especially because there has been such a vast number of miracles before our own day that it has been impossible to hold them in our memory or write them down; not even the greatest eloquence can retrieve them for the telling. So we propose to limit our narration to what we have seen with our own eyes or what we have learned from reliable people with sure accounts to give. And yet who can really try to make known those things which the effigies and models worked in wax that are to be found in this church reveal to those who behold them? Anyone can be amazed at the sight. Let him believe that many have been revived through the merits of the Blessed Virgin Mary, and let him be in no doubt that innumerable people have had their sight restored. Let him also believe that those who have been mortally wounded by swords and pierced by lances, knives and arrows have been restored to perfect health. May you see those hit in the throat able to breathe, others struck in the chest, with their lungs burst asunder, giving thanks for their recovery to the Blessed Virgin. You may wonder at people whose entrails have poured out and yet live, at others whose intestines or groins have been run through and yet they bear witness to their deliverance. And who can properly describe with due praise and admiration the prisoners who carry their heavy chains, more often doing so from afar rather than nearby? Everyone is saved from dangers both on land and sea. They are led out of prisons. They are restored to health. This is so of all those who come to the door of the Mother of gentleness and mercy, and with a faithful heart do not hesitate to knock earnestly on it. She hears everyone and answers their prayers. She cures all people. She succours all people. For the Son will deny nothing that his Mother wishes to obtain. She chose, indeed she pre-elected, the church of Rocamadour, situated in Quercy, which she adorns with many signs and makes radiant with miracles. She makes it famous through her proclamations, and she has made it renowned above nearly all the other churches in the world. O what an amazing and quite stupefying thing! Who could fail to be astounded, when he considers the situation of this place and the rough terrain, that it is somewhere made beautiful by such a great spirit and light? Gentle Virgin, star of the sea, perform your works there as you wish and receive the supplications of those who supplicantly beseech you. She cures those she wants. She takes hold of and frees those she wants. She fills those she wants with all goodness and enriches them with knowledge. But what am I saying? Those she wants? Surely she wants everyone to be saved? Surely she does not choose one person and neglect another? How can she appear hard of heart to one person and soft to someone else? My answer is that she is only hard towards the indolent, whereas she is always gentle in turning her gentle eyes towards sinners who have not yet converted. She looks favourably upon the devout, and she receives those who are humble, because she gives grace to the humble through the grace of her Son. So let those whose minds are injured run to the fount of mercy. Let them run so that they may be pardoned the wrongs they have done. Let those come who are physically ailing, because she heals those who are both contrite in their hearts and suffering in their bodies. Let them come and witness the amazing sights, and let them put their faith in things that are incredible. I do not believe that there is anyone so hard-hearted that he would not shed tears and be filled with devotion if he came devoutly to the oratory of the Blessed Virgin. But I am attempting to make a single collection of the pick of the Virgin's miracles, and so I beg my reader not to act as a critic of my work but as a corrector, for the love and honour of her whose many great works I am making known.

The end of the prologue

Chapters of the first part

1. Two young men unharmed in the water
2. A priest revived by the power of Our Lady
3. A woman who broke her vow is punished by divine vengeance
4. Some thieves unable to do injury to a pilgrim
5. An excommunicate who presumed to enter the Virgin's church
6. A thieving pilgrim deprived of the use of his tongue
7. A mortally wounded woman cured by the Blessed Virgin
8. A knight's wife and daughter restored to health
9. A knight's house saved from fire
10. A Lombard rescued from a fire and later freed from chains
11. Someone else miraculously rescued from an unheard-of punishment
12. A noble who escaped from a precipice
13. A youth saved from shipwreck and hanging
14. A knight cured by the Virgin after being run through with a lance
15. A shrivelled arm cured by Our Lady
16. A blind boy given his sight
17. A man whose lost teeth were restored
18. A man freed from his chains
19. A bull given to St Mary which brought back its herd
20. A woman with dropsy restored to health
21. Three blind people cured
22. A crippled woman cured
23. A small child, blind since birth, who gained its sight
24. A knight who harassed a pilgrim and was assailed by infernal fire
25. A lady cured of a polyp

26. A mute woman to whom the power of speech was restored

27. A ship which was saved and some wine which did not spill

28. A mad woman who recovered her senses

29. A man who was struck by an arrow and could not be healed

30. Another man who was run through with a lance

31. Desperate men aboard ship freed by the Queen of Virgins

32. A knight whom an enemy was unable to harm

33. A girl deaf and dumb since birth

34. A piece of wax which fell onto a lute

35. A demoniac freed from a demon

36. A woman who could not sink

37. A priest cured by the sign of pilgrimage

38. A cripple cured by a vision

39. A deaf and dumb woman who was cured

40. A man restored to health with his horses

41. The horrible illness of a woman

42. Robbers who left what they had stolen with its rightful owner

43. The Virgin's messenger who cured a scrofulous woman

44. A swollen girl who was also cured

45. Knights deprived of the power of speech

46. Men who were appointed to fight in single combat

47. A thief who stole from a pilgrim of the Blessed Mary

48. A knight cured of a lump

49. Another wounded man for whom there was no hope

50. A prisoner's broken chains

51. A young man hurt by many lethal wounds

52. A very serious illness

53. A captive freed by his mother's faith

I.1. Two young men unharmed in the water

Recently a large party of Gascons made the journey to the church of the Blessed Mary of Rocamadour in order to pray. When they had performed their solemn devotions and were on their way home, they came to the River Tarn. As they tried to board a boat they found that there was no room for two of their number because it was too full. These two grew indignant, and being impudent, as well as physically strong, they jumped into the boat on top of their companions. But as it is written, *A haughty* spirit *comes before a fall:*[1] divine retribution and the nod of the gracious Virgin caused them both to fall into the water and sink to the bottom. The water was like a raging torrent. Accordingly, their companions became desperately afraid and mournful, and with one voice they called upon the Blessed Mary for assistance. Meanwhile the skilled efforts of nearby fishermen achieved nothing. Time and time again the pilgrims pressed them to continue their search, but they were unable to find the two youths anywhere. The pilgrims had lost hope that the two were still alive, and were planning to withdraw because such a long time had elapsed, when, marvellous to relate and contrary to all expectation, the two men appeared on the river bank, free from mortal danger and the depths of the torrent; they were unharmed, and not one part of them was wet. When their companions and some other pilgrims who had arrived on the scene asked what had happened, they replied: 'The compassionate Virgin, in whose service we have been exerting ourselves, did not abandon us. She gave us her protection, taking hold of us when we were in the water, preventing us from being injured, and then lifting us up out of the waves.' Those who heard this were astonished. They made a careful inspection and found that the two men were as dry as if they had never disappeared under the waves. But when the two mentioned the possibility of going back to the glorious Virgin to give thanks, they were dissuaded from doing so by their companions. Other pilgrims who had been there, however, and had seen it all, came to the church of the Blessed Virgin and, glorifying the Lord, gave consistent accounts of what had happened.

I.2. A priest revived by the power of Our Lady

Every year a priest called Bernard of Lasvaux,[2] an inhabitant of Quercy and a chaplain of the holy Mother of God, would visit the church of Rocamadour with his parishioners on the Feast of the Nativity of the Virgin.[3] He used to celebrate Mass, and the people solemnly took communion. When he became weighed down by his earthly body, he yearned to be released

---

[1] Proverbs 16:18.
[2] Lot.
[3] 8 September.

from it so that he could live in Christ. As this man saw matters, to live had been Christ and to die was gain.[4] Going the way of all flesh, he fell ill. His flock had cherished and trusted him when he was in good health, and now that he was sick they diligently visited him and tended to his needs. For his part the priest would encourage the good people to better things; as it says in the Bible, the saints *go from strength to strength*.[5] And to amend the ways of the wicked he would warn them about eternal punishment. So it came about that he reached his dying moments. Making a good end, he breathed his last and reposed with his fathers in Christ. This was around the ninth hour of the day. The exequies were performed and the night was spent in vigil. On the following day a Mass was solemnly celebrated for his soul. Deprived of the good shepherd, the priest's flock were afraid that they would be devoured by greedy wolves. And so with a combination of speaking, sobbing and weeping they begged the Virgin to bring their father back to life and restore him to them. They prayed with great perseverance. Demonstrating their devotion and exercising their faith, they cried out as one: 'O Virgin, Lady of Rocamadour, Lady of mercy and compassion, give us our good father back.' And because the only-begotten Son of God said to his disciples *Whatever you shall ask in my name God will give you*,[6] he heard their prayers through the merits of his Mother. When the dead man had been lifted off the ground and was being carried to his grave, he got up from the bier as if he were waking from a deep sleep. He spoke to the people there with kind words and comforted them like a father. To those who persevered in faith he promised the joys which he had already tasted. And he added words of warning to his soothing message. Everyone exultantly danced for joy, praising the Lord for his great works and singing wonderful hymns in honour and celebration of his glorious Mother. Later on the priest, who was grateful for the benefit done to him, returned to the church of the glorious Virgin of Rocamadour, just as he was in the habit of doing but now with greater devotion. He brought with him the bed on which he had lain dead and, recounting the miracle, gave thanks.

I.3. A woman who broke her vow is punished by divine vengeance

In the region of the metropolitan city of Vienne there lived a woman who had been blind for a long time, having lost the sight in both eyes. Hers was a mournful existence. Nevertheless, she was solicitous about her health and

[4] Cf. Philippians 1:21.
[5] Psalms 83:8.
[6] John 16:23.

placed the greatest hope in the Virgin of Rocamadour; and she was not ashamed to wear out the Virgin and her Son with her continuous prayers. She would add that she would go to the Virgin's church if the light in her eyes came back. The merciful Lady of pity listened to her prayers, and the blind woman was not frustrated in her desire. She recovered her sight. Seeming to forget the benefit she had received, however, the woman put off performing her vow. The Mother of the Lord, as if impatient at her delay, inflicted a harsher wound upon her, thereby forcing her to come to her church. For when one day the woman was having a meal, the meat she was eating contained a bone which was sharp at both ends and became lodged in her throat. What was the miserable wretch to do? From the outside one could hear gasps and sighs, but scarcely any voice. This woman, who had once been deprived of the sight in her eyes, was now deprived of health throughout her body. On the inside she was in agony: an exceptionally sharp pain affected the vitals of her heart and ate away at her insides. Her body was so afflicted in this way that she wanted to die rather than be tortured thus any longer. She took no food for sixteen days and was never able to get any rest. Constantly bewailing her guilt with tears and groans, she beseeched the Virgin she had offended to be merciful towards her once more. 'O star of the sea, you gave sight to this wretched woman. How long will you persist in your wounded love? This wounded woman is now nearly finished. If you deny her a sign of your mercy, she won't be able to live much longer.' All those present felt miserable and shared in the woman's misery. And everyone prayed for her. The Virgin became milder because of their prayers: she knocked the bone from the woman's throat and restored her to her former health. To avoid being punished again for delaying, the woman set out on her journey and came to the church of the Mother of God. There she showed the bone as a token of the miracle and praised the mercy of the glorious Lady for the benefit conferred by both the first and the subsequent sign.

I.4. Some thieves unable to do injury to a pilgrim

Because the fame of the glorious Virgin of Rocamadour is talked about and is growing all over the world, it has not only reached peoples in the West but also those in the East. In the city which is commonly known as Acre there lived a blacksmith called John. Crossing great distances by sea and journeying far by land he finally came to this church, which was his goal. Once he had solemnly performed everything that he had vowed to do, he set out to make the pilgrimage to the shrine of Saint James.[7] One day, when he had slipped away from the group he was in because he wanted to empty his bowels, three robbers who had concealed themselves in a hiding-place seized him, cruelly dragged him off, and tried to grab hold of his possessions. O kind Virgin, he

---

[7] Santiago de Compostela in Galicia.

calls on you for help. Where are you? Why do you not come to the assistance of your servant, who truly serves you, in this moment of danger? Look, his things are being taken away, and he is being severely whipped and beaten. And still you do not help him. What was the pilgrim to do as he saw his property being carried off? John had confidence in the Lord and in his merciful Mother. He fixed his eyes on the heavens, and with groans and heartfelt contrition called upon the star of the sea, above all others, and more earnestly committed himself and his property to her care. The wicked men pressed on with their foul crime. Yes, they pressed on, but they could not prevail. For they were unable to lead away the mule which the pilgrim was using as his transport, even though they pushed it, hit it, and inflicted wounds upon it. Marvellous to relate, when they touched John's money, their hands suddenly became paralysed and shrivelled. Overcome by great fear and trembling, they threw themselves face down at the pilgrim's feet and prayed that through his prayers and the merits of the Blessed Virgin they might be able to recover their health. The pilgrim prayed and the robbers were healed. After he had completed his pilgrimage and performed his vow to St James, John returned to the church of the glorious Virgin to give thanks for the benefit he had received. He recounted this miracle and in addition showed everyone the scars on the mule to reinforce their belief in the story.

I.5. An excommunicate who presumed to enter the Virgin's church

A young man who was physically healthy and strong, and who lived among the bands of Gascons,[8] came to the church of the Blessed Mary without receiving penance and priestly absolution. He rashly presumed to enter the church, and just as rashly went up to the holy altar without shame. But the Virgin, the Queen of all the kingdoms, whose temple he had profaned and whose sanctuary he had violated, would not tolerate such impropriety and handed the man's body over to Satan to make him an example to others. The wretch was therefore seized. Calling out with piteous cries and miserably tugging and tearing at himself, he railed at those who were trying to restrain him. Everyone found him unpleasant and terrifying. He thundered in a clear and shrill voice, which resembled the sound of a loud trumpet, that everyone was beating him because of his insolence. He constantly roamed around the church and could not be moved away. Whenever the church was open he would go inside and disrupt the services, because scarcely anything could be

---

[8] The phrase is *Guasconum fretus caternis*, which seems an oddly indirect expression if the author simply meant to say that the young man came from Gascony. It is possible that *caternae* refers to mercenary bands, Gascony being among those areas that were recognized as recruiting grounds for groups of this type. On the other hand the reference to the priest and the payment of tithes would suggest a more domestic setting.

heard above his din. The devil who possessed him gave him such strength that his throat never grew hoarse and his screams never abated. He remained like this for four days, taking no food. And for four nights he did not sleep at all. He was a constant nuisance to everyone with his crying out, the frothing at the mouth, and the grinding of his teeth. What more is there to say? Everyone was afraid when they heard him and anguished when they saw him. The monks and those who looked after the church were disturbed by this new and unfamiliar form of punishment, especially since this is usually a house of mercy, not of vengeance. They made diligent inquiries about the background of the man on whom the devil was now exercising his evil art. It was discovered that he always disobeyed the Church's decrees: he was an excommunicate who was not afraid to go into a church despite the prohibition; he was thoroughly stubborn in all his dealings with priests, even his own pastor; and to cap all his criminality, he used to lay claim to his local church's tithes and keep them for himself. The monks said to one another, 'We believe that this has happened so that the glory of the Blessed Mary should be made perfectly plain to everyone through him. For just as it is in her church that he is raging and pounding, so it is through her that he will be restored to health.' On their advice it was arranged for the man to be taken back home, where he was reconciled to his priest and restored the tithes and other things he had taken. Finally he was given penance by his own priest and absolved in the proper fashion. Immediately, as if in an instant, the demented man became well. He had only recently been raging; now he extolled the glorious Virgin with wonderful praises, honoured her, and affirmed that he had been snatched from the demon's clutches through her merits and kindness. Without further ado he returned to the church of the Blessed Virgin and gave thanks, establishing an annual payment to be made in return for this and other benefits.

I.6. A thieving pilgrim deprived of the use of his tongue

Not long afterwards, a man from the Toulousain arrived with other pilgrims (there are large numbers of pilgrims every day). Entering the church, he placed his offering on the altar and then walked down to his lodgings with his companions to have some food. *Because he was a thief, and as he had the money box,*[9] he kept back some of the offerings which had been sent for the Blessed Virgin. To prevent him from perishing for such a crime when examined at the Last Judgement, he was deprived of the use of his tongue in the here and now. The anguish of his companions was immense. Raising a cry to the heavens, and with tears and sobs, they called upon the most Blessed Virgin on behalf of their friend. They proposed that they would have nothing to eat until the merciful Virgin took pity on their companion. Those living in

[9] John 12:6.

the village rushed up, sharing in the pilgrims' suffering and crying alongside them. With raised voices they called on the Mother of compassion and mercy. After the thief was taken back to the church he revealed the money box containing the sums entrusted to him. When his companions and the crowd of people which had gathered saw this, they realized that he was being held bound thanks to his covetousness for money. The money was handed over. Immediately the mute man began to speak. He acknowledged his own guilt and praised the glorious and everlasting Virgin, who takes pity on sinners.

I.7. A mortally wounded woman cured by the Blessed Virgin

A knight was chatting and joking with his wife, whom he absolutely adored. Being an upright woman, the wife straightforwardly interrupted the conversation with these words: 'I would like you to tell me whether you are sticking properly to our marriage bond. Is there a mistress whose love you prefer to mine?' The knight was a jocular and frivolous young man, and so he replied with a smile, 'Do you think I'm happy with you on your own? Do you believe that I haven't got all manner of girlfriends?' She then said, 'If I really believed what you are telling me I would take this knife (for she had a knife in her hand) and stick it in me.' She was pregnant, and the baby was due soon. But the knight compounded what he was saying by adding 'I don't believe you would harm yourself because you thought what I'm saying was true.' The woman found it impossible to bear so much shame any longer and was unable to restrain herself. Heedless of her sex, she drove the knife in and stabbed herself in the stomach. The knight was overwhelmed by this sudden and unexpected mishap. He pounded his chest, tore at his face and hair, and in a voice choked with tears called himself a wretch. And he was indeed speaking the truth: he had been fortunate with his wife, and now he had lost both the mother and the unborn child she was carrying in her womb. All those present added their anguish to his. Their sorrow was roused both by the man's grief and by the thought of the death of a woman whose life had earned the greatest respect. Who could reasonably fail to hold back his tears when he saw the pregnant woman dying in misery and the foetus not yet brought forth? No one pulled the knife which had transfixed her body out of the wound because they reckoned that she would die when it was extracted. Her husband – still a husband and not yet a widower – was covered in tears. Directing his prayers towards the Lord, he called upon his merciful Mother: 'Lady, you who are my salvation, my consolation, pre-eminent against my worthlessness and tribulation, the Lady who has led me through life to this moment, I bear witness to you and call upon you to bear witness yourself to my clear conscience and pure innocence. I bear witness to you, Lady, and I confess in front of all these people that I have never sullied the marriage bed with adulterous intercourse nor looked at other women. I have kept my heart clean and innocent of all desire for female company. So now, Lady, I am regarded as guilty of all this even though I have done none of it. My wife's death is making me die. I won't be able to live when the greatest part of me has died. O, my wife, my darling wife, is there anyone who can make me die in your place? I will be living but not alive because I will be living in constant mourning and my body will waste away. O, I wish my spirit could fail along with my body! Has there ever been anyone who has felt the wound in someone else's body as I am doing now? But surely we were one body in Christ? Of course we were. My body has been run through, and I am in pain. Who will heal me? Virgin, Lady and powerful Queen, you do not reject those who place their hope in you. Show us your gracious and calm face, and work an act of mercy. Virgin, you hear the prayers of the humble: come to my aid, heal this woman's wound, and give her back her health. It would be better for her to die rather than have her end dragged out and make her carry on in agony any longer. Virgin, Virgin, I commit myself to your judgement. You weigh everything in the scales of mercy: do not treat my hasty words, those stupid words I uttered, as a done deed, for I am innocent of doing wrong. Lady, I will not be able to repay you adequately, but I will make an offering before your holy altar of a wax model of my wife weighing as much as she does.'[10] Without further delay, and in the expectation of the Lady's mercy, he pulled out the knife, which had passed through the woman's spine. Everyone wept and confidently pleaded for help from on high. The Queen of Heaven, who is prompt to help those who beseech her with vows, granted their petition. The woman who could not be healed by doctors' medicines was cured by the Blessed Virgin and restored to her former health.

I.8. A knight's wife and daughter restored to health

The Premonstratensian order has an abbey called Bucilly[11] in the diocese of Laon. It so happened that an old church there collapsed because of its great age. It came crashing down, accidentally burying an adjacent house which was home to a knight, his wife and children. As they hurried to escape, the woman and her daughter were buried under the house's beams and stones from the church. Friends and neighbours ran to the scene and eventually moved some of the stones away. They carefully pressed their ears to the rubble and could hear the girl, who sounded on the point of dying. They set about working with greater urgency, and the girl appeared. Her whole body was ravaged by the sharpness of the stones and the weight of the beams. They grabbed her and attempted to pull her out, but she was trapped by a beam.

---

[10] For the practice of offering life-size/weight models see Bautier, 'Typologie des ex-voto', pp. 254–6. See II.31; II.32 below.

[11] Aisne. See *DHGE* 10.1029–31; Cottineau 1.525. Bucilly became a Premonstratensian community in 1148.

She was making indistinct noises like someone who was dying, and she could not be moved. There was an enormous crowd of people there. They strove with all their might and main to dislodge the beam and free the girl, whose innocent blood was pouring out. They tried without success, for neither strength nor skill was of any use. Losing hope for her well-being, they drew back one after another. But through the mercy of the glorious Virgin, a knight arrived who told the girl's father that she would be freed if he made a promise to visit the Lady of Rocamadour. The father freely and willingly listened to this advice. Immediately, and as if without any effort, he and a handful of others pulled the half-dead girl free. He saw that the Virgin's assistance was at hand and bringing him aid, and so he set about getting his wife out as well. They searched for the wife and she was found, covered in many wounds. The husband pulled her clear, even though she was weighed down under a large pile of wood and stones: this was not the result of human strength but the work of the glorious Virgin. The wounds of the mother and daughter were bound. The lethal injuries were completely healed through the Virgin's medicine. And within a short space of time the two were restored to their former health.

I.9. A knight's house saved from fire

There is an imperial castle called Stollburg,[12] in the diocese of Würzburg, which divine punishment caused to be struck by lightning and burned to the ground because of the sins of its inhabitants. Below the castle and within its outer wall there lived a knight called Riculf, who had been to the church of the Blessed Mary of Rocamadour a long time before. He saw the fire spreading everywhere and his house being covered by burning debris which was falling from the buildings higher up. There was such a mass of flaming brands on the roof of the house that four carts would not have sufficed to carry them away. The houses next to his were on fire everywhere. In his anxiety he loudly called upon the Blessed Virgin from the bottom of his heart: 'Virgin, Lady of Rocamadour, did I not commit myself and my property to your power and protection when I came to your church? Surely I alone won't be able to escape from such a great fire, especially now that my clothes are on fire and the shield which is covering me is almost burned away? Star of the sea, the merciful provider in times of need, come and help me, for I have no faith in my own strength.' Immediately the Lady acted favourably towards her faithful servant, sending down such a heavy fall of rain onto the house that it extinguished the brands within moments, saved the building and spared all the knight's belongings. He came to the church to

---

[12] Or Stolberg (Unterfranken). See C. Tillmann, *Lexicon der deutschen Burgen und Schlösser*, 1 vol. in 4 (Stuttgart, 1958–61), ii.1051; iv.41b.

give thanks, and duly gave thanks to the glorious Virgin as was fitting and proper.

I.10. A Lombard rescued from a fire and later freed from chains

A man from Lombardy was accused of a serious crime in his lord's court and was sentenced to be burned to death. Mindful of the fact that he was to be condemned unjustly and without cause, he poured out his prayers to the Lord and called upon his compassionate Mother with these words: 'O Lady, if I am reckoned to be guilty of this quite wicked offence, may my prayer be execrable to you, may I be overcome by the fire, and may I receive no assistance.' An immense pyre was constructed from pieces of wood, and the innocent man was thrown into its midst. He kept the thought of the glorious Virgin of Rocamadour in his heart and the sound of her name on his lips, crying out to her to come to his aid. His prayers deserved to be answered, as events demonstrated. For although the flames were very high and spread all around, they did him no harm, and he was scarcely touched by them at all. In fact, as the flames enveloped him they actually cooled him down. When those who were responsible for his ruin saw that he was not being consumed by the fire, and that not a hair on his head was singed, they had him thrown back into prison. They had him placed in shackles and bound with other iron chains secured with bars and bolts. And they posted guards to watch over him. That night, as he called on the Lady of all from the depths of his prison, she who had freed him from the fire now showed her favour towards him once more. For she appeared surrounded by an abundance of light and accompanied by many companies of virgins, and she filled the cell with a wonderful fragrance. She released him from his chains and told him to leave a free man. His guards spotted him moving off and carrying his chains, and yet they stood by dumbstruck *like dumb dogs unable to bark.*[13] When he had passed through the first and the second door, he came to a third which, like the earlier ones, was also open to him.[14] Although there were many watchful guards stationed at each of the doors, not one of them laid a hand on the man, who was able to walk past his enemies as if he were moving among his servants. He made a pilgrimage, carrying a substantial weight of iron – just as is on display today in the church – and giving thanks.

I.11. Someone else miraculously rescued from an unheard-of punishment

In Gascony there lived a faithful servant of the Blessed Mary who made annual pilgrimages to the church of Rocamadour to pray. This man was

[13] Isaiah 56:10.
[14] Cf. Acts 12:10.

slandered in his lord's court and accused of the gravest of crimes. He was accordingly thrown into prison and bound with iron chains and heavy shackles, for his lord had sworn that he should die from the squalid conditions in his gaol and from the debilitating effects of hunger. But the Mother of mercy disposed otherwise. When those who had tied the man up left him alone, he was released through our Virgin's compassion and was able to walk around in his cell. When the tyrannical lord heard about this, he had a tomb dug inside the gaol, to be surrounded by a strong wall and sealed by means of enormous beams skilfully forced together. When the lord could not think up any further savage treatment, the prisoner's hands and feet were bound and a chain was placed around his neck. Then they threw him into this tomb, leaving an air-hole just big enough to allow him to breathe. But in the middle of the night, as the prisoner wept and prayed, he was freed through the merits of the Blessed Virgin. He climbed up a ladder to the upper part of the tower, and from there he jumped down a great distance, yet without coming to any harm. When he reached the outer wall he became fearful because he did not have a ladder to get over it, nor could he find an entrance to slip out through. He called on the Mother of God and she came to his aid. She shattered the wall in front of him, and taking him by the hand led him safely and joyously to the church. And he brought with him a wax tower shaped like the one from which he had escaped.

I.12. A noble who escaped from a precipice

In the land of Count Amelius,[15] in the valleys of Maurienne, a noble was being rather careless as he was riding with his companions across steep mountain slopes and along deep valley floors. It so happened that the horse he was riding veered off the path and came towards a precipice, falling down with such a crash that it was cut clean in two on the sharp rocks. The knight was afraid that he would fall as heavily, and thought that he was close to death. He quickly called upon the Lady of Rocamadour, and she immediately came to his aid. She held onto him as he fell and placed him unharmed at the bottom of the valley. His companions had spent a very long time mournfully and tearfully searching for him on the way down when they finally came across him praising the Blessed Virgin. He told them that he had escaped thanks to the merits of the Queen of mercy, the Queen of Heaven and Lady

---

[15] Albe, p. 120 n. 55, read *Amelii* as a corruption of *Amedei*, so that the reference would be to Count Amadeus III of Savoy, who died on the Second Crusade in 1148. This is possible, but it does not support Albe's conclusion that the story cannot be dated any later than that year. In 1172 the count of Savoy was Amadeus's son Humbert III: see C. W. Previté Orton, *The Early History of the House of Savoy (1000–1233)* (Cambridge, 1912), pp. 316–52.

of Rocamadour. After that he came to the church of the one to whom he owed his liberation, gave thanks and recounted the miracle.

I.13. A youth saved from shipwreck and hanging

A youth from Gothia[16] was setting about crossing a river with his mother. But he was pushed into the water by the evil enemy, who always envies and opposes the good, and he sank into the depths of the torrent. With great wailing and weeping his mother called on Our Lady, crying out for her son to be restored to her. Boatmen searched for the lad but were unable to find him. Nonetheless the mother believed that the Blessed Virgin was with her: she alternately offered up to her soothing prayers and wearying cries, like those of a mad woman. The mother wept bitterly but did not lose hope. Surely the Lord was listening to her prayers and was moved by the tears which rolled down her cheeks? It is clear that he was moved, but he caused there to be such a delay, so I believe, in order that faith and devotion should grow and so that the assistance given by the Mother of God should be more clearly and publicly demonstrated to all the faithful. It was around the first hour of the day when the evil spirit overcame the youth. The Mother of God kept him safe under the surface of the water, just as if he had scarcely fallen in at all. By now it was evening, and the mother was continuing to pray, when contrary to all hope the lad who had fallen in appeared in the middle of the stream. He seemed to be held still there; the strength of the current was unable to move him. He was lifted out of the water and taken back to his mother. Everyone shouted out their praises of the glorious Mother of God. When the cunning enemy saw that his wickedness had not prevailed, he continued to persecute the young man because of the great setback that he had suffered. After the youth had reached full manhood, it happened that he was taken prisoner during an expedition and, led off to execution, he was hanged on the sort of gibbet used to string up thieves. He hung there for three days without suffering,[17] and he called on all those there with these words: 'She who long ago brought me out from the water's depths is now holding me up as I hang here: I am untouched by pain and the effects of hunger and thirst. She is deservedly renowned all over the world, and wishes to be glorified through my example.' What an extraordinary and uplifting scene! People gathered

[16] The area north-east of the eastern Pyrenees as far as the Rhône.
[17] For other examples of failed hangings, see *Liber Miraculorum Sancte Fidis*, I.30, pp. 134–6; *Book of Sainte Foy*, pp. 99–101; 'Liber miraculorum sancti Aegidii', cc. 12, 15, 21, 22, 27, *Analecta Bollandiana*, 9 (1890), pp. 394–5, 402–3, 407–8, 410–11, 420 (see also 'Miracula beati Egidii', c. 2, *MGH SS* 12.317–18); William of Canterbury, 'Miracula gloriosi martyris Thomae', VI.126, p. 515. The motif of the man miraculously saved from hanging was prominent in *Mariales* – collections of Marian miracles not linked to a specific shrine – which were popular from the twelfth century onwards: see Ward, *Miracles and the Medieval Mind*, pp. 155–65, esp. 156, 163.

from all around when they heard that he was still alive; and hanging there he spoke to them, apparently in no pain. He moved all of them to love of the most glorious Virgin as he cried out her praises. What more is there to say? He was taken down from the scaffold and visited the church of Rocamadour to give thanks.

I.14. A knight cured by the Virgin after being run through with a lance

William, a knight from Redon,[18] had been run through the stomach by a lance, which went in right up to the spine. Doctors sewed up his entrails, bound the wounds and applied poultices. But their skills were not enough to make their patient well. Whatever he ate would come out of both orifices, and his insides were growing putrid. So when the doctors' attentions failed to heal the injured man, they became afraid of his friends and, declaring that he would be dead within three days, seized the first opportunity to run away. Deprived of all human help, the knight asked for assistance from the Lord. No one had any faith in the possibility of his recovery, but he continued to place his hope in the glorious Virgin of Rocamadour. While his relatives and friends wept, he raised his eyes towards heaven and devoutly poured out his prayers to the Lord: 'Lord, you made everything out of nothing, you make the weak well, you recall those who wander from the true path because you are the way and the truth. Grant me life through you, for it is death not to live in you, so that in life I may give you praise. Queen of the world, the gate to heaven, Lady of Rocamadour, Mother of mercy, you show compassion and pity towards others. Deign to answer my humble prayers so that I can announce the glory of my recovery in your church.' After he offered up this prayer in a flood of tears he was overcome by sleep. For the Mother of mercy had placed her restoring hand upon him, and was already healing his wounds with her caress. The knight's friends were immediately summoned, and he confidently declared that he was feeling much better and more comfortable than the day before, and the day before that when he had been treated by the doctors. Soon Mary, the worker of good deeds and the giver of health, made the man able to stand up and walk, to the glory and praise of her name. And so he came to the church and gave thanks to God and his glorious Mother.

I.15. A shrivelled arm cured by Our Lady

Count Robert of Meulan[19] fell off his horse and landed on his right arm, which became dislocated at the shoulder joint. It was put right thanks to the skills of doctors. After some time had passed, he happened to fall on the same

---

[18] The Latin *Rotonensium* points to Redon in Brittany (Ille-et-Vilaine), not the Rouergue as suggested by Albe, p. 122, n. 59.

[19] Robert III (1166–1207). Meulan is west of Paris.

arm, which was dislocated more seriously than before at the same joint. Doctors applied poultices which did absolutely no good, and they lost hope that the arm would get better; it hung down behind Robert's back as if it were shrivelled up, and nothing the doctors could do would make it lift up. Robert directed his prayers to the glorious Mother of God, saying: 'Lady, you do not scorn the groanings of the afflicted. Remember not the sins of my youth or my wickedness,[20] and recall your mercy. Give me back the strength in my arm, to the extent that I may give thanks in your church at Rocamadour.' As he said these and similar things, he had his arm lifted up, placing his hope in the Virgin's mercy. Suddenly, and to the great astonishment of all those present, he began to move the arm and to wave it around, while also declaring that he was cured thanks to the merits of the glorious Virgin, which was true.

I.16. A blind boy given his sight

In the town of Houdain,[21] which is in the province of Rheims and the diocese of Arras, a man called Robert, known as 'the Lean', had a son, to whom he had given the same name. When the boy was two days old – if that – he became permanently blind. His parents were distraught at the blindness and vowed to carry their son to the church of the Blessed Mary of Rocamadour. So they set out on their journey. When they had been travelling for eight days, the child, who had never seen anything, gradually began to make things out. Moreover, he started to reach out his hands when something was held up to him. But because he still had fairly small pupils, he could not fix his gaze in the same way that someone could who had been able to see from birth. The parents reached the church which is dedicated to the glorious Virgin and, presenting the child who could now see, glorified and praised God for his wonders and exalted his glorious Mother.

I.17. A man whose lost teeth were restored

During a battle a knight who was in his sixties was hit in the mouth by the hilt of a sword and had four of his front teeth knocked out. To prevent himself from becoming an incoherent-sounding object of universal derision, he eagerly prayed to the glorious Mother of God for the teeth to be restored. Amazing to relate, the teeth were soon made good; they were a different colour from the rest, in that they were as white as ivory. He came to the church and demonstrated the miracle. And to commemorate what had happened he brought with him four silver teeth to match the number of those he had lost.[22]

---

[20] Cf. Psalms 24:7.
[21] Latin *Hosden*. Albe p. 126 n. 64 suggested Hesdin, but this was situated in the diocese of Thérouanne. Houdain (Pas-de-Calais) fits the reference to the diocese of Arras.
[22] For anatomical *ex votos* see Bautier, 'Typologie des ex-voto', pp. 256–9; cf. I.25; II.33 below.

I.18. A man freed from his chains

Boso of Allinges[23] captured Richard of Geneva without just cause, threw him into a prison and bound his feet with iron shackles. All the time that Richard was in the dungeon he had the glorious Mother of God constantly on his lips and in his heart, humbly begging to be set free and led out of the prison through her merits. But because the delay served to make his devotion grow and his faith increase, it was only on the eighth night of his captivity that he was freed and got away, carrying his chains with him. From there he came to the church of his liberator at Rocamadour, gave thanks and recounted the miracle.

I.19. A bull given to Saint Mary which brought back its herd

In the region of Grenoble[24] there was a man who owned a large number of cattle. Wishing to propitiate the gracious Lady of Rocamadour he promised to give her a bull, the head of its herd. A short time afterwards an enemy of his arrived with his henchmen and seized all the man's property, taking it to a fortified place and stationing guards. Now that the wheel of earthly success, which had previously made the man prosper, was turning against him, he grieved for the loss of the means to perform his vow and entreated the Virgin with tearful prayers. Something amazing then happened: in the middle of the night, while a guard stood and watched, the insensible and irrational animal acted as if it were capable of reason by knocking the bolt from the gate, leading the herd away with it, and bringing them to the front of their owner's house. The man was overjoyed at his unexpected good fortune. And when he came to the doors of the church of the blessed and glorious Virgin, it was not the man who led the bull, but rather the bull who led the man – like a guide who knew the way, never deviating from the path to the left or right.

I.20. A woman with dropsy restored to health

In the diocese of Cambrai, in the bourg of Valenciennes,[25] there lived a woman named Hathvidis, the wife of Walter of Beaurain.[26] She had been suffering from dropsy[27] for about seven years, and she could not be cured by

---

[23] Haute-Savoie. See L. Blondel, *Châteaux de l'ancien diocèse de Genève* (Mémoires et documents publiés par la Société d'histoire et d'archéologie de Genève, 7; Geneva, 1956), pp. 355–67.

[24] Following Albe's interpretation (p. 128) of *Gramnovolensibus partibus*. The more usual Latin form for Grenoble was *Gratianopolis*.

[25] Nord.

[26] There are several places of this name in north-eastern France.

[27] For this term, which referred to swelling of the tissues, see Finucane, *Miracles and Pilgrims*, p. 104.

doctors' treatments. Although she was favoured by her youth and looks, and although her family background and wealth suggested that she was fortunate, the illness sufficed to rob her of all happiness. Indeed, everyone despaired for her well-being, apart from the woman herself, who would spend night and day, day and night, in constant mournful prayer, asking the Blessed Mother of God to make her well. Because, of course, she lived a long way from the church of Rocamadour, she would habitually prostrate herself on the ground and pray in the direction in which she heard it lay. One day, when she had gone out to pray, staggering and sliding on one foot as she went, the gracious Virgin took pity on her and opened up the fount of her mercy. For the fluid under the woman's skin and inside her body began to pour out of her natural places like a spring. And whereas up to that point two people could scarcely put their arms around her on account of her great size, now her navel seemed to be sticking to her spine because she was so very thin. But why labour the point further? She soon recovered her health, bringing joy to her family who joined her in praising the Blessed Virgin.

I.21. Three blind people cured

In the diocese of Clermont, not far from the city itself, there lived three blind people in the same village. Two of them were taken to the church of the Blessed Mother of God in the company of many of their neighbours. One of these was granted the ability to see through the merits of the distinguished Virgin in her very church. The other started the journey home with his friend who could now see and the other pilgrims. He complained mournfully that the Virgin of all was treating him more slowly than she usually did others; and in disparaging the good which had happened to the other man he seemed to be envious of it, reckoning that he would be dishonoured if he returned home blind while his companion could see. So he carried on behaving in this way, by turns crying and complaining. But he did not despair, and placing his hope in those up above he constantly asked for help from the heavenly Virgin. And it so happened that this man, who hitherto had needed to be led by a guide, now became his own guide, thanks to the mercy of our Virgin; he became able to walk ahead of the group and lead the others. He rejoiced at being able to see, and praised the Mother of God. When the pilgrims were approaching the village which was their journey's end, the father of the blind person who had stayed behind was at his plough when he heard rumours about those who had been given their sight. He left his oxen and, without even going back to his home, set out on the road with his son. He duly arrived at the church of the Virgin. There he confessed that he had sinned in putting off his journey. He kept up vigils and prayers day and night, night and day, pleading on behalf of his son. After three days his prayers were deservedly answered, and the blind son gained his sight.

I.22. A crippled woman cured

There is a well-known church in Burgundy dedicated to St Anthony.[28] It came around to the time of the year when the feast of this saint is celebrated. The people were prohibited from doing any menial work and were instructed to observe the feastday in proper fashion. A common woman, however, shut herself away in her house, well out of sight, to perform some task or other. At the usual time she was about to have a meal with her husband, and was reaching out with a bowl, when her hand suddenly seized up. Her nails stuck into her palm, punctured the skin and damaged the adjacent nerves. She therefore sought guidance, and took up position in front of the altar of the holy and venerable Anthony. There she stayed without a break for thirty days and nights asking to be given her health, but without success. Her hopes dashed, she made up her mind to seek more efficacious, and indeed greater, assistance from the Lady of Rocamadour. At that time several knights from that area were going to the church of the Blessed Virgin. She attached herself to their company and set off on her journey with an anxious sigh. No less a man than the prince of Lorraine[29] happened to be at Rocamadour on a visit to the church. Hearing that a very large number of pilgrims had arrived, he ascended to meet them. When he saw the woman he was moved by pity, and foregoing his horse he took hold of her by the arm and led her to the church. He made up his mind – and declared openly – that he would not abandon her until she had recovered. It was around the ninth hour of the day. Everyone was touched by the women's wretchedness, and they all prayed on her behalf to the Mother of the Lord, asking her to be moved by pity. The prince too knelt down in front of the altar, tirelessly held onto the woman's arm, lifted up her hand and called on everyone to pray for her. While the Lord's praises were being sung in the hour of Compline, blood started to flow out of the woman's hand like a stream, and little by little it began to straighten. And her arm, which had become withered, made a noise similar to the sound of a fence being broken. Now that she had recovered her health, she joyfully returned home.

I.23. A small child, blind since birth, who gained its sight

A man from Galicia[30] journeyed to Rocamadour with his wife, who was already quite advanced in years, to ask for a child. He was granted what he

---

[28] Saint-Antoine de Viennois (Isère). 'Burgundy' would seem to be used here to include southerly areas that lay within the old kingdom of Burgundy, as opposed to the later duchy and county.

[29] Most probably the Duke Matthew I of Lorraine (1139–76) featured later in the collection (III.9).

[30] The Latin, *Gallicanus*, is ambiguous. It may simply refer to someone from Gaul. Albe, p. 132 n. 80 suggests 'Welshman'.

asked for, but the baby boy was born permanently blind. The mother, who had hoped for the joy of a child given by God, became an instrument of lamentation. But she weaned the child and brought him up. And hoping for assistance from heaven, she set out with him on pilgrimage to the church where she had obtained him with her prayers. When she was passing through a village called Hermet,[31] she heard the church bells summoning the people to prayer. Dropping to the ground in front of a cross – there was a crucifix at the crossroads there – she directed her prayers to the Lord: 'Lord, you gave *your maidservant a son.*[32] Graciously listen to my prayer and grant my desire. You deigned to create the child from nothing; you can give sight to him in his blindness. Queen of the world, Lady of mercy, the fount of life, you were gracious in giving me the boy. Make him better by pouring into him the light by which he might see.' What more is there to say? An enormous amount of blood flowed out of the boy's eyes. And when the bleeding stopped he was able to see. Many of those who had seen the blind boy as he passed through the village joined him and came to the church of the Blessed Virgin of Rocamadour, where they praised the glorious Mother of the glorious Lord.

I.24. A knight who harassed a pilgrim and was assailed by infernal fire

A pilgrim bound for Rocamadour and Santiago de Compostela was passing through Poitou. He was wearing a cap on his head. He ran into Harduin of Maillé,[33] who greeted him and said that he wanted to buy the cap off him. The pilgrim rejected the price put on the cap, explaining that he needed it both for when it was hot and when it rained. Filled with indignation and anger, the knight moved away. But whipped up into a rage by the furies of hell, he then retraced his steps and went back up to the pilgrim, addressing him more coarsely with the intention of wresting the cap off him and paying less than it was worth. When the pilgrim did not respond in the way he wanted, the knight was unable to restrain his violent passion, and so he kicked the other man in the chest and threw him to the ground. The pilgrim was injured. With a deep sigh he called on God to take vengeance on the wrongdoer. For the supreme judge and just arbiter, who said *Vengeance is mine, I will repay,*[34] did not put matters off to the next day. As the night following the incident approached, he caused the knight to feel burning – what is called the infernal fire[35] – in his foot. The knight's servants looked for the pilgrim most carefully, but he was nowhere to be found. The great

---

[31] Lot.

[32] I Samuel 1:11.

[33] Indre-et-Loire. Strictly speaking Maillé was on the borders of Touraine and Poitou. See *Atlas de la France de l'an mil*, ed. M. Parisse and J. Leuridan (Paris, 1994), pp. 60–3.

[34] Romans 12:19; Hebrews 10:30.

[35] Ergotism, often referred to as *ignis sacer* ('holy fire').

fierceness of the burning heat consumed not only the foot but the lower leg right up to the knee. The knight was afraid that his whole body would burn away, and so he had his leg amputated at the knee. Straight away the fire crossed over into the other foot and began to consume him with great intensity, until finally he lost both feet and was left maimed. The hand of the Lord stretches over him to this day.

I.25. A lady cured of a polyp

Lady Domna, from the city of Plasencia,[36] suffered from a polyp for four years and more. Since she could not be cured, she promised to give a silver nose to the holy Mother of God of Rocamadour if she saw fit to restore her health. After the woman made this vow, or rather as she was in the act of making it, the Lady of Heaven cured her, as if greedy for gain.

I.26. A mute woman to whom the power of speech was restored

A noble woman, Paschors of Romans,[37] had for a very long time lost not only the faculty of speech but also the ability to make any sound at all. She therefore came to the church of the most Blessed Virgin of Rocamadour, where, crying and praying deep down in her heart, she took up position by the corner of the altar. The guardian of the church twice pushed her away from the altar because she was being a nuisance, but she bore the repulse with patience and made her way back to it through the midst of the pressing throng. When she came back for the third time, all the people prayed on her behalf and with her for the Mother of the Lord to be moved by pity, so that the chain holding her tongue might be loosened and her voice and speech be restored to her. The younger ones in the crowd did this because they observed her appearance, for she was beautiful to behold; but those with deeper understanding and greater devotion did so because they were amazed by the woman's steadfastness. But the guardian who was mentioned above was not mollified by the woman's tenderness, and failing to take heed of the fact that he was a man he had the temerity to strike her on the head with his rod in an attempt to drive her away from the altar. Yet this strong woman had her hope fixed in the Lord and was greedy for health, and she could not be budged from the altar. While the *Magnificat* was beginning during Vespers, however, her mouth opened and with a clear voice she began to glorify God. Many nobles who were present were filled with tears of joy. And lifting up their voices to the heavens they praised the Lord, praiseworthy in his works, and proclaimed the kindness of his Mother, which should be made known everywhere.

[36] León in northern Spain. Piacenza in northern Italy is another possibility for *Placentina*.
[37] Drôme.

I.27. A ship which was saved and some wine which did not spill

Roger Thevin, from Caen,[38] bought some wine at La Rochelle[39] in Aquitaine and loaded it onto his boat. As the vessel ploughed through the waves, in a convoy with ten other merchant ships, he set its sails to the wind. While they were sailing on the Atlantic a contrary wind whipped up into a gale. At times it would plunge them down towards the depths of the abyss; at other times it would lift them right up towards the sky. They were driven this way and that. Their anchors broke, the oars snapped, and everything presaged their death. Driven by the ferocity of the storm and the swirling wind, the ten other boats struck some rocks, where they broke up. Scarcely a handful of sailors and some merchants managed to escape the shipwreck; all those still on board were lost. Realizing that it was a matters of moments before he too was dead, Roger feared for his safety and sought the support of the Blessed Mother of God of Rocamadour, promising to give her a silver chalice[40] if she saved him and his property. Straight away his boat, which was being propelled headlong towards a cliff, reversed towards the open sea as if it were being pulled back by thousands of ropes. Steering a favourable course, and aided by a wind blowing in the right direction, the boat finally reached the port which was its destination. When Roger emptied the wine into other containers, he discovered that none of it had been lost even though the bands on some of the casks had rotted away and those on some others had been broken. For he had entrusted the cargo to a faithful and strong guardian who preserved what was hers by means of her great power and did not allow anything to be ruined. Bringing the chalice and other items, Roger came to the church of the glorious Lady of Rocamadour and recounted the miracle.

I.28. A mad woman who recovered her senses

A mad woman from Auxerre was securely tied up and led around the shrines of the saints, which are numerous in those parts. Denied the saints' intervention, she did not recover her health. Her relatives were pained by her raging madness and took it very badly. Since the physician's arts could do nothing to help her, they directed both the focus of their desire and their devotion towards the greatest of the great, the Lady of Rocamadour. They had not yet finished their prayer when the woman regained her senses. She came to the church and gave thanks.

---

[38] Calvados.
[39] Charente-Maritime.
[40] Cf. I.42 below, in which another liturgical object, a thurible, is offered by a merchant.

I.29. A man who was struck by an arrow and could not be healed

During a mêlée between some knights,[41] Henry of Mâchecourt[42] was hit near the eye by an arrow. Not one of his surgeons could find the iron arrowhead, even though they cut away the bone and explored the wound from the shoulder up to the eye. Gradually the flesh inside grew putrid, and as time wore on the knight became more and more seriously ill. His jaws were oppressed by the weight of the pain and were hardly able to chew. And he could take nothing except some liquid every now and then. His veins contracted, and his complexion, which before had been quite pleasant, grew drawn and pale. Then all the strength in his body and all his energy disappeared; he was like a plant whose roots were decaying before they had fully grown. Since he had lost all hope of recovering by human means, and by now preferred the idea of dying to facing this constant agony any longer, he set off on a journey to the distinguished Virgin of Rocamadour, who is accustomed to healing the sick and recalling them to their former health. Reaching the church, he performed the appropriate pious devotions and then, on the advice of the brethren, returned home, now weaker than before. He did not doubt the Lord's mercy, however, nor the gentleness of his mild Mother. While he was staying in his house, eagerly going about his prayers and free to devote himself to his devotions, his whole spirit began to burn and he felt an itching in his wound. When he looked at the scar in a mirror he found that the iron from the arrow was coming out. This was extracted gently and painlessly by an iron smith, and the knight was immediately restored to his former vigour and perfect health.

I.30. Another man who was run through with a lance

Guirmand[43] of Kleve,[44] a castle situated in the archdiocese of Cologne, was struck in the left eye by a lance. He pulled the shaft out of his head, but the iron tip remained lodged in the wound. Everyone despaired for his life. He alone did not lose confidence, because at the very moment that the eye was struck he had commended the healing of the wound to the Blessed Mary of Rocamadour, whose pilgrim he had once been. The iron tip, however, had lodged so firmly in the bone at the back of the head that it was only after breaking two pairs of tongs that it was finally pulled out with the greatest difficulty. Thus restored to health, Guirmand attributed the miracle to Our Lady, his liberator, and came to the church.

[41] The Latin is *concursu militum*, by which the author may have meant a tournament.
[42] Aisne.
[43] For MS variants of the name, see Albe, p. 138 n. 100.
[44] Rheinprovinz. See Tillmann, *Lexicon der deutschen Burgen und Schlösser*, ii.983–4 s.v. Schwanenburg.

I.31. Desperate men aboard ship freed by the Queen of Virgins

Helias *Bellus Homo*, from Belvès[45] in Périgord, was returning from Jerusalem when he was caught in a storm in the Mediterranean. The sea was thrown into confusion as the waves swelled, and the ship was in danger of being destroyed. The sailors despaired for their lives as they struggled against the ferocity of the waves. Now that the ship was all but lost, they found no means of rescue other than prayers and alms, especially since the vessel's equipment had failed and it was being carried straight towards some rocks. They prayed to God, the liberator of all; they begged for help from the saints; they made vows to give alms to the most renowned of churches. But the sea did not grow calm. O death, how bitter, oppressive and irksome you are for almost all mortals! Yet when things are going well, how rarely does anyone remember you? Daily we are beaten with scourges and weighed down by tribulations; we are just dust and ashes, rotten flesh and worms, but in scorning the fact that we are men we exalt ourselves. We are worthless and useless serfs, yet at the hour of our death we fail to ask for the anger of the just judge to be appeased, as if we had acted well in all respects. Helias was one of those in danger. It is said that when all the others had closed their eyes for fear of dying and had no idea what to do, he gave them this advice: 'Brothers and lords, there is one source of help that we should seek after that from God. Let us together call upon the blessed and glorious Lady of Rocamadour. Let us honour the liberator of all by making vows and promising gifts, and we will then merit her assistance. For my part, if thanks to her helping grace I am worthy to be taken back home, then I will offer a silver ship, weighing one mark, at her holy altar.'[46] Immediately all those in the ship knelt down to entreat the glorious Virgin. With contrition in their hearts they made their vows, each according to his means, and described what they had promised to the others. And lo, the Lady of the winds, the soother of storms, the ruler of the waves, the restorer of all creatures, ordered the wind and sea to be calm. The ship was carried by favourable winds towards the harbour of safety and repose and reached the longed-for shore, by the grace of God who lives and reigns everywhere. Amen.

I.32. A knight whom an enemy was unable to harm

William of Civrieux (a castle situated in the region of Lyons)[47] was attempting to protect and rescue his lord, who had been taken prisoner by his enemies, when he was struck by five lances and thrown from his horse. He too was taken captive, and was handed over to one of the sergeants, who had

---

[45] Dordogne.
[46] For other marine *ex votos* see II.1; II.37 below.
[47] See Albe p. 140 n. 105. To his suggested identification might be added Civrieux in Ain.

a mortal hatred of him, to be killed. Realizing that he would not be spared and that he was on the very point of dying, the knight briefly called upon Our Lady, Our Lady, Our Lady of Rocamadour. And she came to his aid. For when the sergeant drew his sword and brandished it over William, he was unable to touch him even though he was quite still. Again and again the sword was waved around his head, but each time it came down on the ground. Reckoning that William was benefiting from divine assistance and could not be put to death using any weapon, the sergeant declared that he would be slowly starved to death. But the divine design is far removed from human resolution. For the Blessed Mother of God saw to it that a powerful knight on the opposing side was taken prisoner. And William, whose wretchedness and squalor had been a source of triumph to his enemy, was handed over in exchange for this other powerful man. In this way both men returned free to their homes.

I.33. A girl deaf and dumb since birth

On the day before the feast of Pentecost,[48] Huga, a girl who had reached marriageable age and had been deaf and dumb since birth, came to the church of the Blessed Mary of Rocamadour. With her were her father, Peter of Laroque,[49] which is in Quercy, and her mother and sisters. Wearing away her heart in humble contrition, Huga spent that day and the following sleepless night in prayer. At the hour of Matins the Mother of God looked down favourably on the girl. She became able to hear the church bells; and on recognizing Gerbert, the guardian of the church with whom she had been staying, she called out to him using his name. When those who had gathered for the feastday heard that the girl was speaking clearly and distinctly, they believed that this was greater than all the manifestations of heavenly power that they had witnessed. In a loud voice they praised God, who grants his faithful so many great and astounding benefits through the suffrages of his most glorious Mother, Our Lady.

I.34. A piece of wax which fell onto a lute

Peter Ivern, from Sieglar,[50] used to make his living by playing musical instruments. It was his custom to arrive at churches and pour out his prayers to the Lord, after which he would play upon the strings of his lute and sing the Lord's praises. One day he was in the basilica of the Blessed Mary of Rocamadour and had been plucking at his strings for a long time, every now and then singing along to his instrument, when he looked up. 'Lady,' he said,

---

[48] I.e. in May or June.
[49] Possibly Laroque-des-Arcs (Lot).
[50] Rheinprovinz, near Siegburg.

'if my playing and singing please you or your Son, my Lord, then grant me a piece from the countless measures of wax which are hanging here.'[51] As he prayed and sang in this way, and in full view of those who were present, a little piece of wax dropped onto his instrument. But the monk Gerard, who was guardian of the church, accused him of being a magician and caster of spells; and indignantly retrieving the piece of wax he put it back in its original spot. Yet Peter reckoned that this was God's work, and he carried on singing with patient forbearance. Sure enough, the piece of wax which had landed on him the first time dropped down once more. The monk grew impatient and angry, took the piece, and secured it more firmly in its original position. For a third time the Lord, who is forever constant and immutable in what he does, performed the same act as he had already done twice before. All those who were there and saw this were seized by *amazement at what had happened to him*.[52] Praising God as one, they raised their voices to the heavens. Peter began to weep with joy and returned the piece of wax which he had been given to God the giver, praising him *with timbrel and dance, with strings and pipe*.[53] To honour and praise the Lord's name, and to commemorate the miracle, he made an annual offering to the glorious Virgin of Rocamadour of a piece of wax weighing more than a pound. This he did for as long as he lived.

I.35. A demoniac freed from a demon

A noble squire from Montréal,[54] his mother's only child, was in the habit of swearing by the limbs of Our Lord Jesus Christ when out playing with others, and of vilifying him as much as he was able. He would also dishonour Christ's Mother, our glorious Lady, with improper words. So it came to pass that, as a means to amend evil people and to extol those who are good, the squire was deprived of all his bodily strength and became both dumb and mad. He was bound with iron chains and sewn into a newly acquired length of cloth; even though he had his hands secured by iron manacles, it took a large number of people to restrain him. Physicians were summoned and laboured long and hard without success. When they had exhausted all their means of healing they pronounced the squire incurable. But his mother, who loved her son as an only child, tearfully prayed to the Lady of Heaven, whom she knew had been offended by him. She asked her to treat the son favourably, and strove by means of constant alms-giving to lift the sin from him. Some nobles, however, conceived a plan which was no less sound

---

[51] The pieces of wax were not necessarily fashioned as candles: see Bautier, 'Typologie des ex-voto', pp. 245–6. For an offering of a weight of wax see below I.53.

[52] Acts 3:10.

[53] Psalms 150:4.

[54] Probably the place of that name in either Aude or Gers. Both are some distance from Toulouse, however.

and decided that the squire should be taken to the church of the most Blessed Virgin of Rocamadour: in this way the one who had offended her majesty with his haughty and abominable talk might there experience her favour. So the mother and the knights brought him here from the Toulousain. They could scarcely get him into the church because he was forcefully repulsed by the great power who dwells therein. Finally he was dragged in and led up to the altar. Weeping profusely and moving everyone else to tears, they stated that they would not withdraw from the altar until the merciful Virgin showed her mercy towards the lad. And so they stood there praying for a long time, trying to incite pity in the Lady, who does not wish for a sinner's death but rather a change in his way of life. She answered their prayers and, breaking the iron manacles around the young man's wrists and releasing the bond which held his tongue, she gave him back his voice and drove out the evil spirit which had possessed his body. Freed from the demon's clutches, the squire sounded out his praises to the Lord and declared that he had recovered his senses thanks to the merits of the most glorious Virgin, by the grace of Christ who lives now and forever more with God and the Holy Ghost. Amen.

I.36. A woman who could not sink

When Gaston of Béarn[55] died, he was survived by his pregnant wife Leefoas,[56] the sister of the king of Navarre.[57] But not long after her husband's death she had a miscarriage and lost a baby boy. The nobles and non-nobles, and all the common people, men and women alike, were greatly troubled by this loss and saw in it a foreshadowing of the future slaughter of the people, the destruction of churches and the desolation of the entire region. Inferences were drawn – mistakenly, as the outcome of the affair was to prove – and the woman was falsely summoned for trial by King Sancho of Pamplona[58] and his royal council, to stand accused of having aborted the baby boy before its natural term. They accordingly decided that she should be subjected to one of two opposing forms of suffering: she would either be burned alive or be tied up and allowed to sink in water.[59] The queen, who was innocent of this

[55] Viscount Gaston V (d.1170). For the aftermath of his death without male heirs, on which this story turns, see J. C. Shideler, *A Medieval Catalan Noble Family: The Montcadas 1000–1230* (Berkeley, 1983), pp. 109–10.

[56] *recte* Sancia. For an ingenious, if not wholly plausible, explanation of the name *Leefoas* as a corruption of *infanta* ('princess'), see Albe, p. 146 n. 122.

[57] Sancho VI (1150–94).

[58] I.e. Navarre.

[59] The author implies that this was a punishment inflicted after guilt was decided, but it is possible that an ordeal to establish guilt was at issue. For ordeals see R. Bartlett, *Trial by Fire and Water: The Medieval Judicial Ordeal* (Oxford, 1986), esp. pp. 16–20. A similar blurring of the distinction between ordeal and execution of sentence is perhaps also evident in III.24 below.

crime, saw that her end was near and prayed to Our Virgin, the Lady of Rocamadour, to come to her aid. And her petition was answered. She was tied up like someone about to undergo a judgement by water, and was then thrown into the depths of the torrent from the very high bridge next to the castle at Sauveterre.[60] An enormous crowd of more than three thousand men and women had gathered to witness this painful, or rather inhuman, spectacle. They all expected her to drown, like someone caught in a shipwreck. Some of them hurled insults, others compassionately prayed on her behalf to the Lord. Thanks to the Lord's mercy, however, and the assistance of his most glorious Mother, the woman was carried along on the surface of the deep torrent and did not go under: she travelled a distance greater than three bow shots and fetched up on the riverbank. And so her people joyfully carried her back, a free woman, to their home. Consequently she made an intricately-worked cloth to praise and glorify her liberator, and she sent it to the church of Rocamadour by entrusting it to Abbot G[61] of Rocamadour, who was returning from Santiago de Compostela.

I.37. A priest cured by the sign of pilgrimage

William, a priest from Chartres, was gripped by a serious illness and did not get up from his sickbed between the feast of St Nicholas and the feast of St Vincent.[62] As he grew weaker and was almost about to breathe his last, he was lifted from his bed and placed on the ground because he seemed to be on the point of going the way of all flesh; this happened three times in one day. His mother, however, who was touched deep down by her son's pain, called upon the kind and merciful Lady of Rocamadour and placed the sign of pilgrimage[63] upon him. Immediately the priest stopped feeling weak and was

---

[60] Sauveterre-de-Béarn (Pyrénées-Atlantiques).

[61] Gerald, abbot of Tulle.

[62] I.e. between 6 December and 22 January.

[63] Albe, p. 148 n. 133, followed by Rocacher, p. 296 supp. n., identifies the *signum peregrinationis* as the *sportelle*, or pilgrimage badge worn by Rocamadour pilgrims. The use of such badges, well attested from the thirteenth century onwards, can be traced back to the period when the miracles were written: see Garnier of Pont-Sainte-Maxence, *La Vie de Saint Thomas Becket*, ll. 5896–5900, pp. 181–2; trans. Shirley, *Garnier's Becket*, p. 157. But the term *signum* in the context of pilgrimage principally referred to the scrip and/or staff which a pilgrim received on departure. See *Le pontifical romano-germanique du dixième siècle*, c. 212, ed. C. Vogel and R. Elze, 3 vols. (Studi e Testi, 226–7, 269; Vatican City, 1963–72), ii.362. For the pilgrim badges of Rocamadour see E. Cohen, 'In haec signa: Pilgrim-Badge Trade in Southern France', *Journal of Medieval History*, 2 (1976), pp. 193–214, esp. 194–8; K. Köster, *Pilgerzeichen und Pilgermuscheln von mittelalterlichen Santiagostraßen: Saint-Léonard, Rocamadour, Saint-Gilles, Santiago de Compostela* (Ausgrabungen in Schleswig, Berichte und Studien, 2; Neumünster, 1983), pp. 43–88, esp. 49f.

wholly restored to health, thanks to the mercy of the great Virgin and thanks, too, to his mother's faith.

I.38. A cripple cured by a vision

Gerbert of Creysse[64] (a castle situated less than two miles from Rocamadour) was so crippled that his knees dug into his chest and his ankles stuck into his buttocks. When he heard about the many and great benefits which the Son of the most glorious Virgin confers upon pilgrims and strangers, through his Mother's intercession and thanks to the renown and suffrages of the church of Rocamadour, he had himself carried to that church in a basket. There he begged for food from those going in and coming out. The day before the feast of Pentecost arrived. Gerbert diligently performed his fasts and vigils, and that holy night he fell asleep, overcome by the great pain in his body. And lo, the Queen of the heavens, the Lady of the earth, appeared standing next to him. She took his head in her hands, while the blessed and excellent martyr George took his feet; they pulled at him and drew him upright. The guardian of the church, Gerbert, was fetched, and the other Gerbert said to him, 'Look, I've been made well. But the crowd filling the church entrance is stopping me from getting inside.' As a result pilgrims came running from all directions, joyously extolling the great works of the illustrious Virgin. Gerbert gestured for them to be silent and, in front of the entire crowd, announced that he was definitely cured, explaining the nature and sequence of what had happened.

I.39. A deaf and dumb woman who was cured

For a long time Polilia, who was deaf and dumb and came from Périgueux, lived in the village of Rocamadour with a poor woman called Juliana. When she wanted to get food, whatever she could come by, she used to stand outside the doors of the villagers' dwellings, tapping on the doorposts or the doors themselves and not stopping until the inhabitants were moved by her wretchedness to take pity on her. When she witnessed the jubilation of the people rejoicing at the fact that Gerbert had been raised upright, that night, indeed that very hour, she sighed in the direction of the fount of mercy; it was with weeping and moaning that she expressed herself because she could not speak. The joy of the man who had been cured drowned out the sighs of this afflicted woman close by. Yet truly the good Mother, the gentle Mother, took notice of her and listened to her prayers. For she opened the woman's mouth and made her tongue eloquent. The second miracle doubled the amount of

[64] Lot.

exultation and praise. Praise be to the God of gods in Sion, worthy to be praised and proclaimed everywhere. And praise and honour be to his glorious Mother.

I.40. A man restored to health with his horses

A young man called Gerard, who was from the monastery of Déols[65] near Châteauroux[66] in the archdiocese of Bourges, was returning from Jerusalem. The roughness of the sea made him feel sick in his stomach. He lost all his bodily strength, and as death drew near he looked like the empty shell of a man. Indeed, so severe was his illness, and so weak did he become, that every day for eight days those around him were ready to kick his corpse overboard. But Gerard raised up his spirit from its depths to direct it towards the heavens, crying out to the star of the sea of Rocamadour, the foremost amongst all the saints. He was swiftly cured and brought safely to the longed-for shore. On the outward journey, however, and while staying as a guest with some people, Gerard had left behind two palfreys for them to look after. He found that one of the horses had been mortally injured, while the other had become swollen because it had been unable to discharge its waste for eight days. On their behalf he made a vow that he would carry two wax horses[67] to Rocamadour. He then led them in perfect health to the church, performed his vow, and finally took them back joyfully and safely to his home region.

I.41. The horrible illness of a woman

Gervada of Salques,[68] which is a mile from Rocamadour, was seized by a very serious and horrible illness. She would froth at the mouth, grind her teeth, and stick her tongue right out. To the horror and alarm of those watching, she would gnaw at herself with her teeth and tear at herself with her hands. In truth the judgements of God are like many hidden depths, but we know that the manifest crimes of mortal men must be punished in this world or the next. This is why we believe that the woman who is the subject of this story was someone who had committed fornication with one man or had been the mistress of several, not to mention what stayed hidden from view; she suffered her punishment in this life because she will not be judged twice for the same wrong and in order that she might rejoice elsewhere in the fact that her sin was washed away by the pain she was then feeling. She was therefore led, or rather carried, to the church of the Mother of God so that

---

[65] See Cottineau, i.956–7.
[66] Indre.
[67] For other animal *ex votos* see II.12; III.8; III.9 below.
[68] Lot.

she could be washed and made clean in the fount of mercy. The kind Virgin, the Lady and Virgin of Rocamadour, who is always ready to assist those who pray and make vows to her, took pity on her pitiable state and answered the prayers of the faithful and of the pilgrims. She restored the woman to health and sent her back home full of joy, by the grace of her Son, Our Lord Jesus Christ, who lives and reigns forever and ever, one God with the Father and the Holy Ghost. Amen.

I.42. Robbers who left what they had stolen with its rightful owner

Ebrard of *Varez*,[69] a citizen of Lyons, packed a large quantity of money into a bag, together with some gold and silver vessels, and set out to do business at the fairs held at Bar. When he reached Bar[70] and had settled into a guest house, he failed to take proper care of his bag, tossing it under a chest and not entrusting it to anyone before leaving to look over the market and what the pedlars had to offer. Some thieves, however, good-for-nothing men dressed up very fine, went inside – either at the same time as Ebrard or immediately after him. Even though they were his fellow guests they picked up the bag and made off with it. Once he had taken a look around the marketplace, Ebrard returned with the intention of fetching part of his money. But he was unable to find the bag. He became alarmed, and his spirit and strength deserted him. He asked for the return of his property from the Blessed Mother of God of Rocamadour; he was a confrater[71] of the church and used to make it an annual offering, and long before he had committed himself and his goods to the Virgin's protection. He promised to give her one of the vessels if, thanks to her assistance, he should be worthy to recover his things. Consumed with sorrow and fearful of succumbing to starvation and penury, in that he had lost not only his own property but also a great deal belonging to others, he made up his mind to live in wretched exile. But thanks to the mercy of the kind Virgin, who does not spurn those who place their hope in her, the thieves made straight for Lyons and went to the lodging which belonged to the man whose money they had taken, entrusting the bag

---

[69] Possibly Véria (Jura): see *Pouillés de la province de Lyon*, ed. A. Longnon (Recueil des historiens de la France: Pouillés, 1; Paris, 1904), p. 27.

[70] Bar-sur-Aube. For this and the other fairs of Champagne, see M. Bur, *La formation du comté de Champagne, v.950–v.1150* (Nancy, 1977), pp. 293–304.

[71] Albe, p. 152 n. 151 (cf. p. 144 n. 116) interpreted this to mean that there existed an organizational confraternity, as was common in the later medieval period. This is very doubtful, not least because of the geographical dispersal of the persons so termed: cf. II. 28, 29 below. Here *confrater* is used in the sense of someone who had entered into a relationship of confraternity with a church, i.e. made special arrangements for liturgical provision, possibly in return for an annual payment or other form of donation. See also Rocacher, p. 295 supp. n.

to their hostess for safe keeping. Being a prudent woman she refused to take responsibility for the bag unless she saw what was inside, just in case they later tried to claim off her silver where there was in fact tin, and gold where there was in fact silver. The vessels were therefore taken out. The woman recognized that they had once been hers, but she gave nothing away. She went out to find some of her friends and brought them back so that they could act as witnesses to the truth. The friends summoned the city judge, and upon seeing that the woman's story was true, they had the thieves put in gaol. In the meantime a search was being made for Ebrard. Finally – for he had left the beaten tracks and was wandering aimlessly – he was found. When he heard about the great benefit which the Lord and his glorious Mother had bestowed upon him, who can adequately describe and who can properly hear how he became exultant with joy and how he gave thanks? He consequently returned home, and then brought an extremely heavy silver thurible to the church of Rocamadour, where he recounted the miracle.

I.43. The Virgin's messenger who cured a scrofulous woman

Bernarda, from the Rouergue, suffered for a long time from a great swelling in her chest. It poisoned her on the inside, and on the outside it gnawed away at her; her whole body was eaten up by decay and it wasted away. On the advice of doctors, who asserted that she would not be able to survive the opening up of the tumour, she was not placed under the surgeon's knife. She therefore decided to go to the church of the blessed and perpetual Virgin of Rocamadour and there ask for her assistance. On the way she met a pilgrim, who asked her where she was going and the reason for her journey. She explained everything in detail, and the man, who had grey hair, said, 'I am the messenger of the most glorious Mother of God, who mediates between God and mankind, and I have been sent to you on her orders to relieve you of this illness by means of our, or rather her, healing power.' Immediately he perforated the tumour by means of an incision, and bloody matter bubbled out of her body like a spring rising up from deep below the ground. He applied poultices, dressed the wound and, bidding her farewell, departed. The woman came to the church and, showing off the scar, recounted the miracle.

I.44. A swollen girl who was also cured

In the region of Maguelone[72] there lived a little girl called Mary of Ganges,[73] whose whole body became swollen. She was so badly afflicted that those who

[72] Hérault.
[73] Hérault.

saw her were amazed that her skin could be so taught without splitting. The young girl's mother felt great distress to see such a painful growth on her little lass, and she resolutely prayed to the Lady of salvation, the Queen of mercy and compassion, the Mother of all goodness, to alleviate the girl's suffering and restore her to health. The mother set out for the church of Rocamadour with her daughter. Before they arrived the good Virgin, the Virgin gentle and loving, took pity on the fact that she was a girl and that she was marred before her time by disease, and made her well.

I.45. Knights deprived of the power of speech

Hugh of Gondeville and Robert fitz Robert[74] were serving under Henry, the king of Britain,[75] as members of his household alongside the great men of his court. When they sailed with the king to Ireland – the occasion being the time when he placed it under his lordship[76] – God disposed that they should lose the power of speech because of the inclement air, the change of diet and the fact that they had to drink water from rivers.[77] They were warned, urged and advised by some of their people who had heard of the unique Virgin of Rocamadour, or indeed had experienced her bounty. Because they were unable to speak, the two men were obliged to make an inner vow that they would take up the scrip and staff and seek out her basilica from far-distant parts. To be sure, the good Virgin, the patronness of the good, who helps those who seek her help by means of vows, listened to their prayers. She restored their ability to speak and made the mute talk once more. But the king took offence at what they proposed to do, and said that this was all a ruse to visit their wives. The two men gave their solemn word to the king and the royal court, and swore on oath, that they would not go home to England nor visit their wives unless they first travelled to the Virgin's church, with her help and protection.

---

[74] Albe's suggestion (p. 156 n. 159) that Robert fitz Robert is to be identified as Count Robert III of Leicester (1168–90), the son of Count Robert II, is untenable: the author here locates his Robert among the king's *familiares* rather than the *primates*, among whom an earl of Leicester would have been included. But Hugh of Gondeville is a well-attested figure who was closely associated with Henry II between the 1150s and 1170s: see R. W. Eyton, *Court, Household and Itinerary of King Henry II* (Dorchester, 1878), pp. 39, 40, 75, 80, 86, 91, 150, 164, 199, 200, 212, 217, 218. For Hugh's role in the Irish expedition see Gerald of Wales, *Expugnatio Hibernica*, pp. 104–5 and n. 194 at p. 318.

[75] This was not a title in formal diplomatic usage. But it may reflect propaganda used by Henry in the pursuit of his ambitions in the various parts of the British Isles. Note too the Arthurian resonance in the title.

[76] Henry's expedition to Ireland lasted from October 1171 to April 1172; see Warren, *Henry II*, pp. 194f.

[77] For the problems with health and weather faced by Henry II's forces in Ireland, see Gerald of Wales, *Expugnatio Hibernica*, n. 180 at p. 316, citing the *Brut y Tywysogyon* and Ralph Diceto. A similar picture emerges from Becket miracle stories set during the campaign: see William of Canterbury, 'Miracula gloriosi martyris Thomae', II.25, pp. 180–1; II.27, pp. 181–2; V.7, pp. 378–80.

I.46. Men who were appointed to fight in single combat

A young man from Verdun called William was ordered in the court of Arnulf, the bishop-elect of the city,[78] to fight a duel with the man who was accusing him of theft.[79] As he was coming out to fight he prayed silently, but with his heart uplifted, for the Lady of Rocamadour to come to his aid: he asked that she would protect him under her shielding hand because he was innocent, and that once honour had been done on both sides she would put a stop to the fight and make peace between them. Scarcely had he finished his prayer when the aggressor, as if acting on the Blessed Mary's advice, declared before those who were presiding over the contest and the others there that he had behaved deceitfully and worthlessly towards his neighbour; he had never witnessed what he had accused the young man of doing. And thus, through the intervention of the eternal Mother of God, innocent blood was spared that day.

I.47. A thief who stole from a pilgrim of the Blessed Mary

Constantina, an inhabitant of Auxerre, was travelling to the church of the Blessed Mary of Rocamadour with two other women pilgrims. In the Limousin, at a spot in the depths of the forest between Saint-Hilaire and La Roche near the bridge at Ahun,[80] she was robbed by an infamous brigand called Stephen of Arfeuille. Constantina had more courage than her companions and tried to cling on to her things with all her strength; casting aside her womanly timidity she put up a struggle in her efforts to resist. For his part Stephen became angry and indignant, violently grabbing her by the throat and striking her three times in the chest with the point of his knife. And yet he was unable to cut even a single thread on her dress. At the urgings, however, of her companions, who were afraid she was going to die, Constantina stopped putting up any resistance. Nonetheless she called upon the Lady and liberator of all. Unaffected by fear of the great Virgin and unmoved by any pity for the pilgrims' sex and extreme poverty, the evil and savage robber grabbed hold of not only Constantina's money but that of the others as well before making off with it.

O the power of the Saviour, worthy to be proclaimed and praised everywhere! This man, who was a rational being, put aside his reason and followed the suggestions of the devil. He was unafraid of spilling his neighbour's blood without cause. On the other hand, a brute beast which

---

[78] Arnulf's predecessor as bishop of Verdun, Richard of Durbuy, died in 1171. Arnulf is addressed as 'elect of Verdun' (that is, he was yet to be consecrated) in a letter of Pope Alexander III dated 23 January 1172: Alexander III, 'Epistolae et privilegia', no. 849, col. 768.

[79] The bishops of Verdun exercised comital jurisdiction in the city.

[80] All places in Creuse.

had formally served Stephen submissively could not now tolerate its master's misdeeds and accordingly attached itself to the woman pilgrim. Stephen had raised this dog and habitually took it around with him. Yet it recoiled from the ferocity of the man who had nurtured it, and it left its master to stay close to the poor woman. Constantina retraced her steps in mournful anguish to Humbald, the lord of La Roche, and described her misfortune to him just as it had happened. Humbald took a large number of men and made a search of the places where robbers hid out. His hopes were frustrated, however, and he returned home. But people recognized the dog, and as a result the identity of the perpetrator of the crime became known. For this reason Stephen's kinsmen tried to hang on to the dog, but it refused to be kept shut up anywhere. In the meantime a more thorough search was made by the leading people of the region: Humbald of La Roche, Guy Bernard the lord of Saint-Hilaire, and the viscountess of Peyrat.[81] Stephen did not manage to stay hidden. Brought out into the open, he was identified by the woman even though he had changed his clothes. We would weary our listeners if we were to recall in every detail the exchange between the two, the woman's offering of proof, the robber's denial. We will instead touch on the more pertinent parts before moving on to other matters. The woman described the colour of the robber's clothes and how much he had been wearing. She also mentioned the knife, which had a white handle. Convicted by these and other proofs, the robber returned the money to each pilgrim. And he paid the price for his guilt by being hanged. As for Constantina, she came to the church of the most blessed and most glorious Lady of Rocamadour and recounted the miracle, showing the knife as proof.

I.48. A knight cured of a lump

Gerard Tosez, a knight from La Trimouille[82] in Poitou, was afflicted by a heavy lump on the lower part of his throat just above the windpipe. The physicians said that they did not know what this was, and that it was incurable. He suffered for a long time and almost lost his voice, so restricted was his breathing: the growth pressed into his windpipe, and his life was in grave danger. Then he turned his back on earthly glory – and he was someone who in the past had exposed himself to the risk of death precisely for that earthly glory – and as a humble supplicant set out on pilgrimage to the blessed and venerable Virgin of Rocamadour. When he arrived he spent a sleepless night in prayer, confessing his guilt with groans of contrition and inviting everyone to offer up prayers to the Lord. After he had performed his vow he set out on the journey home, still confident and untroubled by the fact that he had not recovered his health. What

---

[81] Creuse. There was no viscounty of that name: see Albe, p. 159 n. 170.
[82] Vienne.

happened on the journey? What did the Lady of mercy work upon this sufferer? Before he arrived back home, the growth shrivelled up and disappeared, and he felt no further pain. His people were delighted by what had happened to him and praised the praiseworthy Lady, who cures the sick and gives them back their health, by the grace of her Son, Our Lord.

I.49. Another wounded man for whom there was no hope

Siger of *Subrigien*[83] was run through the chest by a lance blow delivered by Count Theobald.[84] His people were anguished by this and despaired for his life. For his lungs grew putrid, and his insides came out of the wound bit by bit. And in the same way that armour is treated with sulphur in a vat to make it white and clean, so every day for almost a year wine was poured onto the wound in an attempt to loosen it up and force the putrid and pussy matter to ooze out. Siger stayed alive – if indeed this was alive, in that the loss of one's very nature may more properly be called death rather than life – and this wearied his friends, who eagerly awaited his death. O how removed is divine ordinance from human understanding! Siger's kinsmen were actively discussing his death; but deep down in his heart he tirelessly called upon the Mother of the Lord, the bride of Christ, the advocate of those who invoke her, and she saw to it that he regained his health. Once he had recovered, contrary to what everyone had expected, he went to the church of his liberator, where he showed off the scar and gave thanks.

I.50. A prisoner's broken chains

William Raymond, from Albi,[85] was being held in chains in Montpellier.[86] He had placed his hopes of escape in the most glorious Lady of Rocamadour. Calling out to her, he prayed to be released through her merits because he did not have the means to pay the ransom which was being demanded. Early one afternoon, around the ninth hour, he was busily praying and earnestly offering himself up in his heart to the sweet odour of the Lord and his most glorious Mother, when, marvellous to relate, his chains shattered and dropped to the ground while those who were there in the building watched in amazement. He picked up the chains and left the building without being

---

[83] The identification by Albe, p. 161 n. 176 as Zuberg near Regensburg is questionable. The name Siger points to someone from the Low Countries/Rhineland/Lorraine area. *Subrigien* may therefore be Saarbrücken (Saargebiet): see Tillmann, *Lexicon der deutschen Burgen und Schlösser*, ii.918–19; iv.39c.

[84] A specific count of this name is difficult to identify in the German-speaking lands in this period. It is possible that the reference is to the pre-eminent contemporary French count of that name, Theobald V of Blois (1152–90).

[85] Tarn.

[86] Hérault.

challenged or stopped by anyone. He passed safely through Montpellier despite running into a great many people at various points along the way. From there he came with the chains to the church of his patroness, and recounted the miracle which the Mother of God had performed with the help of Christ, who lives and reigns with the Father and the Holy Ghost. Amen.

I.51. A young man hurt by many lethal wounds

The Basques, a fierce people who live from rapine, were besieging the castle of Gerle,[87] in the Rouergue, with the intention of sacking it. A spirited and energetic young man called Gerald Hugh sallied from the castle and rashly launched himself at the enemy. They threw a spear which struck the youth, entering below his left armpit and coming out through his right. Inflicting a lethal wound did not satisfy their desire to do evil; rather, they added a further wound to the first by transfixing him with a ballista dart which struck him on the same side as the previous blow. At that point the young man dropped to the ground. He prayed, as his situation warranted, for the help and support of the glorious Lady of Rocamadour, who saves those who place their hope in her. Realizing that none of his people had come to his assistance, he picked himself up from off the ground and struggled to make his escape, even though he had already lost a great deal of blood and had almost no strength left in him. A member of the enemy force, however, took an exceptionally wide spear – the sort that hunters use to kill boars – and drove it between the youth's shoulders with so much force that he made it come out through the chest. As a result of this the Basques reckoned that their victim would very soon be dead, and they made off leaving him half-alive. Too late those who should have taken Gerald Hugh's side and protected him emerged from the castle, like anxious mice coming out of their holes; and they carried him back within the walls. Surgeons arrived and, on examining the young man's deadly wounds, declared that only heavenly power, not the work of human hands, could cure him. The wounded youth, however, hoped for help from the Lord, whom he knew had restored many people to life through the intervention of his generous Mother; he did not doubt that while there was still breath in him he could receive the gift of life. So what happened? Faith, which was like a grain of mustard in the youth, had its effect. The power of the Queen of Heaven effected an unexpected recovery; the news spread far and wide and was the occasion of praise and acclamation. The young man was restored to health, came to the church, showed his scars, and gave thanks for such a great benefit.

[87] Aveyron. For this place see Albe, p. 162 n. 184.

I.52. A very serious illness

William of Belvoir,[88] the son of Conon the castellan of Meix[89] in the archdiocese of Besançon, was debilitated by a very serious illness. It seemed as though he was putting aside his mortal form to assume a new one, according to his merits. His father, who loved his son as fathers do, shared in the suffering of his misfortune. Realizing that his son was near to death, and knowing that devotion and prayer would aid a recovery more than weeping and wailing, he got down on his knees, just as if he were before the altar of our great Virgin, and vowed that he would take his son to Rocamadour if the Mother of the Lord restored him to health. Until that moment the son had appeared to be on the verge of dying, but immediately he got up from his bed feeling fit and well. Lifting his relatives' gloom, he showed that he was as cheerful and strong as he had ever been.

I.53. A captive freed by his mother's faith

William Fulcher, who came from the bourg of Montpellier, was captured by the Saracens along with sixteen companions and was held in foot-irons for eight months or more on Majorca. Every day he worked without a break. And although he grew weak because he had so very little to eat, his overseer would not tolerate any reduction in his labours; instead he would insistently urge him to work more quickly. Meanwhile, with the passage of time it came around to the vigil of the Assumption[90] of that distinguished Virgin who gave birth to Our Lord, like a star giving out its brilliance. The young man's mother came to Rocamadour with a pound of wax, an offering that she used to make every year for her son. Weeping and wailing she begged everyone to pray for the captive. What was happening to the young man in the meantime? That very day, indeed at the very moment when his mother was making her plaint among us – and this is just as he told it to us – he felt worn out by his work and also by his prayer (for he would frequently offer himself up to the Lord in the depths of his heart). And briefly putting his work aside, he fell asleep. When he woke up, he was astonished to discover that his chains had broken, even though they had been very strong. He rejoiced in the fact that he was free. But he was also afraid that someone might come up to him, and so he circumspectly set out to walk towards the coast, taking great care as he did so. At that time some people from Tarragona were sailing by. When William Fulcher recognized their emblems and banners as those of Christians, he shouted out loudly after them, crying

---

[88] Doubs.
[89] Meix (Doubs) or, more probably, La Tour du Meix (Jura).
[90] The Feast of the Assumption falls on 15 August.

to them as Christians and for Christ's sake to take a fellow Christian to a safe port. They were accordingly moved by pity and took him to Tortosa, the journey taking less than a day and a half. This was a wondrous thing: one sees how one's reward can be granted in this world and how it is not everyone who has it postponed until the next life. For none of the sailors had ever reached that port in anything less than three days, even with the benefit of a full and favourable wind. The young man did not make a detour to see his mother and friends, but came straight to the church, adding a second pound of wax to the first. He recounted the miracle and gave thanks to Our Lady, his liberator, who saves all those who place their hope in her, through her Son the Saviour, who lives and reigns, three Persons in one. Amen.

This is the end of the first part of the miracles of Rocamadour.

The Second Part

The beginning of the prologue of the second part

Even though we cannot commit to writing all the things which we daily see and hear about in the church of the Blessed Mary of Rocamadour, none-theless we will not decide to pass over everything which is worthy of celebrated memory. Although we are unable to pick all the salubrious flowers from the field, at least we may make a not insubstantial collection. And so to the praise and glory of the Lord's name and that of his generous Mother, let us call to mind the man from Burgundy who was grey-haired, illustrious and sound of judgement; the man from the region of Troyes; the woman from Pavia; the woman from Gascony; someone from Nevers;[1] someone from Montélimar.[2] All these regained their sight; not all of them did so right here in our church, but they all claimed that it was through the suffrages of our church, and they had many witnesses with them. Let us call to mind the woman from Beaucaire[3] who recovered her senses; the woman from Burgundy who regained the ability to speak; someone from the Rouergue who had long been crippled and had long lain near the church but was then made upright; a cleric who would cry out and tear at himself, showing no reverence towards the Creator, but who gained the full use of his senses when, as his relatives were leading him away and he was still quite near the church, he turned back to look. Let me also call to mind the innumerable men who were cast into prison but were then freed from their chains thanks to the glorious Virgin, and came to give thanks to the Lady for their liberation. However, the notary was unwell on the days when these things became known, and so he did not write down in the correct manner and with proper headings those miracles which the flowering and immaculate Virgin wished to perform within a short space of time through her Son, Our Lord, the Saviour of all.

[1] Nièvre.
[2] Drôme.
[3] Places of this name are found in Gard, Gers and Tarn-et-Garonne.

Chapters of the second part

28. A great storm at sea

29. A woman who went into labour every day

30. A woman who did not faithfully look after what was entrusted to her

31. A boy cured

32. A youth suffering from paralysis

33. Someone whose hands were cured

34. Pirates prevented from attacking Christians

35. A boy revived and a killer punished

36. A blind woman who became sighted during the carrying of the light

37. A calming of the air at sea

38. The cure of an abbot of Cluny

39. A piece of iron extracted from a wounded man's body

40. A knight who recovered his senses

41. A youth afflicted by an illness in his legs

42. Another knight cured of a deadly wound

43. A fire put out through the merits of the Virgin

44. The faithful custody of the Mother of the Lord

45. An open wound bound and cured

46. A cured cripple

47. Another sick person cured

48. A deaf woman

49. Someone who fell out of a tree

II.1. Three abbots saved from shipwreck

Alexander,[4] the venerable abbot of Cîteaux, the illustrious John, abbot of Beaulieu[5] and father of the count of Brienne,[6] and Itier, abbot of Toussaint de Châlons,[7] were travelling with a large party of regular and secular clergy to visit the pope.[8] They set sail from Venice. Then an enormous storm blew up over the sea. The air became misty; and a violent wind whipped up, filling the ship's sails from the wrong direction and rapidly driving it backwards towards some rocks. The sailors were terrified because they had death staring them in the face. And unable to regain control of the tiny ship's motion, they filled the others on board with fear and desperation. The storm raged and the waves swelled. The sky was clouded over by the heavy rain and thick spray. Calm was nowhere to be found; everywhere there was the violence of the restless winds. What more is there to say? In their distress those on board would have preferred the ship to be dashed against the rocks and smashed to pieces, rather than having their death put off any longer and being obliged to endure such great fear. Nevertheless the abbots told the sailors that they would pay for the ship to be repaired if, thanks to God's clemency and if he so disposed, they got ashore and let the ship be driven against the rocks. But the sailors would not agree to this. And so the anxious abbots lifted up their voices to the heavens through the swirling air, pouring out their prayer to the Lord and vowing that they would each honour his Mother, the glorious Lady of Rocamadour, with an offering of a wax ship. Suddenly the star of the sea, the empress of the winds, the abater of storms, soothed and calmed everything. A gentler wind blew against the ship from the side and pushed it back into the open sea. They sailed with favourable winds and safely reached their destination.

II.2. A knight tied up in an unheard-of way

During the expedition which William, the marquis of Montferrat,[9] led against the Milanese, many men were killed and wounded on both sides.[10]

---

[4] Abbot 1168–78. See *DHGE* 12.866.
[5] Beaulieu-sur-Aube. See Cottineau, i.302; *DHGE* 7.177–8; *GC* 12.615.
[6] *recte* brother of the count, Evrard II (c.1158–c.1190).
[7] Toussaints-en-l'Île, Châlons-sur-Marne. See Cottineau, i.676.
[8] The background to this journey is almost certainly an embassy to Pope Alexander III, on behalf of the emperor Frederick I, led by the abbots of Cîteaux and Clairvaux in early 1169: Holtzmann, 'Quellen und Forschungen zur Geschichte Friedrich Barbarossas', pp. 400–409; Preiss, *Die politische Tätigkeit*, pp. 118–22.
[9] William V the Old (1135–90).
[10] William, a supporter of Frederick Barbarossa, had a long record of conflict with Milan and its allies: see Usseglio, *I marchesi di Monferrato in Italia ed in Oriente*, i.273–4, 287–92, 321, 357, 362–3, 368. It is possible that this incident refers to a

The illustrious knight Bohemond of *Cariz*,[11] from the region of Vercelli, was taken prisoner by the Milanese. The form of captivity which he faced is harsher, indeed more wretched, than other sorts because it is intended to last forever: it is impossible to redeem anyone through entreaties or the paying of ransom, except when the goodness of peace and concord prevail or when one knight is exchanged for another. On the first night of his captivity Bohemond's captors did not have a castle or fortified place in which to put him, so they co-opted an experienced knight from their army with instructions to tie him up in a new and unheard-of way. The savage knight set about dealing with his knightly captive with a vengeance, covering him with a stout rope from his knees down to his ankles – just as if he were being surrounded by a hedge. He also wrapped chain after chain around and around his prisoner, binding him tightly from the lower part of his body to the knees. He secured the knight's feet with iron fetters, and added a third layer of bonds, made from leather, over the two we have already mentioned. In addition, in order to aggravate this new and unprecedented act of savagery, he had a spear driven with great force up to its mid-point between the captive's legs and the rope which was around them, and then ordered four knights to position themselves on top of the spear. He tied a rope around the midriffs of two knights and placed Bohemond between them, tightly bound with the same rope in such a way that it was reckoned that he could not make any movement without disturbing the two men beside him. When the others had gone to sleep, Bohemond called upon the advocate and Lady of all people for help. He had placed his hope of being freed in her, and now he cried out to her inwardly. His prayer stretched out, his devotion grew, and his faith increased, bringing him firm hope. Moreover, the kind Virgin had already untied and freed him, unbeknown to him and without the others feeling anything. Then Bohemond realized that he was no longer restrained by any chain. But he was afraid that if he moved his arm, it would wake up the knights. Nonetheless he gradually overcame his fears and regained his composure. Feeling the upper part of his body he found that there was nothing restricting him, and on moving his hand lower down he was delighted to discover that he was free. He therefore got up, made his way through the enemy camp, and spent that night in barefoot flight through bushes and thorns. In the morning he ran into a pilgrim who, at God's command, led him back home – to the delight of his relatives. Mindful of the benefits that he had received, Bohemond went to the church of his liberator bearing gifts and offerings, and offering up his prayers he recounted the miracle and gave thanks.

conflict, and defeat for William, in 1172 recorded in 'Annales Placentini Guelfi a. 1012–1235', *MGH SS* 18.413.

[11] See Albe, p. 181 n. 12.

II.3. A young man suffering from a fistula

The nephew of Hugh, a chaplain from Sommevoire[12] which is in the region around Troyes,[13] was tormented by a fistula in his leg which resulted in three openings. The ulcers were dreadful and deadly because they gnawed away at the live tissue around his muscles. The young man had fallen into such a weakened state that he did not want to be fed, nor could he be. His body was once in the flower of its youth, but now it had become so reduced in appearance that one might suppose that it had already been long buried. Advice on this matter was sought from Viscount Odo of *Faverecet*,[14] someone who was moved by charity to look after all those in need of help. But he lost all hope of a cure. Nonetheless he said to the young man, 'Put your affairs at home in order and think carefully about your eternal salvation, because whether they cut you open and sear the wound, or whether they leave things just as they are, you will soon end this life on earth.' Bereft of any human assistance, the young man sought help from heaven, wearing himself out with three days of sobbing and prayer. The Lady of Rocamadour dominated his thoughts. He hoped that he would recover through her. And he was not frustrated in his desire. For while he was taking his bandages off, as he routinely did, to examine the ulcers, he discovered nothing more than scars, and to his delight he found that he was cured.

II.4. A countess who had a swelling

A sizeable tumour grew on the face and neck of Mary, countess of Montbéliard.[15] This weakened her so much that she was unable to eat for eight days. Her husband, the count, was moved both by the fact that she was thin from hunger and by the pain caused by her illness. He vowed that he would take her to the church of the most Blessed Mary if she were restored to health. After a few days elapsed she stopped feeling weak and made a complete recovery.

II.5. A miracle involving a mute woman

A woman from Saint-Guilhem-le-Désert near Lodève[16] was a mute whose mouth was twisted back towards her ear and whose arm was shrivelled up. She was taken to the church of the blessed and most glorious Lady of

---

12 Haute-Marne.
13 Cf. Albe, p. 182 n. 15.
14 Difficult to identify. Albe, p. 183 n. 17 suggests Favresse (Marne), but there was no viscounty of this name: see Bur, *La formation du comté de Champagne*, pp. 442–52.
15 Possibly the wife of Count Thierry (d.1162).
16 Hérault.

Rocamadour, and there she recovered her bodily health while the pilgrims, who had gathered there from different regions and countries, looked on in amazement and praised the Lady of the world, the saviour of all people through her Son.

II.6. A knight who mocked pilgrims going to Rocamadour

Philip, a noble knight from Cerro[17] in Italy, used to mock those people from Italy who sought the assistance of the blessed and eternal Virgin of Rocamadour, his argument being that Italy was conspicuous for its renowned and great churches dedicated to the highest Lady and venerable Queen. But one night, as he lay on his bed, an army of demons appeared terrifyingly before him, brandishing burning torches, swords and cudgels, and threatening him with death – an imminent and horrifying death. As he quaked with fear, terrified at the prospect of dying when he least expected it, the Virgin of virgins appeared, more fierce-looking than usual. She had a wooden switch in her hand. Hooking it around the knight's neck and tugging at him, she said: 'Follow me to my house at Rocamadour. Otherwise you will not escape from the demons' assault. Look at the demons' raging. They will vent their malice on you if they are allowed to. They are ready to spill innocent blood; they seize souls and subject them to agonising tortures; they are not happy unless they are committing evil; and they rejoice in the wickedest of deeds. The downfall of the good causes them joy. They are unjust and worthless adversaries who rush to devour those whom they find unarmed and unprotected – unless their victims regain their senses. With them the infamous actions of the wicked are laid bare, and the guilty are thrown into confusion. With them there is always a torturer sitting ready, and there is always a worm eating away. With them there is sorrow and fear, a foul stench and weeping. Theirs is a stinking workshop which both burns and consumes the cold and freezes the hot with ice more severe than that found in winter. To each is rendered according to his actions and proportionate to his wickedness; indeed, they get more than the wicked ways of men deserve.' Philip was moved both by the admonition of the supreme and kind Virgin and by his terror of the foul spirits. And, still in his vision, he replied, 'Know, Lady, that I am ready to undergo everything I deserve'. Straight away the gentle and delightful Virgin warned off the evil angels, and they disappeared. Then she was received into heaven accompanied by many companies of virgins, giving off a wondrous odour and surrounded by incomparable brightness. When dawn broke the knight made his vision known and, fearful of any delay, set out on his journey. He reached the church, poured out his prayers, made an offering and recounted the vision.

[17] See Albe, p. 184 n. 20.

II.7. The same knight's daughter cured

This same Philip had a daughter called Beatrice. She was rich in material
things and fortunate in her husband and children; she was someone whom
the world had fêted, raised up with riches and showered with honours. But
because nothing in this world ever stays the same, and the motion of the
world causes all things to fluctuate, this woman now drooped where once she
had been blooming. Where once she had had plenty, she now stood in need.
Where once she had rejoiced in good health, as if she could not fall ill, she
now grew feeble and weak in payment of nature's debt. This Beatrice was
deprived of her strength, and for about fifteen years went through considerable suffering. Although many doctors laid their hands on her, not one of
them cured her and she was not restored to health. This was because an
abscess which was amazingly large and horrible to behold had taken hold of
the front part of her neck, so that she was unable to turn her head or look
down. She was in pain whenever she ate. And when she tried to form words
she would stutter and her tongue could scarcely move. Again and again
physicians applied various poultices and cataplasms on the outside; and to
treat her from the inside they used herbal potions and spices. Yet they
achieved little or nothing, and so they gave up. What more was there to do?
Beatrice was pronounced incurable: nothing could heal her except heavenly
medicine. At this point, however, we need to consider how the woman was
feeling during all this. She offered herself up as a living sacrifice to the Lord,
acknowledging that the pain she was suffering was an affliction that she
deserved. With sobs and moans, with contrition in her heart and prayers on
her lips, she called upon the Lady of Rocamadour, the Lady of ladies, the
distinguished Virgin, the glory of virgins, the refuge of the wretched. It was in
her that Beatrice had fixed the anchor of her hope of being cured. Because
she was steadfast in her faith, she was worthy to attain what she was seeking;
and the Mother of mercy did not allow her to be troubled any longer by the
distress of her illness. For as Beatrice was sleeping, she appeared in a vision
and instructed her in how she was to be cured. When morning came the
woman told her friends about the vision, whereupon they set about moving
things along quickly, and in accordance with the Virgin's instructions had a
surgeon cut the abscess open and expose the tumour. But the surgeon was
not at all careful, and he cut one of the arteries in the act of opening the
tumour up. Blood poured from it profusely, causing everyone to despair and
filling them with the fear that the woman would die. They were amazed at
how people can sometimes be deceived by what appears to be the excellent
Virgin. But the giver of this advice looked down upon the woman, who for
her part did not lose faith in anything she had been promised and lifted both
her heart and her eyes to the heavens. Nor did the Virgin delay her assistance.
The fluid which was coming out on both sides stopped. The skin was drawn
across and sewn back in its original position. And the woman was restored to

the state of health which she had enjoyed before – or rather to a better state than before.

II.8. Henchmen who wanted to seize a peasant's property

The modest dwelling of Bernard of L'Hôpital d'Aubrac,[18] in the Rouergue, was besieged by soldiers and malign knights who planned to storm it and take what belonged to the owner. What Bernard possessed were the fruits of his own labours and the richness of the land: his food and clothes came from rearing animals. Although he had never contrived to harm anyone, and lived quietly on his land, he strove to hang on to his property with all his might now that he found himself surrounded by enemies. They made a pile of chaff and straw taken from the roof, placed it next to the door of the humble shelter, and set it on fire. The hut began to burn down, and the man and his tiny family were tortured by the heat and smoke. The animals bellowed and broke the ropes with which they were tethered. Then, realizing that it was impossible to resist by means of force because he reckoned that no one would come to his aid, the peasant sought help from the Blessed Virgin, promising that he would take a house made out of wax to her house at Rocamadour. Straight away, as if at Our Lady's command, the evil men left their wicked work unfinished and withdrew. The man then put out the fire – the shelter was only half burned – and saved the hut and the rest of his things, thanks to his liberator.

II.9. Thieves deprived of their sight

Three pilgrims from *Gosa*[19] were passing through the lonely wastelands near Saint-Guilhem,[20] when they were led astray by thieves along remote and impassable tracks, over steep mountains and along valley floors. The robbers treated these innocent people injuriously and attempted to steal the property belonging to these poor of Christ. But the advocate of all mankind, the powerful Lady of Rocamadour, the exceptional star who lights up the world with her radiance, came to the aid of her servants as they called out to her. As was proper, she seized hold of the servants of iniquity, these workers of wickedness, and took away their sight, which is a human being's most cherished asset. She also paralysed their hands and rendered them immobile like statues, out of pity leaving them only with the use of their tongues so that they could ask for mercy and express heartfelt penitence. And so with

[18] Aveyron.
[19] Possibly Gouze (Pyrénées-Atlantiques) or Gousse (Landes). For other possibilities see Albe, p. 189 n. 24. The suggestion of Rocacher, p. 298 supp. n., that the pilgrims were from Gaza is highly unlikely.
[20] Saint-Guilhem-le-Désert (Hérault).

suppliant cries the robbers fell at the pilgrims' knees and asked that they placate the Lady, who is gentle but had been offended by their misdeeds, with their prayers and merits. The pilgrims were moved by the plight of the afflicted men, and their hearts were touched. They got down on the ground to pray, raised their voices to the heavens, and asked the Lady of mercy to take pity on the wretches. Then the unique Mother of compassion, the people's hope for the forsaken who broke the necks of the dragon, the restorer of health, restored the thieves' senses and returned their bodies to their former health. The pilgrims came to the church and recounted not only this miracle but also another one which they had seen along the way.

II.10. A frenzied cleric who was cured

For there was a cleric was who was gripped by a frenzy. For a long time he stayed in the vicinity of the church of the most Blessed Mother of God at Rocamadour. He used to scream and rage, rage and scream. Everyone found him burdensome and intolerable; he would irritate and accost people as they arrived. But his mother was more troubled than the others. She would throw herself down at everyone's knees and pray that they pray for her son; for she was suffering on account of his affliction. She begged and begged that his senses be restored. She persisted in this contrite behaviour for a long time, but she did not deserve to have her prayers answered for as long as she was in the church. She was advised by the monks to go back home and take her son with her, because the worker of miracles often helped people when they were on the journey home. She agreed to this, and so she left, reaching the oratory which is situated in the upper part of the village of Rocamadour. Looking back towards the church of the Blessed Virgin she gave herself up to prayer. Then the young man began to talk to her more calmly than usual, announcing that he would be cured thanks to the merits of the glorious Virgin and his mother's prayers. He showed her his face, which up until then had been a shocking sight to those who looked upon it, and it was now happy and more cheerful. Who can tell what praises and expressions of thanks the mother offered in return for her son's health? O kind Virgin, Virgin the begetter, our justification and our recovery, born of the illustrious line of Jacob, descendant of David, the ivory tower, the virginal flower, the closed garden, the gate open to the faithful, the haven of safety, worthy to be loved and venerated by us all: who can properly praise and extol you? Everyone praises you well enough, but no one does so fully – you who must be praised in all things. Yet, insignificant and unworthy as we are, we must be very afraid of incurring anger as our reward: we wish to increase her praises with our writing, but she deserves more than we are able to say. But she is gentle towards the gentle and humble towards the humble. She will open up our mouths and unlock the treasury of the Holy Ghost, so that we may receive our instruction from so great a teacher, and so that our minds may be infused with what our intelligence is unable to grasp through the drops of dew of the grace of the kind spirit. But because we have digressed somewhat, we should now return to our subject. The mother was leading the boy – he was now entirely restored to health – and had not yet reached Gramat[21] when she ran into the three pilgrims mentioned earlier. She recounted the miracle, describing how the wonderful Lady had worked miraculously on her son and praising her mighty deeds.

II.11. A thief who stole a vase belonging to Our Lady

Sancia came from the town of Avallon[22] in the region of Autun, the place where St Lazarus, whom the Lord raised up from the sleep of death, is said to repose and exercise his patronage.[23] She was coming to the church of the most glorious Virgin of Rocamadour in order to pray. A young man – someone who was depraved in his mind and perverse in his actions, yet physically robust and elegant in form – attached himself to her with the intention of getting food from her along the way. The woman was strong in her nobility, notable for her generosity, and distinguished by her capacity and willingness to do good; and so she did not refuse the chance to look after him. But he plotted to repay the good done to him with evil, looking for a convenient moment to steal some silver vessels which the matron had with her. And because this wicked man had fixed his mind and desire on the doing of evil, he stole three precious vessels and eighty solidi from the lady's bag one night when they had arrived at Uzerche[24] weary from their journey. He then left the hospice as if he had something or other to do in the village. But all that night he spent wandering back and forth, straying off the beaten track. The alarm was raised by the lady who knew him, and a search was made for him everywhere. Because he was unable to make his escape or get away – for the Blessed Virgin was impeding his steps – he was discovered and led back to the lady. He had not stashed away any of the money – money which had been faithfully committed to the care of the faithful Queen. Exulting in the Lord and lifting up her voice in praise of the Virgin, the matron had the man tied up and brought him with her to the church to exhibit him to the compassionate Mother. But the mediator between God and man, the Mother of Christ who bore the sins of mortal men, she who does not want the death of evil people but rather their conversion, sent the man away free and released from his chains.

[21] Lot.
[22] Yonne.
[23] For the church of St-Lazare, see Cottineau, i.221.
[24] Corrèze.

II.12. Doves which multiplied

A man from Toulouse had built a hut to house his doves. Although he
frequently placed younger doves inside it, their numbers did not increase
because some of them were being eaten by wild animals. Realizing that he
was being thwarted and that he would not be getting any reward for all his
efforts, he promised a wax dove to the Blessed Mary if he ceased forthwith to
be deprived of his birds. From that day forth the birds multiplied. And the
man promptly and willingly performed his vow.

II.13. A bishop of Orléans cured

Manasses, the bishop of Orléans of blessed memory,[25] became weighed down
by the burden of his corruptible flesh and could not rise from his sickbed.
The feastday was drawing near on which the Son of God, born of God the
Father before time began, deigned to be born of the Virgin's womb and
appear to us, visible and passible. He was passible in the flesh, through which
he was *made a little lower than the angels*,[26] and he was clothed in human
form whereas his divinity had made him incorporeal, uncircumscribed,
untouchable, impassible. Truly God and truly man, he came down to the
depths of this world in order to illuminate us by his presence. And so the
faithful gathered at the church of Christ. The bishop presided over
proceedings even though he was ill, exerting himself more for the salvation
of his soul than for the health of his body. Indeed the mind of this
compassionate man, who had been placed as a light *on a stand, and it
gives light to all in the house*,[27] was in anguish because he was unable to
perform the bishop's duties which the feast required of him. He called upon
the Lord, the author of our salvation, either to be taken from this world or to
recover his strength so that he could carry out the ministry entrusted to him.
He also prayed to the Mother of compassion, mercy and all goodness – the
branch which was in leaf and blossomed and brought forth the fruit by
which the faithful are nourished, she who gives life to the dying, the joy
and jubilation of those who dwell in heaven – to apply her health-

---

[25] The identification of this bishop is problematic. The Latin *Aurelatensium* (var.
Arelatensium) points to Arles, but no Archbishop Manasses of Arles is recorded
after the tenth century. Albe, p. 194 n. 33 suggested that the toponym might have been
a corruption of *Aurelianensium* (Orléans), in which case the reference would be to
Bishop Manasses (1146–85), still very much alive when the miracle collection was
being written. A possible solution is that the phrase *felicis memorie* was inserted by a
later copyist working after Manasses's death. It is worth remembering that the
surviving manuscript copies of the miracles date from no earlier than the end of the
twelfth century and were produced in northern France.

[26] Psalms 8:6; Hebrews 2:7.

[27] Matthew 5:15.

bringing medicine. He gave instructions to those who were attending to him that he was to be taken into the church. Divine inspiration had conceived in him the hope of salvation, and taking up his spiritual weapons he celebrated the holy mysteries after receiving his bodily health thanks to the patronage of the glorious Virgin. Then he came to Rocamadour and gave thanks.

II.14. A starling restored to its mistress

Almodis,[28] a noble lady from Pierrebuffière,[29] which is in the Limousin, had spent three years nurturing a little bird – the sort which is commonly called a starling. The bird was eager to make the sound of whatever it heard. It would pitch its voice to sing along with the melody when people were singing, insofar as it was able. And it would imitate the movements of dancers and players. It so happened that the matron was moving from one castle to another, and she took the bird with her. Because of the change of location and the unfamiliar surroundings it flew off into some woods. The lady was indescribably upset, not in the least restrained, and unable to suppress her pain. She went into a rage every bit as violent as if she were present at the funeral of one of her children. Many people made a search for the bird, but it was nowhere to be found. Almodis did not hold back her tears, nor could she be consoled in any way; for three days she pined and wore herself out. Yet because to cry and groan for temporal things is something that small and imperfect people do, she lifted up her mind from the depths it was in, and from the bottom of her heart she called out to the Lady, the Queen of Heaven who is mellifluous in hearing people's prayers. In addition she promised that she would go to the church at Rocamadour barefoot and dressed in woollen clothes. Everyone had by now given up hope of the bird returning. But then it flew back, unbeknown to anyone, and was discovered in its cage. Exalting the Virgin with praises, the lady did not put off performing her vow and recounting the miracle.

II.15. A woman who was afflicted by many blows

I love thee, O Lord, my strength,[30] *because all the paths of the Lord are mercy and truth*[31] and *in your wrath you shall remember mercy.*[32] For *mercy triumphs*

---

28 The only securely identifiable Almodis of Pierrebuffière lived either side of 1100, but this is most probably not the woman featured here: *Cartulaire de l'abbaye de Vigeois en Limousin (954–1167)*, ed. M. de Montégut (Limoges, 1907), no. 59. Almodis was a common name among the Limousin nobility.
29 Haute-Vienne.
30 Psalms 17:2 (substituting *virtus* for *fortitudo*).
31 Psalms 24:10.
32 Habakkuk 3:2.

over judgement.[33] You grow angry and yet you are calm. You change all things and yet you do not yourself change. You contain all things and yet you are contained by nothing. You give *grace to the humble* and you *oppose the proud.*[34] Nothing happens on earth without cause, either because God so ordains or because he permits it to be so. Because God's *judgements* are profound like *the great deep,*[35] it is not at all for us to judge why this thing and that thing happened, except when the Lord wishes to reveal the reason. None of the faithful should doubt that the tribulations of the just are many, nor that the powerful Lord can deliver them from all of these. Some of the tribulations the Lord uses as a trial and examination to test whether we love him; others are inflicted to force us away from evil and bring us back to our senses.

There was a time when a heavy scourge subdued the people of the Lord in the Rouergue. For fierce wolves, swifter than these animals usually are, would snatch small children from their mothers' breasts and devour them with their hard fangs. Stephana of *Tienere* – whose brother had already fallen victim to this great and ruinous misfortune, leaving his mother holding on to nothing more than the arm which had been ripped from his body – had gone into the garden to gather some plants. This was on the eve of the Feast of the Assumption of the Virgin of virgins,[36] the clearest star of the sea. The weather was misty. Suddenly two wolves rushed up, making such a din that one would have thought that it was horses which had just arrived. One of them took Stephana by the throat, the other lifted her clothes up to her navel; they covered her with many different and deadly wounds. They then dragged her off to the woods, not along the direct path from the village – where they were frequently chased off by dogs – but over two walls and three hedges, as if they were tossing a sheep. The woods were half a mile from the settlement. The woman was still breathing but on the point of breathing her last. Invoking the power of the Holy Ghost and the kindness of the Virgin of Rocamadour, who can hear our prayers, she commanded the fierce beasts not to tear at her body any longer; and she confidently told them not to attack her any more. Suddenly, and as if at the command of the commanding Lady, the wolves stopped tearing at her, and they also diligently protected her bloodless body from being attacked by other wild animals arriving on the scene. In the meantime people were searching for Stephana with dogs. After spending a night in the open and exposed to the cold, she was found on the following day and taken back to her village. But she had been so ravaged that it was scarcely possible to recognize in her a human form. Worms and bloody matter poured from her lacerated body. She was terrifying to behold, even for

---

[33] James 2:13.
[34] I Peter 5:5.
[35] Psalms 35:7.
[36] I.e. on 14 August.

151

those who were her close relatives. Yet who is there I can call 'relative' considering that they swiftly and mercilessly rejected her? Her tongue could not move to form words. And when food was placed in her mouth it came out of holes in her throat and chest, leaving her with just a distant, thin taste. Because her nerves were contracted and her limbs damaged, her knees became stuck to her chest. And the wounds, from which considerable amounts of flesh had been removed, could not be covered over with her remaining skin.

Although it says in the Bible that *no one ever hates his own flesh, but nourishes it and cherishes it, as Christ does the church,*[37] people decided that this deformed member had to be removed from the body as something useless and putrid. They therefore placed Stephana on a cart and took her by night to a remote village, where she was abandoned outside the houses. When the people there looked at her they thought that she was some kind of monstrosity. *They have all gone astray* from her, *they are all alike corrupt; there is none that does good.*[38] They all closed up the entrails of their charity, heedless of the fact that it is the Lord who makes people live or die. To ensure that she would not have to stay amongst them any longer, and because evil people cannot tolerate the good, they placed her on an ass – or rather tied her to it like a tree trunk – and had her taken far away. As the ass was descending a steep mountain slope, because it wanted to drink from the river which was flowing swiftly down in the valley floor, it lowered its head and the woman, who had been tied only loosely, fell into the water. But the Lady of mercy, the granter of forgiveness, she who had snatched the woman still alive from the jaws of the wild animals, did not allow her to sink. Stephana came up from the bottom, and she was carried along by the current on the surface of the water, fetching up on the bank. She was able to remember things clearly. She turned over in her mind the treatment she had received, and how her relatives had spurned and cheated her. But she was unable to move and so could not reveal what she wanted. She was pulled out of the river and placed in a barn belonging to a noble whose heart had been touched by the Lord. There she lay alone, removed from contact with people because the stench and frightfulness of her wounds were an assault on the sight and smell of those attending to her. Nonetheless the knight looked after her and ordered that wine and oil should be poured onto her wounds, instructing a stablehand that he would repay whatever was spent on her behalf.[39] Meanwhile the woman was recovering, albeit a little, thanks to the attentions of doctors and the fortifying effects of food. She would ponder over and over the leader of all, the ruler of virgins and the flaming bush through whom her Son, the Lord of lords, burned the dragon's mouth. And she hoped to be cured

[37] Ephesians 5:29.
[38] Psalms 13:3, 52:3; Romans 3:12.
[39] Resonances of the care taken by the Good Samaritan and his instructions to the innkeeper: Luke 10: 34–5.

through her. She was right to do so. For the Virgin is the golden vessel and the ivory tower. It is she who brings together all good things. She weakens the head of the ancient enemy. She strikes fear in her foes. She particularly confers the palm of victory on those who love her. She is the mediator of all people, the certain hope of those who beseech her, life for the dying, the way back home for those who have strayed from the path, and finally the bringer of complete health and the medicine of all. The sick woman felt that none of the doctors' medicines or poultices would make her well. By means of hand signals, head movements and whatever weak sounds she was able to make she begged to be carried to Rocamadour. The journey there took a very long time because she was poor and on her back; but finally she was carried to the church she had set her mind on thanks to the compassionate assistance of many people. As we said earlier, she was at that time bent over and could not lift her head to breathe. She persisted in her prayers, fasts, vigils and heartfelt contrition near the altar of the Mother of mercy. And she was worthy to have her prayers answered and be cured.

This all happened in the Rouergue in the year of the Incarnation of the Word 1166. We wrote this in the sixth year after that date, in the reign of Our Lord Jesus Christ, to whom is the power and the glory, with the Father and the Holy Ghost, forever and ever. Amen.

II.16. A cleric cured of melancholy

Matthew of Lectoure,[40] a cleric from Gascony, was in the first flowering of youth when he was overcome by melancholy. Both his parents brought him to Rocamadour – not without some difficulty. He used to go into rages and scream. He would tear both his clothes and those of others. And he regularly tried to throw himself headlong off the cliff – and would have done so had he not been restrained. If it happened that he had a book in front of him, he was devoid of all knowledge, as if he had never learned his letters. But because we are ordered to devote ourselves to prayers, fasts, alms and other works of mercy, in that *the prayer of a righteous man has great power in its effects*,[41] the Mother of mercy opened the entrails of her compassion and cured the young man. Consequently both he and his parents were filled with inexpressible joy, and praised and thanked the glorious Mother of God.

II.17. A knight who escaped from his enemies

Peter Bromadans, a knight from Beauvais,[42] was captured by his enemies and imprisoned at Combles.[43] He was secured with iron fetters. He called upon

40 Gers.
41 James 5:16.
42 Oise.
43 Somme.

the advocate of all, the Lady of Rocamadour, who after God breaks both the chains of sin and those around bodies. And he experienced her favour. He climbed up from the dungeon at the bottom of the tower to the top floor. He then jumped out through a window down to the ground. Because he was being pursued, and they were getting very close, he was forced to go into the church which was next to the tower and close the door behind him. Surrounded and unable to get away unobserved, he climbed up into the rafters of the church and broke his fetters with an iron implement. Pouring out a prayer, he launched himself into the midst of his enemies. But what did the Lady of all clemency do? What did she arrange to happen to her knight, who was not presuming in his own strength but rather hoping for help from above? She restrained the strong assailants and prevented them from getting their hands on him. And she made the fast sluggish to prevent them from running after the knight and grabbing hold of him. Thus he escaped their clutches in the Lord's name.

II.18. A blind man who regained his sight

William Boarius lived in the castle of Auribeau,[44] in the region around Apt.[45] He was strong and physically robust, a peasant who did manual work to earn his living. He brought up his young children and provided for their worldly needs. Because it is not allowed to make judgements unless matters are entirely clear, we should leave what is not firmly ours to the judgement of God, whereas we should not pass over what shines with a brighter light and is clear to everyone. The William who is the subject of this story lived quietly from the fruits of his labours, as we learned from his own lips: he did not have it in mind to harm anyone, and he did not take from his neighbours what was theirs. Nonetheless the hand of the Lord fell heavily upon him: he was deprived of his sight, and for six years or more he remained blind. Those people for whom God was present in all things groaned deeply; those whose hearts were far removed from him showed no regard or compassion, remaining impenitent and as hard as stone. The skill and hard work of physicians did not work on him, failing to restore to him any degree of sight. They were astonished how it could be that only his sight was affected when the rest of his body was perfectly healthy. Now that the head of the family was blinded, the household went without and wasted away from lack of food. The man's wife would raise her voice in lamentation and bemoan the fact that she was alive because she was faced with the sight of her small children going without the necessities of life. She had often heard from many people about the great benefits which the Lord, the restorer of all mankind, deigned to bestow through the glorious Virgin and Lady of Rocamadour. So the story

---

[44] Vaucluse.
[45] For a different identification see Albe, p. 204 nn. 56–7.

goes, she said to her husband, amidst all the other prayers which she frequently poured out to the Lord, 'Why is it that we should be the only ones to go without God's favours? Why is he harder on us than on everyone else, when he said *Seek and you shall find, ask and it shall be given, knock and the door will be opened to you?*[46] So let's ask for his help, apply ourselves to our prayers, and clear our consciences so that we may be fit to be heard. Let's honour the Lord with what is left of our meagre property. Let's call upon the Queen of angels, after God the only effective hope for mortal beings, she who gives to all in abundance and is not tardy about it.' The woman was completely burning with desire and inspired by the Holy Ghost. She made a candle measured against her husband[47] and said to the Queen of kings, 'We will honour your house of Rocamadour, o gentlest of the gentle, with this wax candle if you remember your accustomed compassion and take pity on our wretchedness, commanding that the darkness in my husband's eyes be taken away and that he may see. Failing that, if you continue to close off your kindness from us and put off taking pity, we will take the candle we have made in your honour and burn it in this fire here.' O the power, or rather the sweetness, of our supreme Virgin, worthy to be proclaimed everywhere! She does not blush; she is always the flower of modesty. Immediately she made the man able to see and inexpressibly happy that he could recognize his family. Friends and neighbours rushed up from all directions. They lifted their voices in praise of the Virgin who mercifully works wondrous deeds. And their spirits were roused to love, serve and fear her. When they found a convenient time, they came to the church with the candle which was mentioned earlier, gave an account of the miracle, performed their vow and gave thanks.

II.19. A similar story of a blind woman who gained her sight

There was also a woman, whose name I have not discovered, who came from Burgundy. She was pregnant, and she went into labour in the hospital of St John the Baptist in Jerusalem.[48] During the birth she lost the use of her eyes. After her purification, her husband took her through Jerusalem, the city of the highest King, and brought her to that noble church where our salvation

---

[46] Matthew 7:7; Luke 11:9.

[47] For this practice, involving measuring a length of wick against someone's body or body part for incorporation into a candle, see Bautier, 'Typologie des ex-voto', pp. 246–50; Finucane, *Miracles and Pilgrims*, pp. 95–6; Sigal, *L'homme et le miracle*, pp. 96–7.

[48] For the hospital of the Order of St John in Jerusalem, see J. S. C. Riley-Smith, *The Knights of St John in Jerusalem and Cyprus c.1050–1310* (London, 1967), pp. 331–5. The hospital was notable for the provision made for gynaecological cases. For descriptions of the hospital which are close in time to the miracles, see *Jerusalem Pilgrimage 1099–1185*, ed. J. Wilkinson with J. Hill and W. F. Ryan (Hakluyt Society, 2nd ser. 167; London, 1988), pp. 266–7 (John of Würzburg), 287 (Theoderic).

hung on the cross and where the faithful flock from all over the world to adore the life-giving cross of the Lord.[49] Both of them prayed in this place of prayer, where the Lord of all died and was buried. But their prayers were not answered, and they were denied what they wanted. Turning their minds to the Lady of Rocamadour, the most blessed of all the blessed, the man and woman promised that they would take up their scrip and staff and set out for her church. And straight away the woman's eyes opened. They praised and glorified the star of the sea who lights up the blindness in our minds with the radiance of her humility and repairs our bodies in all their many different infirmities.

II.20. A disaster in the East

In the year of the Incarnation 1169,[50] in the East, in the Promised Land, an earthquake destroyed many cities, churches, towns and villages as a punishment for men's sins. The ground opened up and swallowed countless thousands of people. Others died buried under fallen buildings. Down the ages no one has heard tell of God's vengeance causing so great and so rapid a loss of life. In the midst of all those perishing in this sudden destruction there was a man called Herman, whose family came from Vienne but who had been brought up in Antioch. He found himself in the church of St Peter in the castle of Cursat, which belongs to the patriarch of Antioch.[51] When he saw the flashes of lightning and heard the sounds of thunder, when he witnessed a fissure in the ground swallowing more than 140 people alive – just counting those who were in the church – and when he found himself sinking as far as his neck, he called upon the most compassionate Mother of the Lord who exercises her patronage at Rocamadour. And immediately he sensed that his prayers would be answered. All around the dying were moaning and dropping down into the depths of the earth. But thanks to the aid of Our Virgin, who takes pity on everyone's plight, he was pulled out of the ground and got out alive even though he had been trapped by the earth and was on the point of suffocating. This dreadful event happened on the

---

[49] The church of the Holy Sepulchre. For the significance of this church in particular and Jerusalem in general in twelfth-century Christianity, see Hamilton, 'Rebuilding Zion', pp. 105–16; *idem*, 'The Impact of Crusader Jerusalem', pp. 695–713.

[50] *recte* 1170. See Mayer, 'Das syrische Erdbeben von 1170', pp. 474–84. The fullest contemporary account in a Latin source is William of Tyre, *Chronicon*, XX.18, ed. R. B. C. Huygens, 1 vol. in 2 (Corpus Christianorum, Continuatio Mediaeualis, 63; Turnhout, 1986), ii.934–6; Eng. trans. (based on an older edition) in William of Tyre, *A History of Deeds Done Beyond the Sea*, trans. E. A. Babcock and A. C. Krey, 2 vols. (New York, 1943), ii.370–1.

[51] Cursat (or Qusair) in Syria was the seat of the Latin Patriarch Aymeric of Limoges, who had been driven from Antioch in 1165 to be replaced by an Orthodox patriarch (who in fact died from injuries sustained in the earthquake): see B. Hamilton, *The Latin Church in the Crusader States: The Secular Church* (London, 1980), pp. 45–6.

Feast of the Apostles SS Peter and Paul,[52] around the sixth hour. The Lord Jesus Christ took pity on his faithful. He lives and reigns three and one with the Father and the Holy Ghost. Amen.

II.21. A cowherd overcome by an illness in his legs

The church of Cluny has a priory in the Auvergne called Sauxillanges.[53] There one of the cowherds was overcome by an illness in his legs and was confined to his bed. A long time passed and he found no remedy to effect a cure. A lot of people tended to him, and they applied many poultices, but these availed him nothing. The prior of the monastery, however, persevered with this work of mercy, asking the man whether he wanted to be cured. When the cowherd replied that he wanted his health more than anything else, the prior said, 'If you give some of your property to the Blessed Mary of Rocamadour and go on pilgrimage to her church, then you will get your health back without delay. She is the real medicine and truly heals those who are sick. She is worthy to receive whatever she wants from her Son. She can be placated despite our worthlessness, and she can hear our prayers in our time of tribulation.' The sick man yearned to be well. Because he had been worn down he eagerly promised that he would take heed of the prior's advice. And from that moment onwards he was cured. But when the following day dawned the peasant behaved in a wholly unrefined manner: he dismissed the benefit that he had received from the Virgin and, setting his hand to the plough, resumed his work. When the prior summoned him, he lied before the Holy Ghost and imputed the strength he had regained in his weakened limbs to the doctors' plasters and medicines. And he irreverently failed to show any reverence towards the Virgin who had healed him. The prior became angry and indignantly replied, 'Why were the cataplasms so ineffective for such a long time? Why was it that you were bedridden for so long, forced to spend your days in inactivity, when all that time you were using exactly the same medicines as now? Do you think that you can escape the clutches of the Almighty who sees everything? Or do you think that you can hide from the eyes of God, who probes men's hearts and knows their thoughts, *that they are vanity?*[54] *All things are naked and opened unto the eyes of him with whom we have to do.*[55] He rightfully withdraws his benefit from the person who is ungrateful. Your illness will return and you will not escape the Lady whose power lifted you up from your sickbed.' The prior went away. The man who had been sick – even though he wanted to pretend that he had not – was now struck by an even greater pain and immediately fell ill. He sprawled on the ground and shouted out piteously that he was a wretch.

---

[52] 29 June. The date is corroborated in other contemporary descriptions of the disaster.
[53] Puy-de-Dôme. See Cottineau, 2.2963.
[54] Psalms 93:11.
[55] Hebrews 4:13.

The illness which bit and gnawed away at the upper and lower parts of his legs was so virulent that he did not believe that any mortal man had ever undergone such excruciating agony. He said that he would rather die than suffer unbearably strong pain like this. Finally the prior went back to see him and caustically asked which path he preferred: either have his health and go without a portion of his property, or put up with the torture, keep his property, and stop his lamentations and complaining. The man drew a deep sigh and answered the prior by stating that he would rather be dead than have a limitless amount of money. To this the prior responded, 'So hand over the key to your chest [for the cowherd had a chest full of corn] and let me have for free what is inside, as well as the rest of your things.' The man replied, 'It's all there, And I shall carry out my vow to the Blessed Mother of God.' The prior appeased Our Lady with his prayers, and the man recovered his health.

II.22. A dean who suffered from an acute fever

Matfred,[56] the venerable dean of Mauriac,[57] was suffering from an acute fever, and his people were losing hope that he would get well. Although he was on the verge of dying he fixed his gaze upwards and earnestly prayed to the mediator between God and man, she who bore our salvation, the supreme glory of virgins, to take pity on him in his illness and restore him to health. The sound of his prayer could not travel very far because he was short of breath. But nonetheless it was not long before there were signs of recovery. For although the critical phase of the fever had not yet passed, he got up felling quite well – to the delight of his people and the amazement of others. He praised the Lord and extolled his magnificent Mother, who saves those who put their hope in her and gloriously attends those who rely upon her.

II.23. Another occasion when this same man was gripped by fever

On another occasion Matfred was riding with Lord Renard,[58] the abbot of Cîteaux of blessed memory, when he was seized by a tertian fever. Arriving at the church of Obazine,[59] he took to his bed, worn down by the accession of

---

[56] *recte* Manfred. See *Chronique de Saint-Pierre-le-Vif*, pp. 212–18; Geoffrey of Vigeois, 'Chronica', c. 68, p. 320; *Tulle*, p. 339. Manfred of Escorailles was related to the abbot of Tulle and other senior ecclesiastics in the region: see Dufour, *Les évêques d'Albi, de Cahors et de Rodez*, p. 65.

[57] Cantal.

[58] *recte* Reynald, abbot 1133–50. See *DHGE* 12.866.

[59] Corrèze.

the illness.[60] A large number of heavy coverings were therefore placed on top of him. His limbs had become so frozen with cold that he was convinced that the heavy mass of blankets over him scarcely weighed anything. In fact, to increase the weight he begged two monks who were there by the bedside to lie down on top of him. He was colder than wintry ice, and yet his spirit was burning; he conceived a loftier hope as to how to get well – in that he was someone who had already experienced the Lady's assistance – and eagerly prayed to the Virgin of the heavenly city, the fragrant nard, the myrtle of moderation, the exceptional lily. And suddenly he became better and experienced no further loss of strength. He now felt heavily pressed down by the pile of coverings and the weight of the two monks. These were removed, and he revived when he took some food. Indeed he was not afraid to eat the sorts of things which can exacerbate a fever and are not conducive to health.

II.24. A knight who suffered from epilepsy and paralysis

A distinguished young man from Bazas[61] in Gascony was rich materially and strong physically. As befitted the nobility of his lineage he married a woman from another noble family. He was someone who would have lived prosperously and happily if he had paid heed to the Lord's commands. But because man's clay-like flesh presses down on his spirit and prevents it from being lifted up from transitory things to the eternal, the young man became too caught up in worldly affairs and turned into a gambler. This is behaviour typical of the race to which he belonged; one might even say that their levity forces them to turn out that way. This man would often offend the Lord with his swearing. And he would drive people out of whole regions with his plundering. So it came to pass that God, who can do everything and has greater power than the powerful, brought the power of this man low. He struck him with the rod of his anger and brought his heavy hand down upon him by giving him the falling sickness.[62] The young man's relatives were extremely anguished: they were used to extending their authority over the people in adjacent territories thanks to the ferocity of their lord, but now the tables would be turned and they would themselves be threatened by those very people. O flower of earthly success, how quickly you withered! Up until that moment this man seemed to be soaring through the clouds and considered himself second to no mortal being. But now he lies frothing at the mouth in agony. He gnashes his teeth, he contorts his mouth, and his

---

[60] The background to this episode is probably the visit of Abbot Reynald to Obazine in 1148/9 to formalize its affiliation into the Cistercian order: see *Cartulaire*, no. 532; Barrière, *L'abbaye cistercienne*, pp. 72–3. For Reynald's reputation at Obazine see *Vie de Saint Etienne d'Obazine*, II.11–12, pp. 110–14.

[61] Gironde.

[62] Epilepsy.

eyes stare terrifyingly. He clenches his fists, and there is no use in his limbs as if they were dead. Where is his pride now? Where now his destructive ferocity? O good God, the fount of all goodness, the sweetness of all kindness, who can escape your clutches if you pronounce upon us a sentence which matches what we deserve? Spare the wretched, heal the sick, and take pity on those who are contrite in their hearts. For, since we are all sinners we stand in need of your grace because there is no one unsullied by filth, not even a one-day-old baby. If you were to punish the wicked all at once, who would there be left who could still appear innocent and pure before the gaze of your innocence and purity? If the just man falls and gets back up seven times in one day, how often do the unjust come crashing down – those people whose taste is for worldly things, who are given over to their pleasures, who pay earnest attention to the heaping up of sin upon sin? Lord, your clemency allows us this consolation – this sole refuge for those who are found wanting – that you carried the hundredth sheep back to its fold on your shoulders, and that you would rather a sinner convert than die.

We should not pass over in silence what the knight was doing all this time. Unable to find a doctor who could cure him, he made up his mind to come to the church of the Blessed Mary of Rocamadour. He therefore got a group together to accompany him on his journey; and he made a suppliant and devout pilgrimage to the church, where he keenly set about his devotions, vigils and prayers in an effort to appease the Virgin's anger. In addition he swore on the holy altar that thenceforth he would not commit the sorts of crimes which people held him responsible for, if he were worthy to be given help. 'O unique Virgin, delightful above all others, the rose of patience, our refuge in our misery, do not close the entrails of your accustomed kindness to your knight. Rather, propitiate your Son and, as a token of this, give me my health.' His profuse prayers reached the heavens. Indeed, thanks to his Mother's intercession, the Son of God and of the Virgin cured him and sent him off home, to the delight of his relatives. And for a long time thereafter the man kept firmly to the pact that he had made with the Virgin.

Some time passed. The knight's father-in-law found himself under serious threat from his enemies; and the son-in-law helped to protect him with his followers. In doing so he behaved more soberly than all the others fighting alongside him. His father-in-law summoned him and asked whether he had renounced the knightly life and made his profession as a monk, since he was not acting in the sorts of ways that a knight does; on the contrary, his behaviour was that of a monk. When the son-in-law started to explain that he wanted to observe fully the agreement which he had sworn to the Virgin, who had made him well, his father-in-law jokingly interrupted him, saying 'This promise of yours runs counter to the fact that you are in the flower of your youth and is inconsistent with your knightly status. While you live under arms you should behave like a knight.' What more is there to say? The knight was beguiled by these and other arguments – since we have long since been by nature the sons of anger, and the earth from which we are made swiftly becomes earth – and he broke his vow, becoming like a dog which returns to its vomit. His illness then returned. In full view of the many people who were there he began to foam at the mouth and collapsed onto the ground, falling more heavily than he had done before. His right arm and right hand – the one he used to throw dice – became withered, as did the middle part of his body, which became paralysed. Everyone felt a shared sadness. Wails and cries rose heavenwards. And the anguish which they had once overcome now returned. Those in particular who had been with the knight hurled insults at the father-in-law and said that this great disaster was all his fault. Who can properly describe, and who is in a position to hear described, the knight's groans, anguish and lamentation, the torment in his features, the tearing at his hair? The man screamed that he would be fortunate if he departed this life, in that he had become *scorned by men and despised by the people.*[63] He said that he would have been better off if he had never drawn breath: better that than be afflicted by a destructive illness and daily die a hateful death. His words were filled with pain, softening even the hardest hearts. For who could fight back the tears when they saw so many being shed by this suffering, weeping knight? O misery, misery, how miserably you bear down on the hearts of the miserable! People's minds are deeply sensitive to ruin when the body is being tortured and the breath of life is being driven out. This man would have sunk into despair and abandoned all hope had he not collected himself and hung on through the kindness of the Holy Ghost. Because he had offended both the Virgin's Son, who is propitious to all men, and his kind Mother, who is the reconciliation of those who fall, he had become a rock of scandal and a stone of offence, and he could find no one to whom he might have recourse.

Nevertheless his relatives had formed the hope that he might recover his health. They lifted his spirits and offered these words of consolation: 'There is no kindness like that of the Lord. In the raging of his anger he does not bring death but the means of correction. He strikes with his scourge in this life so that he may save us in the next. As he strikes he grows angry at the proper time so that presently he may offer consolation as he spares us. Most noble of noble men, do not let shame make you waiver about returning to the fount of healing, he who does not punish our every fault because he has long since condescended to the weakness of our mortal passibility.' The knight grew penitent from the depths of his heart, and he followed the course of action which his people were exhorting him to. Arriving at the top of the cliff above Rocamadour, he took off his clothes – he did not blush as he exposed his dishonourable nakedness in full view of everyone – and had a rope placed around his neck. He was then pulled along by two assistants – as one does with a thief – while two others lashed him severely with birches. Humbled in

[63] Psalms 21:7.

the very depths of his being, and afflicted all over his body, he rolled about on the ground at the feet of all the pilgrims. He revealed his wound. In front of everyone he shouted out that he was a liar, a perjurer, and a wrongdoer. Everyone gathered from all directions. They were moved by the knight's wretched state, and they urgently and devoutly prayed for this unhealthy limb, in so far as it was worthy to be made well by Christ, who is the head of all the faithful. Who was so hard-hearted that he was not driven to tears by the sobs of the people crying there? O the pain! No one could be left unmoved, first by the knight's horrifying downfall, which was happening in front of everyone's eyes, and then by the wailing of the countless people who were grieving for their lord's pain. The knight bore his sin openly, bewailing and admitting his iniquity. He had put aside all thoughts of modesty so that his abject condition would make people appreciate the contrition in his heart and his words of confession. O light of virgins, the salvation of all, the medicine of the ill, on whose milk the bread of angels wished to be fed, acknowledge the man who is crying out to you. Virgin, the honour of the world, the Queen of Heaven, radiant like the sun, receive the prayers of those supplicating you and anoint the sick man's injury with the antidote of reconciliation. If the hard hearts of hard people can be touched, how much more do we pray for the waters from the spring to remain flowing – the spring which up till now has supplied drink to the thirsty in abundance. Door to heaven, the compassion of the earth, do not close the entrails of your overflowing clemency, but let the ill man's sore be cleansed and bathed in the drops of your mercy. He has no support; he seeks no refuge other than with you. In this very place, here in your house of prayer, you are used to hearing our prayers and offering your protection; you hear the prayers of those supplicating you, and you do not deny your patronage to those who are unwell. At least be moved by the entreaties of this crowd of people, so that you may be praised and glorified by many.

The knight did not presume to enter the church. Rather, he would kiss everyone's feet and chose to be tormented by punishing himself all over his body for the Lord's sake. He arranged for three solidi of Poitevin money to be paid to the Blessed Virgin every year. He was then completely cured, and he honoured and glorified the glorious Mother of God while everyone else praised God, who is praiseworthy in all his works.

II.25. Dogs which were struck down

Gerard of Le Puy, from the village of Mayrinhac[64] which is a mile away from Rocamadour, had been out hunting and was passing close by the church of the most glorious Virgin with his dogs. Because the mild girl, the most supreme Queen of all mankind, grew indignant, the man's dogs were all

[64] Mayrinhac-le-Francal (Lot).

struck and cast down to their deaths from the cliff. All those who heard about this were amazed. And they became afraid of getting too close to the church, keeping their animals well away so that the Virgin's vengeance would not fall upon them.

II.26. The presumption of a church guardian

Renald Belloz, a guardian of the church, threw a stone at a sparrow which was trying to fly into the most holy basilica of Rocamadour. He lost the strength in his arm, and it remained withered for the rest of his life.

II.27. Another presumptuous man

Peter Guarnier wanted to make some repairs to the outside of the church, and intended to remove a gutter and put a new one in its place. He instructed Gerbert, the sacrist, to move the corner stone, but Gerbert did not dare lay hands on it because he had seen how the presumptuous were punished. He therefore did not carry out the man's wishes. As a result the craftsman became extremely angry, and, being of a restless disposition, he began to demolish the stones in the church wall. Dust from the mortar above him came loose and hurt his eyes. Water was fetched and the eyes were bathed, but he could see very little or nothing. He was taken home and his whole body became wracked with pain. He put his affairs in order, said his goodbyes to his family, and that night went the way of all flesh.

II.28. A great storm at sea

An adolescent from Lyons, who was swarthy and short, was rowing on the Rhône in a boat loaded with wine. He was a confrater[65] of the church of the most Blessed Mary of Rocamadour. A considerable storm blew up over the river, and a contrary wind drove the vessel along and whipped the waves up over it. Realizing that he was in imminent danger, and that it was useless to fight against the rushing waves using either his boatcraft or brute force, he turned his thoughts to prayer – which was the more sensible thing to do. 'O Lady', he said, 'blessed among women, through whom true peace, salvation and life are granted to men, the star of the sea and the Virgin of virgins, from whom was born the Son of God who became visible among us and took pity on our wretchedness, snatch us from the swirling waves and lead us to the haven of tranquillity.' While he was praying in these and similar terms, amazing to relate, the boat made a great crashing noise and disappeared beneath the surface, sinking to the bottom of the river which was four times

---

[65] Cf. I.42 above.

deeper than the distance a ballista can throw its missile. Then, thanks to the mercy of the kind Lady, it was tossed back up into the open air: none of the people on board had come to any harm, none of the boat's apparatus had been damaged, and not one drop of wine had spilled. Everything appeared completely dry. The young man who had experienced this benefit did not want to be blamed for delaying, and so he journeyed to the church of the Lady who had protected him. In addition he and another man, who had experienced the same mortal danger with him, showed some hides and cloths, on which there was no sign that they had got wet, as a token of the amazing miracle. They praised the Queen and Lady of all, who is worthy to be celebrated in all four corners of the earth.

II.29. A woman who went into labour every day

I do not think that I should omit an astonishing and wonderful miracle, the like of which has not been heard of down the ages. A woman from Gothia became pregnant and carried the baby for thirty months: every day she would feel labour pains, but without bearing the foetus. She was her parents' only child, and they were confratres of the church of Rocamadour. They were tormented by great sorrow and constantly grieved for their daughter just as if she were already dead. Those who heard about this new and unbearable sickness were amazed by it; and those who witnessed it were moved to compassion. The Lord's dreadful scourge terrifies everyone, especially when it bears down more severely than usual as if Christ has forgotten his mercy and takes no heed of women's sex. Indeed, in this poor wretch was fulfilled that condemnation passed on the first woman: *in pain shall you bring forth.*[66] This woman would have been happy had she been able to bear the child even though childbirth is impossible without discomfort; she would have joyfully considered the pain to be no pain at all. She waited for death, although death is a bitter thing; and she screamed out that people who died were the lucky ones. Hers was a living death: she reckoned that death would be sweeter than her illness because it would last but a moment. Although everyone in labour experiences some sort of deathly sensation at some point during the delivery, what pain should we imagine this woman suffered, so long in labour as she was? Her agony was greater than any we have heard any woman has experienced in the past. Her parents exerted themselves to move the merciful Mother of God to mercy, in the knowledge that devout and constant prayer penetrates the heavens and appeases the Judge. Because the illness was so unusual, it proved necessary for the faithful doctor to cure it in an unusual way. The woman's navel miraculously opened up – something which was contrary to nature and beyond the experience of mortal men – and the baby boy, by now long dead and decaying, was taken out piece by piece. The

[66] Genesis 3:16.

woman recovered and came to the church to give thanks to Our Lady of Rocamadour, her healer. Being quite without shame, or because that is the way that people from the South[67] behave, she showed off her wound, which was still open, and eloquently spoke in praise of the supreme Virgin.

II.30. A woman who did not faithfully look after what was entrusted to her

Some women pilgrims were devoutly travelling from northern Gaul[68] to the church of the Blessed Mary of Rocamadour. While they were passing through Périgord they spent a night in the home of a poor woman, to whom they entrusted a small quantity of flour, along with their packs, for safe keeping. But there was a serious famine in the area, and the woman was careless in looking after the items committed to her. Driven by a lack of anything to eat, she used the pilgrims' flour to prepare a meal for herself. When she wanted to check whether the food had enough salt in it, she took a knife which she happened to have to hand and put it to her mouth to have a taste. The knife stuck both to her tongue and to the roof of her mouth, and it could not be dislodged. Friends and neighbours gathered from all directions to see the strange sign: some of them condescended to take pity on the poor woman; others took a more severe line, expressing the view that this was manifest and justly deserved retribution on the part of Our Lady, who cannot endure injustices. Different people took different positions. But matters turned out quite unexpectedly. The woman's pain and agonies did not diminish, for the hand of the Lord was striking her. What she had thought would be hidden became visible to everyone: this was praised by the devout as the work of the Virgin, and the dread of lesser people, those with fear, increased. When they had completed their pilgrimage the women pilgrims returned to collect their things. They were moved by the woman's affliction and prayed for her. She was then cured. Afraid of delaying, she went to the church of the most holy Virgin. There she proffered the knife as a token of faith, recounted the miracle and gave thanks.

II.31. A boy cured

William Ulric,[69] from Montpellier, was badly affected when his son became ill. He was advised to send a wax effigy weighing as much as the boy to the

---

[67] *gens braccata* (lit. 'trouser-wearing').

[68] *Gallia comata* (lit. 'long-haired') used in Classical Latin in contradistinction to *Gallia togata*.

[69] Probably to be identified with the Guillelmus Olrici who features in a number of Montpellier documents between the 1160s and 1180s. He would appear to have been a burgess close to William VII of Montpellier, to whom he lent money and whose testament he witnessed in September 1172, and to William VIII: see *Liber*

Blessed Mary of Rocamadour; in this way the boy would be made well. He set quickly to work, placing wax on one side of some scales and the boy on the other. Suddenly the boy – who up to that moment had been regarded as a terminal case – gave a laugh of delight and, more than that, was completely cured, through the merits of the Lady who can do whatever she pleases.

II.32. A youth suffering from paralysis

This same William told us about a young man from Montpellier who was gravely stricken with paralysis and, on the advice of his physicians, was carried to the baths.[70] Whereas only part of his body had been withered up till then, when he was brought back from the baths his whole body was now desiccated and crippled. He was immobile, like a statue, and he could not feel anything. His eyes were permanently closed, his mouth was twisted back, and he could not do anything with his hands: he appeared to be dead yet did not die. His relatives were weighed down by his condition, for he was only breathing and was not properly alive. They devised a plan and used some scales to measure out a weight of wax matching that of the boy with the intention of making an effigy in his likeness to send to the Lady of Rocamadour, the gentlest of the gentle, to ask for the health of the poor wretch. As soon as this was done, the youth came back to life.

II.33. Someone whose hands were cured

This William told another story which reminded us of something that we too had witnessed some time before. A youth from the same bourg of Montpellier had an elegant body and an attractive appearance. People would have thought him fortunate, and he would have been just that, if he had had healthy hands. For they had become so blemished with warts that it pained people to look at them; and he would tuck them away from view as if he were maimed. To be sure, the hands were deformed more than one can credit or indeed describe; they had become more revolting than those of a leper. Since the skills and attention of physicians did nothing for the hands, an artisan was employed to fashion some wax hands, knotted like those belonging to the youth, to be presented to the most supreme Virgin of Rocamadour. O the power of the Lady, of the mediator between God and man, which should be extolled above all others, proclaimed above all others! Whatever human strength lacks the power to do, whatever is beyond the knowledge and skill of wise men, comes to pass through the kindness of the star of the sea. For when the wax hands had been made, and as the next day

Instrumentorum Memorialium: Cartulaire des Guillems de Montpellier, ed. A. Germain (Montpellier, 1884–86), nos. 48, 79, 81, 93, 96, 98, 124, 161, 166, 313, 414, 556.

[70] Montpellier was by the later twelfth century developing a reputation as a centre of medical learning: see Paterson, *World of the Troubadours*, pp. 188–90.

was dawning, the youth's hands looked so completely well that no traces, no indications of his condition, no scars remained on them.

II.34. Pirates prevented from attacking Christians

William of Tortosa[71] and a crew of fifty men were ploughing through the waves in a bireme loaded with merchandise. Two Saracen triremes – with 320 soldiers, the enemies of the Christian name – started to chase them; the Saracens thirsted to plunder their goods and to wipe their memory from the face of the earth. They sped forwards to pierce a hole in the side of the Christians' ship, which would allow them to enter through the breach and slay those on board. Because the Christians could see no means of escape, they rushed to the weapons of prayer and with heartfelt feeling called out to the star of the sea, the Lady of ladies of Rocamadour, who is gracious towards those who invoke her and ready for those who cry out to her. The perfidious Saracens were starting to act triumphantly as if their victory had already been gained, but the Virgin of virgins threw them into confusion. She broke the masts of their ships and tore their sails, and in this way she restrained the impudence of the infidel pirates. This happened around the first hour of the day. As the Saracens were repairing the damage done to their ships, the men from Tortosa hoisted their sails, started to row, and quickly made their escape. But as dusk was falling their pursuers' ships appeared once more. The Saracens hurled insults at the Christians, their screams and trumpets making a terrifying din. They threatened them with imminent death and ruin. The Christians sought refuge in their accustomed weapons – their prayers – and asked for the power of the Virgin, whose splendour they had felt earlier, to assist them again. The more fervent the prayers of devotion are, the quicker the demonstration of mercy comes about. For in the same manner as before – there was no change in the nature of the miracle – the good Virgin broke the masts of both ships, tore their sails and forced the perfidious enemy to come to a halt. O unique palm, who has no peer on earth or in the heavenly court! O the honour of the human race, who displays above all others the privileges of her powers! Just as the sun is brighter than the moon, and the moon brighter than the stars, so Mary is worthier than all created beings. O Virgin who surpasses all virgins, through you is opened to us that gate of heaven which the cherubim closed to mortal men by brandishing a fiery sword, because God born of you joined us to God his Father. The waters of the Holy Ghost covered you in divine dew. And you remain intact because in you your virginity was not taken or diminished in any way. Because you greatly please your Son, Our Lord, in all things, you snatch those who invoke you from danger, you set them free, and you lead them back to the path of truth. For you miraculously freed your sailors so that your name may be praised and your wondrous work proclaimed amongst the nations forever and ever. Amen.

[71] Catalonia.

II.35. A boy revived and a killer punished

Gerberta lived with her five sons in the court of Bertold, which is located within the area controlled by the king of France. Her youngest son was carrying a basket on his head containing bread for sale. It was early summer, and the crops were not yet fully grown. Some distance from his village he came across someone whom he already knew amongst those sowing in the fields – someone ensnared in the net of manifold and manifest crime. This man craftily spotted the youth – whose friend he had once been – and when he had lowered his guard with words of flattery he took him to a remote spot, wrested his knife from him, threw him violently to the ground and cut his throat, leaving only a small area of skin at the back undamaged. As the youth lay dying, he turned the Virgin of virgins over in his heart – he was unable to address her vocally – and repeated exactly what he had learned to say in life. The evil killer was making off with the spoils he had taken from his victim – who was still shaking – when a lady appeared next to the dying youth. She was amazingly beautiful and dressed in many colours. She stroked the youth's head, which was all but severed from the trunk, and touching it with motherly affection made the sign of the cross on it with her hand, putting it back in its original position and stopping the flow of blood. The youth was discovered by some travellers and, to the accompaniment of the wails of his family, carried to his house. The wounds were sewn up, and he was quickly healed. Nonetheless his voice remained hoarse and he had scars on his throat for the rest of his life as a reminder of this memorable happening. On the anniversary of this wicked deed the evil spirit which had enslaved the profane murderer in body and soul led him back secretly to the village to pay the price of his crimes. While he spent the night with some ne'er-do-wells playing dice with gamblers and giving himself up to worthlessness, he was revealed to the spirit of the youth's mother, who saw that he was close by and had joined the gamblers' gathering. When she told her sons, they thought that she was talking nonsense. But they soon roused themselves, took hold of the murderer, and handed him over to the king. Unwilling to let such a serious crime go unpunished, the king ordered the culprit to be hanged so that he should receive due reward for the wicked act he had committed. Then the youth came to the church to give thanks to the Lady of Rocamadour who had given him life. And to demonstrate the miracle he showed his scars and described what had happened to everyone.

II.36. A blind woman who became sighted during the carrying of the light

A woman from the Auvergne had lost her sight for about seven years. She grieved and wept over the fact that along with her sight she had also lost all the pleasant things in life. She came to Rocamadour and poured out her prayers to the Lord. Contrite of mind and clamorous of voice, she mournfully redoubled her prayers to the star of the sea, who is brighter than all other stars. She was more concerned about the sort of sight which can be recovered and lost than about the vision of the Lord which, when the burden of the flesh is laid aside, will endure without diminution. Days passed, and it was getting close to the time when we honour anew the memory of the Lord's Passion.[72] During the hour of Matins in the early morning of Holy Thursday, while praises were being sung to God with psalms and canticles, the woman had to be restrained by the brethren of the church because her spirit had become more fervent and her complaining was sometimes too shrill, and also because they found her voice irritating and excessively loud. Nonetheless she persevered with her prayers, invoking the spring of the gardens, the well of living waters, the guardian of the perfumes, and turning her over and over in her heart. As the office of Lauds was being concluded, the lights in the church were ritually extinguished[73] – an act which signifies the perfidy and blindness of the Jews, which persists to this day – and for a time the church was in darkness, just as the woman was. Then a signal was given and the light was restored – a symbol of the Catholic faith which spreads its clear radiance everywhere – and as the church lit up so was the light in the woman's eyes rekindled. The woman who could now see rejoiced in the God of gods in Sion, who cures and saves those who place their hope in him through the merits of the merciful Lady.

II.37. A calming of the air at sea

Some men from Cologne[74] were rowing their ship in the Atlantic Ocean. The rough weather and the swirling winds made them afraid that they were going to die, especially since the clouds were getting thicker, the claps of thunders and flashes of lightning were becoming more frequent, and the enormous waves were tossing the ship up and down. The sailors threw anchors over the side so that the ship could lie to, but the ropes snapped straight away even though they were fairly new ones. What more could be done? Gripped by heartfelt anguish inside and out, and terrified by the thought of dying, they raised shouts and uttered tearful sighs to the heavens in an effort to placate the divinities of the sky. They asked the lamb who is without blemish, who reigns forever and breaks the chains of death, to give them back their life – just as if they were already dead. They begged the life of the living, the salvation of those who wander, to save

---

[72] I.e. Easter.
[73] The Office of Tenebrae, in which the lights in the church are extinguished.
[74] A MS variant may indicate Boulogne. See Albe, p. 230 n. 99.

them from shipwreck and lead them back to the haven of tranquillity. O Virgin,[75] star of the sea shining clearly through the waves, free us as we face shipwreck and the danger of death. Unique Virgin Mother, grant us your assistance so that we can get out alive from the depths of the storm. Kind Virgin, who bore the maker of the world, be our guide and our path so that, led by you, we may reach the shore. There was now just one anchor left out of all the ones they had been carrying. The sailors released it into the deep and made a vow that they would carry a silver anchor to the church of the most Blessed Virgin of Rocamadour if they were worthy to be saved through her – for there was no other means of salvation. Immediately the air became calm and the raging of the winds abated. The sailors reached harbour without any problems whatsoever. From there they came to the church and performed their vow with humble devotion.

II.38. The cure of the abbot of Cluny

Stephen, the venerable abbot of Cluny,[76] was suffering from a serious illness. He had put his temporal affairs in order, just as if he did not have long to live, and mindful of his salvation he had received the last rites and purified his heart in readiness to journey to the court of the heavenly king. Upset at the prospect of their abbot's death, the senior members of the monastic body approached him with great humility and asked him – because he knew the qualities of all those there – who would be suitable to succeed him in the task of ruling such a large number of monks. But the abbot replied that this was not his decision to make because a new abbot should be appointed by means of a canonically regular election. Nevertheless he told them that he would give them an answer on this and other matters on the following day, if he were still alive. That night he managed to remain alert even though his flesh was being severely whipped by the Lord's scourge. He beheld the God of gods in his heart. And praying earnestly for his bodily preservation, he yearned for the Mother of the Lord – gentler, higher and better than other virgins, she who is the glory of all, the light of the blind, the support of the fallen, the hope of the guilty, the unfailing joy of the angels – to be the mediator between himself and our Redeemer, whom she nobly bore. Because a contrite and humbled heart appeases the King of kings, Stephen was worthy to be heard and to be healed. When morning came, the monks gathered to hear the abbot's reply. He looked more cheerful and physically healthier than usual, which made the astonished monks think that they were seeing things. And he said: 'Let there be prepared for us a more lavish meal than is customary,

---

[75] Rocacher, *Rocamadour*, i.69 points out that the Latin from this invocation down to the prayer to reach the shore scans rhythmically, suggesting that it was taken from an existing hymn or canticle.

[76] Abbot 1161–73. See *DHGE* 13.74–5

because today I intend to feast with our brethren in accordance with what it provides in our Rule.[77] To be sure, the Mother of God, the perpetual Virgin of Rocamadour, ordered that I should be restored to health by her Son so that I may correct my own faults and not allow the excesses of those in my charge to go unpunished.' Without further delay he went at the head of a large number of monks to the church of the mellifluous empress to give thanks for the benefit he had received and to relate the miracle.

II.39. A piece of iron extracted from a wounded man's body

Hubert of Pierrelatte,[78] in Burgundy,[79] was wounded in the chest when an arrow hit him under his right breast. And for three and a half years he carried the iron piece in his body. None of the surgeons could get it out or heal the wound. But in his heart he trusted the Lord, and he called out to the precious pearl of Rocamadour, Our Lady, to come to his aid, seeking her help above that of all others. Sending a wax effigy on ahead to the church, he shortly afterwards went there himself. He entreated the people to help him with their own prayers of entreaty, moving complete strangers with his sighs and tears. But he did not move the Lady of compassion compassionately to give him his health straight away. He then returned home, never losing confidence in the clemency of the Lord and his kind Mother. He summoned one of his servants, an artless man who was rough and unskilled for the task he was going to perform. He ordered him to do what the physicians could not: that is, pull the piece of iron out of his body. The servant refused because he was concerned that his master would die. But the knight was convinced that he would be cured, and is reported to have addressed his dependant in these eloquent terms: 'Take a good hold, and do so with confidence, because I have had a divine revelation and am in no doubt that I will recover my health with your assistance.' The servant picked up a tool and, shaking with fear, inserted it into the wound. He moved the instrument from side to side – the flesh had become rotten deep down – and he came upon the piece of iron without knowing what it was that he was touching. And with the desire born of suffering the knight instructed him to take it out, whatever it was. The servant therefore extracted the iron fragment, to the delight of all those who were there. Soon restored to health, the knight came to the church to give thanks to his liberator, declaring that she had brought about his recovery, and bringing with him a silver effigy with the arrow that had struck him stuck into it.

[77] Cf. *The Rule of St Benedict*, cc. 39–41, trans. J. McCann (London, 1976), pp. 45–7.
[78] Drôme.
[79] Pierrelatte is in the Dauphiné. For the broad application of the term 'Burgundy' see I.22 above.

II.40. A knight who recovered his senses

Raymond, a knight from the region of Toulouse, became mad and unable to control himself. He used to utter blasphemies against God, the salvation of us all, and against his glorious Mother. He was also unable to respond to those addressing him, and would simply mimic them by repeating exactly what he had heard. Besides which, he asserted that he had renounced God and had confirmed his fealty to the devil in a written instrument. Therefore the people who knew that he was troubled, and in particular his family, vowed to give on his behalf a wax effigy weighing as much as he did to the most Blessed Mother of God of Rocamadour. And he recovered his senses.

II.41. A youth afflicted by an illness in his legs

Godfrey, the son of Count Hartmann of Altenburg[80] was afflicted by an illness in his legs for a year. A young man should be in his prime when he is at that age, but this particular youth was so debilitated by his sickness that he could not leave his room. When one limb hurts, the others do so too because the parts of the body are joined in such a way that one part cannot be damaged without injury to all the others. The nobility of Godfrey's birth made him a notable figure, and he had a charming way of speaking which made him loveable; no wonder that his relatives were troubled when even outsiders were affected as well. Medical science was ineffective and quite useless because no remedy existed to make this sick youth better. His family had lost hope for his recovery, particularly because a long-lasting illness is said to be incurable. But even though he lived in the remote parts of Germany, Godfrey had heard about, and believed in, the kindness of the most Blessed Mary of Rocamadour, her manifold generosity and her healing of the sick. He had therefore conceived the hope of getting better. In addition he promised that he would travel to the church of the most Blessed Virgin on pilgrimage and make an annual payment in return for his recovery. He then obtained what he had so long desired. Mouths are opened in praise of the supreme Virgin, her servants dance for joy, the earth resounds, the world echoes because the salvation of the sick, the medicine of mortal men, performs her works whenever, wherever and howsoever she wants, paying out more than is due through her bountiful munificence.

---

[80] Latin *veteri castro*. Albe, p. 234 n. 105, suggests that the author, departing from his normal practice of using established Latin place-names or Latinized phonetic approximations of vernacular names, was here translating Altenburg ('old castle'). This is questionable. But if true, there were numerous places with this name in Germany: see Tillmann, *Lexicon der deutschen Burgen und Schlösser*, i.19–22. One possibility is the royal palace of Altenburg in Thuringia: see *ibid.*, i.20; G. Köbler, *Historisches Lexicon der Deutschen Länder* (Munich, 1992), pp. 9–10; B. Arnold, *Princes and Territories in Medieval Germany* (Cambridge, 1991), p. 77.

II.42. Another knight cured of a deadly wound

Anselm, an Italian knight from the region of Ivrea,[81] had been hit by an arrow between his groin and his navel, the arrow passing through his back. Sensing that he was mortally wounded, he put his affairs in order and made his will like someone who is going to die very soon. He then directed his thoughts and raised his eyes to the heavens. And he is said to have called upon the Lord of the earth with these words, or something similar: 'Redeemer of all men, do not despise me, made by your hands. *Show me a sign of thy favour*[82] according to the depth of your mercy. I know, and I confess, that you cannot fail to be just in your judgements because you are wise; you cannot be corrupted because you are just; and you cannot be evaded because you are present everywhere. The only thing left for me to do, therefore, is to flee to you, to flee from your anger, to flee towards your mercy. I do not ask you to judge me but to take pity on me. I do not wish to ask for trifles because it does not become the great to give small things. In asking for so much, Lord, I have no trust at all in my own merits. Rather, I honour your magnificence. Take pity on me and make me well again. Indeed, if you do not help me, everything which I have at present will soon come to an end. Star of the sea and Virgin of virgins, blessed amongst women, the giver of life to mortal men, who gave birth to the Lord of Heaven, whom Judea brought forth for us as a thorn brings forth the rose, respond favourably to my prayers. Closed door, the spring of the gardens, the storeroom of perfumes, the painted room, stand by me. Glory of virgins, the mediator of mankind, the Mother of salvation, stand by me, I say, ready to answer the prayer of your supplicant. Stand by me with your munificence. Stand by me with an indication of your kindness. If you decree that I should be cured, I will immediately and painlessly be free of this deadly curse. You will not only be praised by me because I have been saved; you will be universally esteemed by everyone throughout the world.' Then the arrow was completely removed. The knight made a quick recovery and came to the church to offer his thanks and praises.

II.43. A fire put out through the merits of the Virgin

Houses in the town of Saint-Geniez,[83] in the Rouergue, were burning down as a punishment for men's sins. The inhabitants could think of nothing to fight the fire, and brute force was useless, because the wind was against them. The weather had been dry: this and the fact that the houses were close together fuelled the flames. The tearful cries of people together calling upon the Blessed Mary of Rocamadour rose up to the sky, and the Lord's anger – a

---

[81] Piedmont.
[82] Psalms 85:17.
[83] Probably Saint-Geniez-d'Olt (Aveyron).

disciplining anger and not a raging fury which destroys everything – turned into a refreshing dew. Through the intervention of the glorious Mother of God, the wind, whose blasts had fanned the flames to an enormous size, now retreated. The fire stopped raging, and disaster turned to good fortune. As the fire subsided, the buildings, which only moments earlier were being torn apart, now remained standing; and the pained lamentations turned to songs of praise. What had been on the verge of destruction was saved by the Lady, who is gracious above all others, through her Son, Our Lord, Jesus Christ, who is God three and one, and lives and reigns forever and ever. Amen.

II.44. The faithful custody of the Mother of the Lord

Peter, a citizen of Tours, was on pilgrimage to the churches of the Blessed Mary of Rocamadour and St James[84] when some bandits tried to strip him of his money and possessions. In the absence of anyone to protect him, he placed all his hope in prayer, and trod ten gold coins – which was all he had – into the ground under his feet because he had *no place in the inn.*[85] He was delivered from his enemies thanks to the merits of the most Blessed Virgin, and he faithfully and devoutly completed his pilgrimage. Returning to the spot, which he had shrewdly made a note of, he did not find his property. As often happens when paths are worn away by traffic, the passage of people and beasts of burden had trodden the ground down, and part of the money committed to God's care had gone. Peter was distressed, and looking up to the heavens he said, 'Blessed Virgin, did I not place my things under your protection? Do not others find that you faithfully protect what they commit to you and keep to your promises, since you give without measure and grant more than they are owed? So what has happened with me? Is it that you are being less kind towards me, when you appear to everyone else as gentler than the gentle? It is your way to give to those who are without, not to take from those who have. I have been exerting myself in your service, and my reward is for you to keep my property? What can one ask from someone who has had nothing entrusted to him? But here, on this open road, I left my things in your charge. So return the sum which I – I alone, with you as my only witness – committed to you.' While he was speaking in this way and rolling his eyes, he spotted his property next to the road. He joyfully picked it up and offered thanks in the church of his faithful guardian.

II.45. An open wound bound and cured

William Berenguer, from Montpellier, had been stabbed with a knife near his navel. When the knife was pulled out, some of his insides came out of the

[84] Santiago de Compostela.
[85] Luke 2:7.

wound. But he did not lose confidence in the Lord's clemency, and he committed the deadly wound to the care of the Blessed Mother of God. What is more, he proposed that he would not allow any remedy to be used on him except the heavenly and divine sort. And, as he told us, he could not marvel enough at the sweetness of the sweet and adorable Lady: he felt no pain in his wound, nor any discomfort while it was healing. The lesion in his entrails was tightly bound, and the wound soon closed up. He was restored to his former strength – or perhaps to greater strength than he had before – and told those who were in the church at Rocamadour what had happened, showing off his scar as he did so.

II.46. A cured cripple

Raymond, from Couserans,[86] had been a cripple since childhood and had lost his strength throughout his body. He was weak and thin, and he had such slender joints that his stiffened limbs and wrinkled skin made him only just resemble a real person. His parents frequently poured out prayers for him in the church of the Lord. While the holy offices were being celebrated, they sought the suffrage of the saints and diligently performed their prayers with true devotion. They did not leave out the supreme honour of virgins, the outstanding star of Rocamadour, praying to her to relieve their son's distress. What is more, they made some candles to present to the Blessed Mary; these were the same length and thickness as the son's legs.[87] The granter of pardon, the restorer of health, had regard to their devotion and did not put off any longer making the boy well.

II.47. Another sick person cured

At the same time, and in the very house where the cripple was lying, there was also someone called Peter who was suffering from a very serious illness. He was on the verge of laying aside his mortal body. Cold and already stiff, he was lifted off his bed and placed on the ground. As his relatives sat around the body weeping, they had a sound idea and hurried to make a candle measured against him[88] before he expired, intending to take it to the church of the Blessed Virgin. Because faith operates alongside works, for *without works faith is dead*,[89] the humble Virgin responded to the steadfastness of their prayer and the frequency of their devotion. And the man, who already seemed to be on the point of dying, immediately got up and was well.

---

[86] Ariège.
[87] Cf. II.18 above.
[88] Cf. II.18; II.46 above.
[89] James 2:20, 2:26.

II.48. A deaf woman

In this same house there was also a deaf woman. As she witnessed the sorts of cures which were happening, and being herself in need of divine aid, she prayed and regained her hearing.

II.49. Someone who fell out of a tree

Amelius, from Toulouse, wanted to pick some nuts from a tree. He climbed to the top, where he shook the nuts with a stick to get at them. But he was careless and slipped. He was afraid of falling – because the tree was sixty cubits or more in height – and so he turned his thoughts to the Lady of ladies, scarcely able to call to her out loud. He then fell down with an enormous crash. No part of his body was harmed except one hand which hurt him. And this pain soon dulled. His body was undamaged and his mind was alert, but he put off giving thanks to his liberator, something which was to be his undoing. Some time later he went to a mill carrying some corn. On entering, he was pushed by a demon and fell into the water. And he would not have escaped drowning had he not been pulled out straight away. Then he came to his senses, clearly and carefully pondering the wiles of the crafty tempter, who is aggrieved at upright people and tries to entice and incite them. Those he is allowed to harm he dashes down to destruction with the intention of having them as his companions in his error and as sharers in his iniquity. Every day he entices the flesh, the flesh in turn lures the spirit, and by consenting to impiety wicked deeds result. In this way the flesh ensures that it will burn in a fire which never dies. The young man did not put off coming to the church to give thanks any longer, for he was afraid of being assailed a third time by a demon now that he had already experienced this twice. He knew perfectly well that he had escaped the demons' attacks on two occasions thanks to the Virgin's merits and assistance, with the help and co-operation of Our Lord Jesus Christ, who is with the Father and the Holy Ghost one divinity, essence and power, the honour and the glory, forever and ever. Amen.

This concludes the second part of the miracles of Our Lady of Rocamadour.

The Third Part

Here begins the prologue

We have considered it a worthy task to bring into the light what we have decided should not be overlooked through negligence or silence, so that God may be praised and loved more fervently, so that his glorious Mother, our powerful Lady and Queen, may be honoured, and for the edification of our neighbour. For something to endure until the ends of time it must be committed to writing. For given that the Creator of all has deigned to restore for the praise and glory of his name, should we, whom he fashioned and whose flesh is clay, refuse to show obedience to the divine will and command? Without him we are nothing, and with him and in him we can achieve much. So why should we not attach ourselves to the tower of strength, the fount of wisdom, the plenitude of all good things? Because we are pressed down by our earthly habitation, which is a weight and not a support, we are unable to fix our bleary eyes on the radiance of the sun. But at least let us pause a while in taking delight in his invisible works and with his help continue the task that we have begun.

Here ends the prologue

Chapters of the third part

III.1. The miraculous voyage of some sailors

At the time of the war between the king of Aragon[1] and Count Raymond of Toulouse,[2] Raymond, a priest and monk from Psalmody[3] in the diocese of Nîmes, was attempting to transport some corn by sea to supply the inhabitants of Montpellier. God permitted the sky to cloud over, the sun to become hidden, and the sailors to be cloaked in darkness. The wind whipped up into a storm and threatened them with shipwreck; there was no obvious means of escape. The waves were becoming so swollen that one would think they were washing against the sky; at other times the waters dropped down into what seemed an abyss. Those on board prayed and stretched their palms up to the heavens, pleading with the star of the sea, the Lady of Rocamadour. With sobs and sighs, cries and even screams they all called out for mercy. Immediately the ship dropped down from under their feet and sank into the depths of the sea, leaving them floating on the surface and clinging to each other in a tight group. As they were tossed around, they were astonished by the force of the waves which came crashing down over them. The icy cold, combined with their great fear, made their throats become hoarse. And already their hearts were gripped by a feeling deep down that their end was somehow near. Why go into more detail? The men closed their lips and nostrils as tightly as they could to stop thin streams of water from getting in, and they did not let their mouths relax as they clung to life because the raging water was coming up to their necks and higher.

So, may they be consoled and raised up by the power of the Father, through which sins are punished, so that they may have the strength to overcome the enormity of the waves. May they be consoled by the wisdom of the Son, who restores what is lacking through ignorance. And may they be consoled and aided by the kindness of the Holy Ghost so that unwanted despair may not overtake them. O gracious Virgin, gentle in your mercy, the substance of their bodies is at stake, and there is no doubt that death is close; they are being asked to pay the debt of perdition. But unless you rescue these drowning men, who are wholly crushed in their minds and bodies, they will soon be overcome by the dangerous and crashing waves. Their death is imminent – a death which is bitter because it is unwanted and sudden, a death not cleansed by confession, a death not fortified by the last rites, a death which is unexpected. This is the death that faces them. Death spares no one, but it is punishing these men more terribly. Mother of the Father and Daughter of the Father, joy of the entire world, order your Son, pray to your Father, to lead them to the longed-for shore of safety. Virgin, the salvation of

[1] Alfonso II (1162–96).
[2] Raymond V (1148–94).
[3] Gard.

the humble and the lily of chastity, lend these men your help. Listen to them as they cry out to you; lift from them the danger of death as they pray. The sea is swelling up, and without a ship their fear is growing. If you delay in helping them then they will be drowned.

The celebrated Virgin, praiseworthy in all things, worked a new miracle, the like of which we have not heard of before. She brought the ship back up from the bottom of the sea and repositioned it under the sailors' feet. She then calmly conducted it – still full of water and without its oars – to the shore. The men, however, were frozen stiff from the enormous cold; they could not move any of their limbs because of both the wintry rain and their drenching in the sea. So before they reached port they prayed that they should be worthy to be warmed up, and their prayers were answered. For they felt the force of a fire inside and out, stronger than a real blaze, through the warming effect of the Holy Ghost. News of the miracle quickly spread in the area. People proclaimed that *great are the works of the Lord, studied by all who have pleasure in them.*[4] And they glorified the light of Rocamadour which is placed upon a chandelier and shines forth in all directions.

III.2. A cured youth

A noble youth from Montpeyroux[5] was hunting a stag. Once he had brought the animal down, he had to struggle to keep his dogs off it, having recourse to threatening cries and blows. The most savage of the dogs leapt at the young man and bit into his arm, causing him such enormous pain and producing so large a swelling – not just on his arm but all over his right side – that people thought he was going to die straight away. He was carried to someone's house. Everyone doubted that he would recover because none of the poultices applied to him did him any good. But he offered up numerous prayers to the Blessed Virgin. Wishing to die at home, he first set out on a journey to the most Blessed Mary of Rocamadour, carried on a horse and supported on both sides by his followers. His arm, which was hanging from the shoulder, was wrapped up in a cloth to give it some support. He was tormented by unimaginable pain. It so happened that, overcome by the agony and by the effort of the journey, he fell asleep as he rode. The most Blessed Virgin appeared to him in a vision, ordering him to free his arm and telling him that he was going to be well. The young man immediately awoke from his sleep and discovered that he was cured. He described the vision to his companions and then with much rejoicing came to the church, where he recounted the miracle.

---

[4] Psalms 110:2.
[5] Various places of this name in Aveyron, Dordogne, Hérault and Puy-de-Dôme.

III.3. A man cured of dropsy

Gerald of Saint-Michel[6] (a castle in Quercy)[7] was a noble and straight-forward man of sound judgement. He was afflicted by a long illness: he was swollen all over his body and diagnosed as having dropsy. He abstained from all bodily nourishment for two and a half months – something which has been unheard-of up right up to the modern day and is almost beyond belief. But to avoid losing track of the truth in any details, we must stick to what we learned from his own lips and from those of many others; this will spare us the backbiting disparagement of spiteful tongues. We heard that all he took was the juice from a couple of cherries and the merest drop of water – and even then very seldom – over that entire length of time. Day in, day out people expected him to die, for the attentions of physicians did nothing to cure him. His condition utterly defeated the experts' knowledge. Contrary to nature, or rather exceeding the bounds of what is natural, his bodily substance came to resemble soil, and he lay like a lopped tree. He was dead yet unable to die. His spirit yearned to join the celestial spirits – to render earth to earth and spirit to God. The anguish of his relatives was expressed volubly: an anguish which was beyond consolation. As far as Gerald was concerned, to die was gain and to live was Christ.[8] He wanted to be free of his earthly flesh so that, according to his merits, he could receive an abode in heaven. Since he lived close to the church of the most Blessed Mary of Rocamadour, both he and his household and dependants lifted up their voices in prayer to the Virgin, who is outstanding in the entrails of her mercy, and fixed upon her as the anchor of his salvation. Gerald would speak in the following terms, not because he was losing hope, but more out of compassion for his people rather than himself: 'I reckon that it would be less of a miracle to bring the dead back to life than to restore me to my former state of health, now that I am fetid and already half-decayed. Nonetheless I have no doubt that my Lady is capable of anything thanks to the grace and power of her Son. But I do not believe that I am worthy enough in his sight to deserve to have my sinfulness concealed and for her to intercede with my Lord; and the hand of punishment has not been laid upon me as heavily as I in fact deserve. I am being scourged for my past deeds, because I used to take delight in adulation and praise while pretending that I did not. But now, in satisfaction of what I have done in the past and as a mark of honour in the future, I have made up my mind to give five solidi to the Blessed Virgin every year for the rest of my life.' Gerald was restored to health, and with great joy he performed his vow and gave thanks to his healer.

[6] Probably the man of this name attested in a number of charters from Obazine in the years either side of 1172/3: *Cartulaire*, nos. 41, 136, 331, 370, 733.

[7] Saint-Michel-de-Bannière (Lot).

[8] Cf. Philippians 1:21.

III.4. The barbarians killed by a falling wall

An enormous army of Brabançons and Basques – a well-armed people who are aggressive and highly skilled in the arts of warfare – laid siege to the city of Mende.[9] The way people saw it, the town did not have sufficient numbers of inhabitants and was not adequately protected by fortifications and walls, so it did not seem able to resist this cruel and evil race.[10] Outside the walls the attackers would launch assaults; they were already dancing with joy and blowing their trumpets as if they were assured of victory. They uttered loud, terrifying cries, and the earth resounded with their shouts. Outside the city there was rejoicing; inside there was grief. Outside there were attacks and ambushes, and people striving to practise every form of treachery; inside there was a public-spirited mood of resistance as people fought for their homeland and homes and to prevent a massacre of their people, the hideous deflowering of virgins, and the hateful violation of wives. One would see mothers in mourning clothes and young girls with unkempt hair screaming hysterically; they would wail as they roamed the streets, carry stones to be thrown from the walls, and urge the men on as they moved forward to the fray. One would also see the hands of the old and those unable to fight stretching up to the sky in ceaseless prayer, asking the Lord for assistance. For the people knew that the question of whether they would be victorious would be decided in heaven. Just as Israel triumphed and the Amalekites were overcome while Moses prayed,[11] so they offered up clamorous prayers, fervent devotion and tearful cries to the ears of the Almighty, asking that they should be worthy to be heard now that they had been brought to penitence. The tears shed by virgins, the unremitting pain, and also the cries of women touched the mercy of the Virgin of virgins, the refuge of pity and graciousness, the Lady of Rocamadour, whose works the people knew overcame and checked the hands of the wicked. But the Virgin delights in the prayers of sinners, and because *the kingdom* of God *has suffered violence,*[12] she was happy to be appeased by their holocaust of prayer so that she might have the opportunity to exercise her mercy. Acting on what was a necessary and sensible course of action, and by common assent, the people of the city decreed that they would give themselves, their property and even the walls of the town to the Blessed Virgin, placing all the civic affairs under her protection. They also decided to make an annual payment to her from their communal resources. The humble Virgin, supreme in her gentleness, answered the citizens' prayers by defending them miraculously and in a way

---

[9] Lozère.

[10] For a closely contemporary account of Mende's need to defend itself against the 'perfidious race' of Basque, Aragonese and German mercenaries, and of the value of its walls, see 'Chronicon breve de gestis Aldeberti', p. 126.

[11] See Exodus 7:8–16.

[12] Matthew 11:12.

which was clear to see. For although the weather was calm and settled – there was no rain falling, no wind blowing, and certainly no earth tremor – a section of the city walls which was more than sixty cubits long collapsed completely, killing the barbarians and destroying their highly-prized and expensive animals: there were no external wounds on the beasts but they were killed from the inside. All this was done so that the power of the Almighty might shine forth more clearly for all to see. An army which had once trusted in its own ferocity and its countless numbers now felt the hand of God heavy upon it. Its members became afraid and withdrew from the unconquered city as quickly as they were able, leaving behind the remains of the rotting corpses as a monument to divine vengeance. Who has the eloquence to relate, and who has the mind to conceive, how the citizens' hearts became enflamed and how their mouths were opened in praise of the Lady of ladies. They did not forget the benefit they had received, and they went to the church of their liberator. They had had made a wax city modelled on their own – as far as the craftsman could manage – and they presented this, offered up delightful praises, and recounted the miracle in all its wondrous detail.

III.5. Money entrusted to Our Lady

A man named Magro, from the area around Nîmes,[13] hid some money and entrusted it to the care of the Blessed Mary. When he returned the following day he was unable to find it; what had happened was that someone had secretly taken it during the night. Whereupon Magro burst into tears, expressing his amazement with moans and groans that he could be cheated of his property when it had been commended to the protection of the most holy Virgin. As he cast his gaze this way and that, looking all around him, someone appeared to him to relieve him of his sadness, handing the coins – not one of which was missing – back to the man.

III.6. Oxen restored to their owner

Among the oxen which Andrew of Île-Barbe,[14] in the Lyonnais, owned were two which were fit to do heavy work and were for that reason very valuable. But it so happened that they were stolen by some thieves, who drove them away to some distant place. Despite all this Andrew was hopeful that he would recover his animals: he had earlier commended himself and his possessions to the glorious Virgin. Confident in the very midst of his enemies, he made a search in unfamiliar areas and finally found what he was looking for. But the robbers recognized him and were whipped into a frenzy; they first tried to run him through with their lances, and then to

[13] Gard.
[14] Rhône.

wound him at close quarters with their swords. But Andrew remained unafraid of the sharpness of their weapons, and no harm came to him. With a clear, resonant voice he praised the name of the Virgin, a name which was prefigured of old by signs and symbols. When the robbers saw what was happening, they were amazed at the turn of events and threw themselves at the man's feet, begging and beseeching him for forgiveness. They handed the oxen back without asking for any payment, and they accompanied him on his return journey to make sure that he got back safely to his own part of the world.

III.7. A punished thief

Three pilgrims on their way to the blessed and glorious Virgin of Rocamadour were passing near Le Puy[15] when they lost their money to some scoundrel who cut their purses. The poor of Christ bemoaned the loss of the means to get supplies, whereas the thief went off cheering and clapping, grasping the money firmly in his hand. But when he tried to open his hand he could not do so at all, because divine vengeance was making it shut tight. As he wondered in amazement at this, he came across a knight. He told the knight about both the misdeed he had committed and the misfortune which had befallen him, and asked him for his advice. The knight grabbed hold of the man, saying 'This sort of remedy is what I know'. He hanged the thief with the reins of his horse, an act in praise of the Virgin and vengeance upon the enemies of Christ. The knight also gave orders that the money be returned to those from whom it had been taken.

III.8. Other thieves who were punished with madness

A gang of sixteen thieves had stolen two cows from someone from Montpellier. The owner spent a long time travelling far and wide in search of his animals, and finally he found them. He also recognized the thieves, who were ranting and raving out of their minds. On discovering this, the man burst into praise of the Virgin, to whom his herd had been entrusted and thanks to whose help and guidance it had been recovered. Everywhere that he went he told people about what he had seen, describing how the thieves had gone mad. Upon his return home he did not delay making the journey back to the church of Rocamadour. He presented an offering of some wax models of cows, and in recounting the miracle told of how those wicked men continued to be punished by the Lord's scourge.

---

[15]   Haute-Loire.

III.9. A cured hawk

Duke Matthew of Lorraine[16] had a hawk which he loved enormously because of its strength. One day the hawk was in pursuit of a duck; it caught its prey but then dropped into the swirling waters of a deep lake. A knight who was a member of the duke's household rushed to help the bird, but was thwarted by the deep water. Instead, he tried to pull both birds out with his sword. However, the hawk received a deadly wound to the head from the sharp point of the weapon. As a result, the knight became afraid of the duke's anger and went into hiding for the time being. For his part, the duke flew into an excessive rage but then repressed his anger, promising a silver bird to the exceptional and venerable Mother of God of Rocamadour if she saw fit to give life to his hawk. And when he had calmed down further he sewed up the bird's wounds. The bird was restored to health and thereafter was in as good a condition as it had been before.

III.10. A cured merchant

Godfrey, a merchant from Regensburg,[17] was off to do business at the fairs held at Turnhout.[18] Travelling as part of a large group, and carrying many wares, he entered land which belonged to Walter Bertold.[19] This same Walter laid an ambush for the merchant and attacked him at the head of an armed gang, grabbing hold of both his property and that belonging to the other people in his party. The merchant realized that there was absolutely no use in pleading with his attackers to be spared or in appealing to anyone's better feelings, and so he resisted the aggressors as much as his strength permitted. But his efforts were to no avail. He received five lethal blows to the head and, what is more, he suffered stab wounds all over his body. He was then left there, half alive. Nevertheless, even though he was unable to open his mouth because of the circumstances in which he found himself, in his heart he turned to and called upon the Lady of Rocamadour, who comes to the assistance of all those who place their hope in her. He knew that he would be made well with her help, and without needing to consult any doctors. He was carried to Brussels, where everyone came to the conclusion that he was not going to live very long. The breath of life stirred faintly in his chest, next to

---

[16] Matthew I (1139–76). See I.22 above.

[17] In Bavaria (Oberpfalz). Latin *Resnenburc*. Albe's identification (p. 259 n. 29) as Rijnsburg in Holland is questionable because the story describes a journey northwards through Brussels and Mechelen (see later note) towards Turnhout, which is north-east of Antwerp. Another possibility is Regensberg (Oberfranken) near Forchheim.

[18] In modern Belgium (Antwerpen).

[19] Probably to be identified as Walter Bertold of Mechelen (Antwerpen). See E. Warlop, *The Flemish Nobility before 1300*, trans. J. B. Ross and H. Vandermoere, 4 vols. (Courtrai, 1975), ii.436 n.123, 513 n. 78.

his heart. For nine days and more he uttered not a word, because he was weakened by the considerable loss of blood and the depth of his gaping wounds. He was unable to recognize or even focus on anyone. He lay there half-dead, his ruddy gore striking terror into those who looked at him. Unsurprisingly so. For a man who had once presented a pleasing and manly appearance, and who had been robust, was now drained of blood and misshapen: he looked the very picture of a dead man, and he smelled of death. *But when it pleased God who separated* him *from his mother's womb and called* him *by his grace*[20] to magnify his power among the peoples and to bring the dead man back to life, he completely and immediately restored the merchant to health: not by means of the trifles of physicians, but thanks to his Mother, Our Lady, the most powerful of queens. On account of this the man came joyfully, devoutly and without delay to the church of Rocamadour to give thanks the more fully for his health and to recount the miracle. In this he was sent by him who lives and reigns, one God, with the Father and the Holy Ghost. Amen.

III.11. A crippled knight who had blasphemed against the church of Rocamadour

Senorez, a knight from Longas[21] in Périgord, wished to receive a fitting reward from God, who repays all good things, in return for undertaking physical toil. So he went on pilgrimage to Jerusalem, and he also applied himself to visiting other saints' shrines which the faithful of Christ are accustomed to frequent in their devotion. Finally he came to the church of the unique Virgin, the Mother of the highest King, at Rocamadour, which was not very far from his own part of the world. When he came upon the many wax models which were pierced in various ways by different sorts of weapons, he did not place faith in what he was seeing. What is more, he added that these were deceitful pretences, asserting that these things had not been brought by pilgrims but rather fraudulently placed there by the monks' servants. When he returned home he pointed out that he had not seen this sort of thing in the Valley of Jehosophat,[22] in the Church of the Ascension,[23] nor in the many other renowned churches dedicated to the Blessed Virgin. And he used this observation to argue strenuously against what people generally, and indeed truthfully, say about the basilica at Rocamadour. It accordingly happened that because he mockingly disparaged this house wherein holiness resides forever, where the Mother of God dwells with her Son and which she makes famous by her many works of mercy, spreading the

---

[20] Galatians 1:15.
[21] Dordogne. Cf. Albe, p. 260 n. 37.
[22] Our Lady of Jehosophat in the valley of Kidron, which was a community of Benedictine monks: see Hamilton, 'Rebuilding Zion', p. 108.
[23] Situated on the Mount of Olives: Hamilton, 'Impact of Crusader Jerusalem', p. 701.

beams of the light of its fame near and far, Senorez was struck down in all his limbs and became paralysed. This was an act of vengeance on the wicked and in praise of the good. O, the glory of the world, and the pomp of vanity! O, the alluring seductiveness, the pernicious superstition! A town may be adequately defended by its walls, but if there is an opening anywhere its enemies will enter in and capture it. In the same way, this knight, who frequently gave of his property and served the Lord, and who was someone reckoned to be steadfast against the wiles of demons, had a reputation for perfection; but the armour about his mouth was pierced and lay exposed to the enemy, who found a place to enter. Struck for having offended against Christ, the very corner-stone of the faith, the knight's mind wavered and he reconsidered what he should do. He concluded that the worst offence he had committed had been to be blasphemously dismissive and scornful of the church of Rocamadour. Then indeed he came to his senses. And after he had been punished with his illness for a long time – more than two months – he was brought to repentance and prayed for forgiveness. But he did not deserve it yet. The sheep was infirm, and *its mouth* had *spoken vanity,*[24] and guile was found in its mouth. Nevertheless *God is faithful, and he will not let* it *be tempted beyond* its *strength, but with the temptation will also provide the way of escape, that* it *may be able to endure.*[25] So let the ill sheep experience the solace of comfort, let its mind be strengthened, because *through many tribulations we must enter the kingdom of God.*[26] Thus the Lord calls the wandering sheep; thus he looks upon those who are penitent. He is the *good shepherd* such that he laid down *his life for his sheep.*[27] If this were not so, the sheep would have continued to wander lost in the wilderness, nor would it have been lifted up from the inconstancy of its ignorance and blindness. It had caused its own downfall, but it could not raise itself up again on its own. It was therefore carried back to the fold, recalled from death by the Passion of Christ after having long lain in the stinking dung and long been entombed in hell.

May Our Lord Jesus Christ see fit to exercise his mercy on his knight. May he see fit to make him well through his strength and power. For the knight repents, wishing that he had kept silent rather than say what he did. If such harsh vengeance be imposed for a mere blasphemous utterance, then how are the infamously guilty to be punished? Merciful Lord, who erased the doubt of your apostle Thomas when you showed him where the nails had entered, forgive this man who sinned through ignorance and uncertainty rather than as a deliberate act. The fact that he was slow in coming to his faith will make many others more certain in theirs and encourage them to revere the generosity of what you have done. Virgin, the honour of virgins, the certain deliverance of the sick, listen to what the ill knight desires even though it is

[24] Psalms 143:8, 11.
[25] I Corinthians 10:13.
[26] Acts 14:21.
[27] John 10:11.

late that he is sighing to you from the depths of his heart. May he avow that you are all-powerful and can do whatever you wish, because you are close to the power. You do not have regard to the height and size of your houses, nor is it in fine pictures on walls, decorated with gold, that you take delight. Rather, you humbly look after the humble in your own humility and perform renowned miracles through your power. The knight was not ashamed to announce publicly that the church of Rocamadour is raised high through you and is adorned by you; through you it is famous for its miracles and the various cures of the sick. While he was making this devout confession, the knight's sinews grew stronger and his joints eased so that he was able to stand up and return to perfect health. He praised the Lord and glorified the gentle Mother, his advocate, of Rocamadour. This he did far and wide, proclaiming the name of her who should be proclaimed everywhere.

III.12. The mill that remained undamaged

The nuns of Saint-Pierre des Chasses,[28] which is in the diocese of Auvergne, own a mill on the River Allier. There had been heavy rainfall: the clouds had thickened, the snows had melted, and there was flooding. The river rapidly became very swollen and fast-flowing, destroying stone bridges and sweeping away even very sturdy buildings which stood on its banks. The stewards of the aforementioned mill were afraid of the oncoming flood, especially because the strength of the raging torrent was carrying off everything in its path. So they placed the mill under the protection of the Blessed Mary of Rocamadour, promising to take a mill made out of wax to her basilica. The mill duly stood firm, and no part of it was damaged.

III.13. An epileptic man is cured

A citizen of Milan called Brancus was laid low for four years by the falling sickness.[29] He prayed to the Blessed Virgin; and his prayers were answered. He then came to the church of his liberator, with his father, and recounted the miracle.

III.14. A knight who broke his vow and was punished by the reappearance of a fistula

Raymond, a knight from *Largentiere*[30] in Gothia, lived near the church of Saint-Guilhem.[31] He suffered from a fistula on his thigh near his genitals.

---

[28] See Cottineau, i.719.
[29] Cf. II.24 above.
[30] Albe, p. 264 n. 47, suggests Largentière in Ardèche. But this is neither near Saint-Guilhem nor, strictly speaking, in Gothia. Possibly the reference is to Jonquières near Aniane.
[31] Saint-Guilhem-le-Désert (Hérault).

And because it is a very serious matter to use the iron or fire on that part of the body when it is affected by some grievous injury, the knight ran the risk of dying. All his people, therefore, lost hope that he would recover, for the illness was very virulent. But he alone prayed to the sole star of the sea, the advocate, the Lady of Rocamadour, stating that he would go on a pilgrimage to her house before a year was out if he became well thanks to her intercession. Truly, the humble and gentle Virgin, the Virgin praiseworthy in all things, restored the knight to health. And he then spent a year happily at home, breaking his vow and putting off coming in the way that had been agreed. The Queen of mercy deceives no one, nor does she suffer anyone to deceive her. She saw to it that the knight's illness returned, making him suffer even more grievously than before and bringing back the pain. He recognized that he was guilty and bemoaned his iniquity: while contrition filled his heart and deadly suffering gripped his body, he would cry out that he deserved to be in agony. He had reckoned that he would not be punished for the delay, and that the Lady of ladies, who forgets nothing other than the injuries done to her, would not take heed of the deadline which had been fixed. If he had known that he would be afflicted a second time by the very illness which he had escaped once already, then he would most definitely not have gone over the time limit for performing the vow. He was anxious and in pain. Again and again, over and over, he devoted himself to prayer and to offering himself totally as a sweet sacrifice to the Lord. She who had once raised up this suffering man did so again, repeating the benefit and duplicating the miracle. Fearful of any delay, he came happily and healthily to the church, glorifying the glorious Lady and singing her praises everywhere.

III.15. A house that did not burn down

The Brabançons had set fire to the town of Alès,[32] which is in the region of Nîmes. As the raging fire was consuming everything in its path and driving all the people away, Lawrence of Valence[33] saw that his house was threatened by the flames on three sides. His body began to tremble, and his family started to shed copious tears. Calling out in a loud voice he begged and entreated the glorious Mother of God that his home be freed from the flames. A marvellous thing then happened: the more fiercely the fire blazed, the less powerful it became despite its strength. The evil ones were frustrated in their wicked design. And the house remained standing, undamaged and untouched, in the midst of the burning embers of all the others.

---

[32] Gard.
[33] Probably the place of that name in Drôme.

III.16. Another instance of houses that did not burn down

Similarly William Bataile saw that the houses which abutted his own home on all four sides were ablaze, and that the flames were licking against his house. For a strong wind was driving the fire towards it. He prayed to the Virgin of virgins, of whose church he was a confrater. And she protected his house, keeping it undamaged by the fire thanks to the power of her virtue. The worker of miracles and marvellous deeds did the same thing for someone called Peter – if I remember his name correctly – to her praise and glory. This was during the very same fire, in that same town and at the same time. The three men accordingly came to the church of Rocamadour bringing three wax houses, and they recounted the miracle.

III.17. A man rescued from drowning

During the war between the king of Aragon and Count Raymond of Toulouse,[34] William Goirans of Montpellier took a boat across the River Gard.[35] With him were eleven companions, men who were very accomplished warriors. Then twenty-two Brabançons, part of the count's mercenary force which thirsts for human blood, launched a daring attack on William and his party. The latter went into a tight formation and put up a stiff resistance in hand-to-hand fighting, forcing their opponents to withdraw. The Brabançons turned and fled in order to give the impression that they had been defeated; and by alternating between rearguard actions and rapid retreat they were able to draw their incautious pursuers towards an ambush laid by their people. For almost four hundred men had taken up hidden positions in order to *shoot at the upright in heart*.[36] With a triumphant shout they jumped out and fell upon their foes like wolves upon lambs. William's group fled, with their enemies in hot pursuit, and they came to the river which was mentioned earlier. Those being pursued knew that they would be unable to escape the strong current, but they were afraid that it was a matter of moments before they faced death at the end of a sword. So they leapt into the fast-flowing water. While William was trying to swim against the powerful current, he was hit by an arrow and mortally wounded, whereupon the force of the stream carried him right back to where his enemies were standing. But the divine will, as opposed to human efforts, had disposed that it was not yet the time for him to be taken prisoner by his

[34] Cf. the dating element in III.1.
[35] Albe, p. 266 n. 55, interpreted *flumen de Gradibus* as referring to the Ebro in northeastern Spain. But there is no suggestion that the conflict between Alfonso II and Raymond V extended south of the Pyrenees into Aragon. The identification with the Gard makes better sense, as it flowed through parts of the Midi that were contested by the two sides.
[36] Psalms 10:3.

enemies or be killed: so the current pulled him back out into deep water. Because William had swallowed a great deal of water and had lost a lot of blood, with the result that his bodily strength was reduced, he sank below the surface. His life was in grave danger. His thoughts turned to the Lady of Rocamadour, foremost of those who dwell on high, who like a gentle mother warms her young under her protecting wings. He was already a heartfelt devotee, and now he wanted her to bring necessary and rapid assistance. Indeed, the powerful current had swallowed up seven of his companions, and there was no reason to suppose that he would be spared by heavenly intervention given that he was being repeatedly struck by the force of the swirling waves. Yet this man, someone who totally burned in his love for the unique and desirable Virgin, conceived the hope that he would escape. And he was carried to a dock, thanks to the help of the Lady of all. What a marvellous and unheard-of thing! Those who saw what happened were astounded, and those who heard about it were amazed; they all joined in extolling the powerful Lady, the merciful Queen, with shouts of praise. What was more, those who inspected William's injuries said that he was incurable. What use was it to them, they argued, that he had just been pulled out of the water if he quickly lost all the blood in his body and died? But he managed to lift his family from out of their gloom by saying, in so far as he was able to talk, 'Let no one doubt that she who freed me in an ineffable manner from the raging waters, who was able to do so much in the midst of the waves, can do just as much in restoring my health!' The arrowhead was pulled out, and the man was then carried home. The gentle Virgin of virgins came to him and brought him succour. For within the space of five days he was restored to full health: this was without any doctor seeing him, and without his experiencing any discomfort or pain. This sort of great and manifest miracle caused a great many people to be fired by a desire for the Virgin of virgins; they extolled her great works with lavish praises, and fervently declared that this surpassed the other wondrous deeds that they had seen.

III.18. A man freed from his chains on the Feast of the Assumption

The lord of Mozac,[37] a castle in the Auvergne, captured the town of Rochefort[38] and set it on fire. Many people he put to the sword; many others he had chained up and thrown into prison. Among this latter group there was a prisoner called Peter, known as 'the Bald'. He was grievously tortured by his gaolers, but he did not have what they were trying to extort from him. Afflicted in his body, and humbled in his heart, he placed his trust, after that in God, the hope of the living, in the kind Virgin, who works her

[37] Puy-de-Dôme.
[38] Rochefort-Montagne (Puy-de-Dôme).

miracles most particularly and frequently at Rocamadour. Time passed, and the Feast of the Assumption drew near – an outstanding day of universal joy on which he directed all his prayers to asking to be freed. On the night of the feast, after he had finished praying, his limbs became somewhat more refreshed with sleep; and in a vision there appeared to him the Virgin, the Lady of the sublime, who told him in a clear voice to follow her and leave as quickly as possible. On hearing these words of freedom he quickly opened his eyes and caught sight of the Lady of lords drawing away. He could still feel that he was being restrained by his bond, so he hesitated and failed to act with sufficient resolve. But he then became more confident, and walked out unhindered through a door which always used to be locked. Next he launched himself from a great height to the ground below, and thus unharmed he returned joyfully home, thanking the Virgin of virgins who works our salvation here on earth through the Saviour of all mankind, her one Son, Our Lord, who grants to each as his faith and love demand through the suffrages of the kind Virgin.

III.19 A woman working on Saturday evening

One Saturday evening, as darkness was falling, a woman from Figeac[39] failed to stop the manual work she was doing. On the contrary, she carried on busily sewing. She removed a needle from the material and pressed it between her lips – something one sees often. She then turned her attention to something else and lost her concentration, and when she took a deep breath she also sucked in the needle, leaving part of the thread which was attached to it hanging out of her mouth. The needle became stuck fast in the woman's mouth. She pulled on the thread, but far from extracting the needle this made it stick even more firmly; the poor woman only made the existing wound bigger by tugging on it, causing her yet more agony. The woman's misery and the grieving of her family attracted a crowd of people from all around. They were all stupefied and amazed. And turning to one another, they said, 'Surely this woman's suffering is what she justly deserves? Surely the Lord is just and is justly angered? It must be the case that she is being punished on her own as a warning to the rest of us; she alone is being beaten so that many others might pull back on the reins of their temerity and inobedience, and so that the Lord's precepts, promulgated by the masters of the Church, might be adhered to more diligently in a spirit of fear and reverence.' Later, because the woman knew of no means of escaping her plight, and at her own heartfelt entreaty because her calamitous circumstances had long urged such a course of action, she was taken to the church of the Blessed Virgin of Rocamadour. There all the pilgrims felt compassion towards her, and everyone shared in her pain and suffering. When God's

---

[39] Lot.

praises were being sung in the church at the last hour of the day, the man giving the sermon summoned them all to pray together on behalf of the suffering woman. And she prostrated herself with great humility in front of the altar, her eyes raised heavenwards, tears streaming down her face, and her hands outstretched. She fixed her mind on the cross of Christ and in a supplicant manner begged for forgiveness. The Mother of the Father, yet born of the Father, overflowing with the grace of mercy, brought relief to the suffering woman in her wondrous gentleness. For in full view of all those present she lit up her house: she pulled the needle, reddened with rust, from the woman's throat, causing a great deal of blood to flow out. And the woman was soon returned to her former state of health.

III.20. An ill man is cured

Gerald, a carpenter from *Panesac* in the region of *Axensi*,[40] was afflicted by a very oppressive pain in the left-hand side of his chest in the area around his heart. He therefore took to his bed, even though he seemed quite healthy. The illness was very serious, with the result that he was unable to take any food for seven days. He could barely focus his gaze on anyone, and he was scarcely able to inhale and exhale, so restricted was his breathing. His family and those who knew, or rather loved, him were therefore reduced to tears. Arrangements were begun for his funeral, and everything necessary for the burial was made ready, because everyone was of the opinion that Gerald would very soon depart this life. His spirit groaned under the weight of the mass of his flesh, and was almost succumbing to the burden; but for a little while it found some rest in Christ, and it fervently prayed and longingly begged for the protection of the gentle Lady of Rocamadour, worthiest of all created beings, the highest beneath her Son. The Queen who responds favourably to petitions received the prayers of the supplicant, and she did not delay giving him his health: suddenly she restored the strength to his limbs and through the power of her clemency raised him up from his bed. He was cured, to the amazement of all those there who were dumbfounded by what had happened. As they gathered round Gerald declared that he had been protected by the Virgin, as was plain to see. And they all glorified and praised the Lady who saves those who place their hope in her.

III.21. A paralysed woman is cured

Guillelma of *la Boisera*,[41] from Grenoble, was crippled by paralysis in the middle part of her body. She was ill for a long time, and nothing that anyone

---

[40] Places difficult to identify. Albe, p. 271 n. 65, suggested Dax or Aix for *Axensi*. See also Rocacher, supp. n., p. 304. Another possibility is that *Axensi* refers to Auch, in which case *Panesac* would be Panassac (Gers).

[41] Possibly La Boissière (Jura), Bossey (Haute-Savoie) or Bossieu (Isère).

could think of, nor the treatments of doctors, could do anything to cure her. She was in the flower of her youth, but her great illness had made her thin and shrivelled before her time. She had heard stories, and had learned from those with actual experience, about how the glorious Mother of God and perpetual Virgin at Rocamadour performed great and various cures for those who were unwell. Accordingly her hopes revived, and she poured out her heart in earnest prayer, persisting in her fervent entreaties and unremitting devotion, and never ceasing from asking to be given her health. In addition, she vowed that she would come to the church which is especially honoured by the special Lady. And immediately she was cured.

III.22. A squire who miraculously escapes from prison

In the region of Vienne a castle called Anjou[42] was being fiercely and closely besieged by the vassals of Count Gerard.[43] A squire named Peter, who had a house inside the castle, was fighting back with all his strength when he was captured by the besiegers. He was then bound with heavy foot-irons and hidden away in the palace at Vienne, with a large number of men set to guard him. But he had faith in the Lord, who raises up those who are contrite in their hearts and remedies their faults. Peter prayed for the noose around his neck to be worn away, and asked that he be worthy to be freed from so many bolts and bars. The palace in which he was being held in chains is reputedly so high and so strong that it is reckoned to be impregnable. Although it had stood for a long time – too long – it scarcely ever happened that its dungeons lacked prisoners; and over the years no one had ever managed to escape, either by ingenuity or force of arms. Nonetheless, the higher and stronger the fortifications stood, the more the prisoner persevered in the idea that his prayers – and not his own merits – would lead to the Lord, the liberator of all, taking him from the prison and returning him back home. In addition, and before all the thousands of other saints, he invoked and called out to her who after her Son holds the highest rank in the heavenly court: she who is full of mercy for those who invoke her, the kind Lady and advocate of Rocamadour. And he also declared that he would visit her church. Then, growing weary from the effort of praying and overcome with fatigue, he took a short rest and fell asleep. He then heard a voice telling him that he would be able to get away if he did not delay. So he got up in the silent dead of night and, fearful of the guards who were keeping a close watch, he carefully inched his way to the first door, which opened to him of its own accord.[44] In the same way he got through a second, third and fourth door, reaching a fifth which was the outermost one on that side of the palace and which he opened

[42] Isère.
[43] Girard, count of Mâcon and Vienne. See C. B. Bouchard, *Sword, Miter, and Cloister: Nobility and the Church in Burgundy, 980–1198* (Ithaca, 1987), pp. 276–8.
[44] This and the following sentence evoke Acts 12:10.

without difficulty. The site was on top of a steep incline, and for this reason the descent was very hazardous. There was neither ladder nor rope, nor anything which could support someone climbing down. Moreover, the wall of the palace was as smooth and slippery as its builder had been able to make it. But Peter was afraid of delaying and, committing his body and his spirit to the care of the Blessed Virgin, he eased himself slowly down the wall, coming to no harm. Then he was able to pull on the gate of the outer wall, which was locked with bolts and bars; and he managed to undo it just as if it were not bolted at all. After that he crossed through the town and found his exit blocked by the last gate of all. Without using any implement, but with the assistance of the Virgin, he broke the large mass of chains with his bare hands. Then he moved down into the outskirts of the town, still restricted by his foot-irons, and from there he made his way back to his people. Once home he was delayed by the blandishments of his friends, with the result that he put off going on pilgrimage to his liberator's church for longer than he ought to have done. For they gave him their word that they would accompany him on his journey so that they could all arrive together and give thanks in the church of the kind Virgin.

III.23. This same man and another are imprisoned anew and again freed

The evil of wicked men had not yet abated, and the raging fury had grown among the malignant, when the count of Vienne's scouts hastened to take up position in front of the aforementioned castle and tried to draw out the forces which were inside. Amongst the defenders who went out to do battle were the Peter we have just been discussing and his brother Rogonus. As they fought in hand-to-hand combat they were overwhelmed by the strength of their enemies and taken prisoner, after which they were thrown into the dungeons of the palace at Vienne. Peter was told that he would have no bread to eat until he made arrangements for the return of the foot-irons which he had stolen from there. They were brought back, and while they were being fastened on him by his tormentors, Peter said, 'The Lady of Rocamadour, the tenderest of the tender, who recently used her wondrous power to rescue me from these very chains, will have the power to perform the same miracle a second time.' He was therefore taken to the deepest part of the dungeon, where he wracked his body with fasting and fortified his spirit with diligent prayer, seeking no rest except in the Lord. His brother, the knight Rogonus, was seriously wounded: he had received four blows from lances, three from spears, and had taken a sword blow to the foot. For this reason he was placed under guard in an upper part of the palace, where he lay half-dead. Although he had lost a great deal of blood and was in a very bad way – his body was much weakened – he too was fervent in his spirit and remained steadfastly constant in his mind. The greater the need in which he found himself, the more fully he asked for divine aid and a work of mercy. The Lord therefore bestowed his grace on both men in full view of their guards. One Sunday they hauled Peter out of his dungeon and put him next to his brother in the upper storey to allow him to recover his strength. They spent that day together in prayer. And as they more diligently called out to the most Blessed Virgin, the fount of all benevolence which flows bountifully on everyone, they had a presentiment that her goodness would bring about their liberation. Able to talk openly to one another, they agreed that they would get away the following night while the guards were asleep, with the help of the worker of great wonders. And this is what happened. For that night, after the guards had fallen into a deep sleep, the two men got up silently and opened the door – which actually made quite a lot of noise – before lowering themselves down from the top storey by means of a rope. One of them was led out through the gates by some city watchmen who took pity on him. The other one was hidden by an inhabitant of the town in his house. On the third day, once the men who had been searching everywhere for the fugitives had returned, the man hiding him gave him a change of clothing and accompanied him for a mile out of the town. He still had his foot-irons attached to one of his feet, but he managed to get back home safely. Hurrying, therefore, to perform their vow, the two men came to the church of the most Blessed Virgin of Rocamadour. They showed their foot-irons and their wounds, which were still open, recounted the miracle and gave thanks.

III.24. A woman saved from the fire

At Saint-Sever,[45] a quite well-known town in Gascony, there was a great mortality among people of both sexes and those of tender years. Even though we daily witness the deaths of those who are paying the debt of the flesh, it is only when one of our friends passes away that we become astonished and mournful, as if we had had no advance knowledge that he would die. For by reason of the original sin, when Adam took a bite from the apple, created beings must die. Those people of Saint-Sever whose friends and neighbours were unexpectedly dying accused a woman called Lombarda of being a sorceress who was responsible for the deaths – indeed, they said that she was the very cause of them. They placed her in foot-irons and threw her into prison. And they condemned her without a proper judgement and any formal pronouncement of the death penalty; she was not properly convicted, nor had she made a confession. They then set about looking for a means of execution which would enable them to wipe the woman's memory from the face of the earth and to ensure that people would be unable to find anything good to say about her when they called her to mind. For three days they sweated and toiled, and hurriedly went about their evil work, since they had

[45] Landes.

made up their minds that the innocent woman was to be burned alive. You could see people busily hewing at wood with their axes; some were leading horse-drawn wagons and carts back and forth, others were ceaselessly carrying material on their shoulders, and yet others were gathering wood into a pile. You could also see people fetching torches and bringing sulphur, pitch and wax, and whatever else might make the fire burn, to throw onto the pyre. As one they all raged against this solitary woman, as if with her death they could avenge the deaths of their relatives. They violently gnashed their teeth like rabid dogs. They punished this woman, who did not deserve such treatment, with deceitful and idle words, with their senseless reasoning and their stupid malice. To cap the madness of their vile intent, they sought out forms of torture which surpassed anything known before; in their cruelty they rejected the sorts of torments which they had used on earlier victims so as to add to the punishment inflicted on her.

In the meantime the woman had been shut up in a dark prison and bound with a weight of iron. She recognized the wrongs that she had done and confessed the sins that she had committed. She placed her trust in the Lord, to whom she offered herself up as a sacrifice. Over and over she declared that she deserved to die for all the things that she had done, even though she was innocent of the crime which had recently been imputed to her, in that she had never planned such a grave and great wrong nor put it into effect. Whoever makes known, and makes no attempt to conceal, the contempt in which he had held God and the negligence that he had shown towards himself or his neighbour, will without doubt experience the effects of God's merciful clemency. Let us therefore ordain a communal lamentation – people of all ages, both sexes, and every rank. Let us raise our voices in mourning and pour out tears and moans into the ears of the Lord of hosts for the injustice done to this woman. Let us prevent the anger of the clement Lord through confession and penitence. For the clemency of God mercifully disposes all things, and as soon as we change our ways he stops being angry and turns to compassion. Let us have pity on ourselves and open up the way for his justice and mercy. Let us sow with our tears so that we may reap in the joy of the next harvest. Indeed the soul which is not corrected by the Lord's scourge is beyond curing. Consequently it is a serious matter to be struck by a blow, but it is much more serious to be punished and fail to amend, as it is written: it is terrible to fall into the hands of the living God, for *the face of the Lord is against them that do evil, to cut off the remembrance of them from the earth.*[46] Nor does anything escape God's hearing, for he did not even ignore the mournful voice of this little woman as she wept and moaned. For where can anyone hide when the Lord fills everything and is everywhere present? He sees through us whether we wish it so or not; he lays bare the secrets of our hearts and knows the thoughts of men.

---

[46] Psalms 33:17.

The context of what has just been argued – its rationale – is as follows: the woman we mentioned earlier was shut away in the depths of her prison, calling out with devout and assiduous prayers to those up above to take pity on her. She also insistently prayed for mercy to the Lady of Rocamadour, the most gentle of all after her Son, the most prompt in responding to entreaties; Lombarda had visited her church less than two years before. This, or something similar, is what she said: 'Queen of the heavenly host, the hope for our salvation and the fount of mercy, the consolation of us all in our tribulation, the protection of the contrite when they are oppressed, you would not deign to listen to my prayers if you knew that I was actually guilty of the crime of which I have been falsely accused. I know full well, and it makes me ashamed to confess, that I have lived my life in a heedless and corrupt manner, and I have been unabashed in breaking the Lord's commandments so many times that I have lost count. But if I am considered guilty of such a grave crime as this, then do not give me any protection.' The woman filled her time with mournful vigils and fasts, and the day which had been set for the execution arrived. She was taken from the prison and led to the pyre. Despite the fact that she was a woman, the women gathered there did not blush when they saw her nakedness out in the open. O the shame of it! It was the Tuesday of Pentecost, when the Holy Ghost appeared to the disciples in tongues of fire. By contrast, it was an evil spirit which was at that time inciting these people against their neighbour. A crowd of more than twenty thousand people, men and women, had flocked from all directions to witness the spectacle: some of them were praying for the woman, some hurling abuse at her. And it was the abuse which was the louder. As Lombarda wept copiously and called out in a loud voice to the Blessed Virgin of Rocamadour, she was thrown into the midst of the flames. A youth who had good sense beyond his years was shaken by the unseemliness of the woman's confusion and nakedness, and he tossed her the short tunic that he was wearing as an act of respect for God and the others. This served to cover some of her body, though most of it remained exposed. The woman made the sign of the holy cross and confidently called out the name of the Lady of Rocamadour. She then submitted herself to the dangers of the pyre, passing over it without being burned at all and, even more remarkably, without feeling any heat from the fire. For the flames coming from the large pile of different sorts of material fell back at the sound of Mary's name; the fire stopped burning and gave her the courage to enter. As she passed through the fire it *did not touch* her at all, *nor did it trouble* her.[47] Then all those present, both those hostile towards the woman and those who were her friends, joined in singing a hymn and glorified the Lord, the liberator of all those who place their hope in him. The woman immediately set out on pilgrimage towards the basilica of the most Blessed Virgin, her powerful and

[47] Daniel 3:50.

excellent saviour. This she did accompanied by a large party of noble women. On the eighth day she arrived, and showing off the tunic recounted the miracle before the Lady of ladies, giving thanks to her who performs her works in all things through her one Son, Our Lord, Jesus Christ, to whom is the power and the glory, forever and ever. Amen.

The end of the miracles of Saint Mary of Rocamadour

BIBLIOGRAPHY

Primary Sources

Alexander III, 'Epistolae et privilegia', *PL* 200.69–1320.

Anna Comnena, *The Alexiad*, trans. E. R. A. Sewter (Harmondsworth, 1969).

'Annales Placentini Guelfi a. 1012–1235', *MGH SS* 18.411–57.

Augustine, *The City of God against the Pagans*, trans. H. Bettenson, intro. J. O'Meara (Harmondsworth, 1984).

Bede, *The Ecclesiastical History of the English People*, trans. B. Colgrave, ed. J. McClure and R. Collins (Oxford, 1994).

Benedict of Peterborough, 'Miracula sancti Thomae Cantuariensis', ed. J. C. Robertson, *Materials for the History of Thomas Becket, Archbishop of Canterbury*, vol. 2 (Rolls Series 67:2; London, 1876), pp. 21–281.

Bernard of Clairvaux, *The Letters of St Bernard of Clairvaux*, trans. B. Scott James, new intro. B. M. Kienzle (Stroud, 1998).

The Capture of Constantinople: The "Historia Constantinopolitana" of Gunther of Pairis, trans. A. J. Jaeger (Philadelphia, 1997).

Le cartulaire de l'abbaye cistercienne d'Obazine (XIIe–XIIIe siècle), ed. B. Barrière (Clermont-Ferrand, 1989).

Cartulaire de l'abbaye de Conques en Rouergue, ed. G. Desjardins (Paris, 1879).

Cartulaire de l'abbaye de Vigeois en Limousin (954–1167), ed. M. de Montégut (Limoges, 1907).

Cartulaire de l'abbaye d'Uzerche, ed. J.-B. Champeval (Paris, 1901).

Cartulaire des abbayes de Tulle et de Roc-Amadour, ed. J.-B. Champeval (Brive, 1903).

La Chanson de Sainte Foy, ed. E. Hoepffner, trans. P. Alfaric, 2 vols. (Publications de la Faculté des Lettres de l'Université de Strasbourg, 32–3; Paris, 1926).

Chronicle of the Third Crusade: A Translation of the Itinerarium Peregrinorum et Gesta Regis Ricardi, trans. H. J. Nicholson (Aldershot, 1997).

Chronicles of the Age of Chivalry, ed. E. M. Hallam (London, 1987).

Chronicles of the Crusades, ed. E. M. Hallam (New York, 1989).

'Chronicon breve de gestis Aldeberti', ed. C. Brunel, *Les miracles de saint Privat suivis des opuscules d'Aldebert III, évêque de Mende* (Collection de textes pour servir à l'étude et à l'enseignement de l'histoire, 46; Paris, 1912), pp. 126–34.

Chronicon universale anonymi Laudunensis, ed. A. Cartellieri and W. Stechele (Leipzig and Paris, 1909).

Chronique de Saint-Pierre-le-Vif de Sens, dite de Clarius, ed. and trans. R.-H. Bautier and M. Gilles (Sources d'histoire médiévale, 3; Paris, 1979).

The Cistercian World: Monastic Writings of the Twelfth Century, trans. P. Matarasso (Harmondsworth, 1993).

The Coutumes de Beauvaisis *of Philippe de Beaumanoir*, trans. F. R. P. Akehurst (Philadelphia, 1992).

Decrees of the Ecumenical Councils, ed. N. P. Tanner (London, 1990).

Les deux rédactions en vers du Moniage Guillaume: Chansons de geste du XIIe siècle, ed. W. Cloetta, 2 vols. (Paris, 1906–10).

Dialogus de Scaccario, ed. and trans. C. Johnson, rev. F. E. L. Carter and D. E. Greenway (Oxford, 1983).

Dudo of St Quentin, *History of the Normans*, trans. E. Christiansen (Woodbridge, 1998).

Eadmer, *The Life of St Anselm, Archbishop of Canterbury*, ed. and trans. R. W. Southern (London, 1962).

English Historical Documents: Volume II, 1042–1189, ed. D. C. Douglas and G. W. Greenaway, 2nd edn (London, 1981).

'Epistolarum regis Ludovici VII et aliorum ad eum volumen', *RHGF* 16.1–170.

The Etablissements de Saint Louis: Thirteenth-Century Law Texts from Tours, Orléans, and Paris, trans. F. R. P. Akehurst (Philadelphia, 1996).

Feudal Society in Medieval France: Documents from the County of Champagne, trans. T. Evergates (Philadelphia, 1993).

Fulbert of Chartres, *The Letters and Poems*, ed. and trans. F. Behrends (Oxford, 1976).

Fulcher of Chartres, *A History of the Expedition to Jerusalem 1099–1127*, trans. F. R. Ryan, ed. H. S. Fink (Knoxville, Tennessee, 1969).

Galbert of Bruges, *The Murder of Charles the Good*, trans. J. B. Ross (New York, 1959; repr. Toronto, 1982).

Garnier of Pont-Saint-Maxence, *La Vie de Saint Thomas Becket*, ed. E. Walberg (Paris, 1964); English translation: *Garnier's Becket*, trans. J. Shirley (London, 1975).

Geoffrey of Vigeois, 'Chronica', ed. P. Labbe, *Novae Bibliothecae Manuscriptorum Librorum*, 2 vols. (Paris, 1657), ii.279–329.

Gerald of Wales, *Expugnatio Hibernica: The Conquest of Ireland*, ed. and trans. A. B. Scott and F. X. Martin (Dublin, 1978).

Gervase of Canterbury, *Chronica*, ed. W. Stubbs (Rolls Series, 73:1; London, 1879).

Gesta Francorum et aliorum Hierosolimitanorum, ed. and trans. R. M. T. Hill (London, 1962).

Gesta regis Henrici secundi, ed. W. Stubbs, 2 vols. (Rolls Series, 49; London, 1867).

Gregory of Tours, *Glory of the Confessors*, trans. R. Van Dam (Translated Texts for Historians, Latin Series, 4; Liverpool, 1988).

—— *Glory of the Martyrs*, trans. R. Van Dam (Translated Texts for Historians, Latin Series, 3; Liverpool, 1988).

—— *Life of the Fathers*, trans. E. James (Translated Texts for Historians, Latin Series, 1; Liverpool, 1985).

Gregory the Great, 'Life of Benedict', trans. C. White, *Early Christian Lives* (Harmondsworth, 1998), pp. 161–204.

Guibert of Nogent, *Autobiographie*, ed. and trans. E.-R. Labande (Les classiques de l'histoire de France au moyen âge, 34; Paris, 1981); English translation: *Self and Society in Medieval France*, trans. J. F. Benton (New York, 1970; repr. Toronto, 1984).

—— *The Deeds of God through the Franks*, trans. R. Levine (Woodbridge, 1997).

Le guide du pèlerin de Saint-Jacques de Compostelle, ed. and trans. J. Vielliard, 5th edn (Paris, 1997); English translation: *The Pilgrim's Guide to Santiago de Compostela*, trans. W. Melczer (New York, 1993).

Herbert of Bosham, 'Vita sancti Thomae, archiepiscopi et martyris', ed. J. C. Roberston, *Materials for the History of Thomas Becket, Archbishop of Canterbury*, vol. 3 (Rolls Series 67:3; London, 1877), pp. 155–534.

Herman of Tournai, 'De miraculis S. Mariae Laudunensis, de gestis venerabilis Bartholomaei episcopi et S. Norberti libri tres', *PL* 156.961–1018.

—— *The Restoration of the Monastery of Saint Martin of Tournai*, trans. L. H. Nelson (Washington, DC, 1996).

Hugh Farsit, 'Libellus de miraculis B. Mariae Virginis in urbe Suessionensi', *PL* 179.1777–800.

Jerusalem Pilgrimage 1099–1185, ed. J. Wilkinson with J. Hill and W. F. Ryan (Hakluyt Society, 2nd ser. 167; London, 1988).

John of Salisbury, *The Letters*, ed. and trans. W. J. Millor, H. E. Butler and C. N. L. Brooke, 2 vols. (Oxford, 1979–86).

Lambert of Wattrelos, 'Annales Cameracenses', *MGH SS* 16.509–54.

Liber Instrumentorum Memorialium: Cartulaire des Guillems de Montpellier, ed. A. Germain (Montpellier, 1884–86).

Liber Miraculorum Sancte Fidis, ed. L. Robertini (Biblioteca di medioevo latino, 10; Spoleto, 1994); English translation: *The Book of Sainte Foy*, trans. P. Sheingorn (Philadelphia, 1995).

'Liber miraculorum sancti Aegidii', *Analecta Bollandiana*, 9 (1890), pp. 393–422.

The Life and Miracles of St Ivo, trans. S. B. Edgington (St Ives, 1985).

The Life of Christina of Markyate, ed. and trans. C. H. Talbot (Oxford, 1959).

Medieval Iberia: Readings from Christian, Muslim, and Jewish Sources, ed. O. R. Constable (Philadelphia, 1997).

Medieval Popular Religion, 1000–1500: A Reader, ed. J. R. Shinners (Peterborough, Ontario, 1997).

'Les Miracles de Notre-Dame de Chartres', ed. A. Thomas, *Bibliothèque de l'Ecole des chartes*, 42 (1881), pp. 505–50.

Les Miracles de Notre-Dame de Rocamadour au XIIe siècle, ed. and trans. E. Albe, rev. intro. and notes J. Rocacher (Toulouse, 1996).

Les Miracles de saint Benoît, ed. E. de Certain (Paris, 1858).

'The Miracles of the Hand of St James', trans. B. Kemp, *Berkshire Archaeological Journal*, 65 (1970), pp. 1–19.

'Miracula beati Egidii', *MGH SS* 12.316–23.

'Miracula ecclesiae Constantiensis', ed. E.-A. Pigeon, *Histoire de la cathédrale de Coutances* (Coutances, 1876), pp. 367–83.

'The Old French Continuation of William of Tyre, 1184–97', in *The Conquest of Jerusalem and the Third Crusade: Sources in Translation*, trans. P. W. Edbury (Aldershot, 1996), pp. 11–145.

Orderic Vitalis, *The Ecclesiastical History*, ed. and trans. M. Chibnall, 6 vols. (Oxford, 1969–80).

Otto of Freising and Rahewin, *Gesta Friderici I. Imperatoris*, ed. G. Waitz and B. de Simson (MGH Scriptores rerum Germanicarum in usum scholarum, 46; Hanover and Leipzig, 1912).

Peter Abelard, 'Historia Calamitatum', trans. B. Radice, *The Letters of Abelard and Heloise* (Hardmondsworth, 1974), pp. 57–106.

Peter Tudebode, *Historia de Hierosolymitano Itinere*, trans. J. H. Hill and L. L. Hill (Philadelphia, 1974).

Le pontifical romano-germanique du dixième siècle, ed. C. Vogel and R. Elze, 3 vols. (Studi e Testi, 226–7 and 269; Vatican City, 1963–72).

Pouillés de la province de Lyon, ed. A. Longnon (Recueil des historiens de la France: Pouillés, 1; Paris, 1904).

Ralph Diceto, *Opera Historica*, ed. W. Stubbs, 2 vols. (Rolls Series, 68; London, 1876).

Raymond of Aguilers, *Historia*, trans. J. H. Hill and L. L. Hill (Philadelphia, 1968).

Readings in Medieval History, ed. P. J. Geary (New York, 1989).

Rigord and William the Breton, *Oeuvres de Rigord et de Guillaume le Breton, historiens de Philippe-Auguste*, ed. H.-F. Delaborde, 2 vols. (Paris, 1882–85).

Robert of Auxerre, 'Chronicon', *MGH SS* 26.219–76.

Robert of Torigny, *Chronica*, ed. R. Howlett (Rolls Series, 82:4; London, 1889).

The Rule of St Benedict, trans. J. McCann (London, 1976).

The Song of Dermot and the Earl, ed. and trans. G. H. Orpen (Oxford, 1892).

Suger, *Vie de Louis VI le Gros*, ed. and trans. H. Waquet (Les classiques de l'histoire de France au moyen âge, 11; Paris, 1929); English translation: *The Deeds of Louis the Fat*, trans. R. C. Cusimano and J. Moorhead (Washington, DC, 1992).

Sulpicius Severus, 'The Life of Saint Martin of Tours', *Soldiers of Christ: Saints and Saints' Lives from Late Antiquity and the Early Middle Ages*, ed. T. F. X. Noble and T. Head (London, 1995), pp. 1–29.

Thomas Aquinas, *Selected Writings*, trans. R. McInerny (Harmondsworth, 1998).

Thomas of Monmouth, *The Life and Miracles of St William of Norwich*, ed. and trans. A. Jessopp and M. R. James (Cambridge, 1896).

The Usatges of Barcelona: The Fundamental Law of Catalonia, trans. D. J. Kagay (Philadelphia, 1994).

Vie de Saint Etienne d'Obazine, ed. and trans. M. Aubrun (Publications de l'Institut d'Études du Massif Central, 6; Clermont-Ferrand, 1970).

Walter Daniel, *The Life of Ailred of Rievaulx*, ed. and trans. F. M. Powicke (London, 1950).

Walter Map, *De Nugis Curialium*, ed. and trans. M. R. James, rev. C. N. L. Brooke and R. A. B. Mynors (Oxford, 1983).

William fitz Stephen, 'Vita sancti Thomae, Cantuariensis archiepiscopi et martyris', ed. J. C. Robertson, *Materials for the History of Thomas Becket, Archbishop of Canterbury*, vol. 3 (Rolls Series 67:3; London, 1877), pp. 1–154.

William of Canterbury, 'Miracula gloriosi martyris Thomae, Cantuariensis archiepiscopi', ed. J. C. Robertson, *Materials for the History of Thomas Becket, Archbishop of Canterbury*, vol. 1 (Rolls Series 67:1; London, 1875), pp. 137–546.

William of Jumièges, Orderic Vitalis, and Robert of Torigni, *Gesta Normannorum Ducum*, ed. and trans. E. M. C. van Houts, 2 vols. (Oxford, 1992–95).

William of Malmesbury, *Gesta pontificum Anglorum*, ed. N. E. S. A. Hamilton (Rolls Series, 52; London, 1870).

—— *Historia Novella*, ed. E. King, trans. K. R. Potter (Oxford, 1998).

William of Newburgh, *Historia Rerum Anglicarum*, ed. R. Howlett (Rolls Series 82:1; London, 1884).

William of Poitiers, *Gesta Guillelmi*, ed. and trans. R. H. C. Davis and M. Chibnall (Oxford, 1998).

William of Tudela and an Anonymous Successor, *The Song of the Cathar Wars: A History of the Albigensian Crusade*, trans. J. Shirley (Aldershot, 1996).

William of Tyre, *Chronicon*, ed. R. B. C. Huygens, 1 vol. in 2 (Corpus Christianorum, Continuatio Mediaeualis, 63; Turnhout, 1986); English translation: *A History of Deeds Done Beyond the Sea*, trans. E. A. Babcock and A. C. Krey, 2 vols. (New York, 1943).

Secondary Works

Abadal i de Vinyals, R., 'A propos de la "domination" de la maison comtale barcelonnaise sur le Midi français', *Annales du Midi*, 76 (1964), pp. 315–45.

Abbott, E. A., *St. Thomas of Canterbury: His Death and Miracles*, 2 vols. (London, 1898).

Aigrain, R., *L'hagiographie, ses sources, ses méthodes, son histoire* (Paris, 1953).

Albe, E., 'La vie et les miracles de S. Amator', *Analecta Bollandiana*, 28 (1909), pp. 57–90.

d'Angomont, T., 'Sur les miracles de saint Privat véneré à Mende', *Revue du moyen âge latin*, 23 (1976), pp. 13–26.

Arnold, B., *Princes and Territories in Medieval Germany* (Cambridge, 1991).

Atlas de la France de l'an mil, ed. M. Parisse and J. Leuridan (Paris, 1994).

Aubrun, M., 'Le prieur Geoffroy de Vigeois et sa chronique', *Revue Mabillon*, 58 (1974), pp. 313–26.

Aurell i Cardona, M., 'Le personel politique catalan et aragonais d'Alphonse Ier en Provence (1166–96)', *Annales du Midi*, 93 (1981), pp. 121–39.

Barlow, F., *Thomas Becket* (London, 1986).

Barrière, B., *L'abbaye cistercienne d'Obazine en Bas-Limousin: Les origines – le patrimoine* (Tulle, 1977).

Bartlett, R., *Trial by Fire and Water: The Medieval Judicial Ordeal* (Oxford, 1986).

Baumel, J., *Histoire d'une seigneurie du Midi de la France, I: Naissance de Montpellier (985–1213)* (Montpellier, 1969).

Bautier, A.-M., 'Typologie des ex-voto mentionnés dans des textes antérieures à 1200', in *La piété populaire au moyen âge* (Actes du 99e Congrès Nationale des Sociétés Savantes, Besançon, 1974; Paris, 1977), pp. 237–82.

Benjamin, R., 'A Forty Years War: Toulouse and the Plantagenets, 1156–96', *Historical Research*, 61 (1988), pp. 270–85.

Bisson, T. N., *The Medieval Crown of Aragon: A Short History* (Oxford, 1986).

—— 'Unheroed Pasts: History and Commemoration in South Frankland before the Albigensian Crusades', *Speculum*, 65 (1990), pp. 281–308.

Blondel, L., *Châteaux de l'ancien diocèse de Genève* (Mémoires et documents publiés par la Société d'histoire et d'archéologie de Genève, 7; Geneva, 1956).

Bonnassie, P., 'La monnaie et les échanges en Auvergne et Rouergue aux Xe et XIe siècles d'après les sources hagiographiques', *Annales du Midi*, 90 (1978), pp. 275–88.

—— 'Descriptions of Fortresses in the Book of Miracles of Sainte-Foy of Conques', in his *From Slavery to Feudalism in South-Western Europe*, trans. J. Birrell (Cambridge, 1991), pp. 132–48.

Bouchard, C. B., *Sword, Miter, and Cloister: Nobility and the Church in Burgundy 980–1198* (Ithaca, 1987).

—— *Strong of Body, Brave and Noble: Chivalry and Society in Medieval France* (Ithaca, 1998).

Boussard. J., 'Les mercenaires au XIIe siècle: Henri II Plantagenêt et les origines de l'armée de metier', *Bibliothèque de l'Ecole des chartes*, 106 (1945–46), pp. 189–224.

—— *Le gouvernement d'Henri II Plantagenêt* (Paris, 1956).

Brown., P. R. L., *The Cult of the Saints: Its Rise and Function in Latin Christianity* (Chicago, 1981).

Brown, S. D. B., 'Military Service and Monetary Reward in the Eleventh and Twelfth Centuries', *History*, 74 (1989), pp. 20–38.

Bull, M. G., *Knightly Piety and the Lay Response to the First Crusade: The Limousin and Gascony, c.970–c.1130* (Oxford, 1993).

—— 'The Diplomatic of the First Crusade', in *The First Crusade: Origins and Impact*, ed. J. P. Phillips (Manchester, 1997), pp. 35–54.

Bulles., B., 'Saint Amadour: Formation et évolution de sa légende (XIIe–XXe siècle)', *Annales du Midi*, 107 (1995), pp. 437–55.

Bur, M., *La formation du comté de Champagne v.950–v.1150* (Nancy, 1977).

Caitucoli, C., 'Nobles et chevaliers dans le *Livre des miracles de sainte Foy*', *Annales du Midi*, 107 (1995), pp. 401–16.

Cheirézy, C., 'Hagiographie et société: L'exemple de saint Léonard de Noblat', *Annales du Midi*, 107 (1995), pp. 417–35.

Chibnall, M., 'Mercenaries and the *Familia Regis* under Henry I', *History*, 62 (1977), pp. 15–23.

Clayton, M., *The Cult of the Virgin Mary in Anglo-Saxon England* (Cambridge Studies in Anglo-Saxon England, 2; Cambridge, 1990).

Cohen, E., 'In haec signa: Pilgrim-Badge Trade in Southern France', *Journal of Medieval History*, 2 (1976), pp. 193–214.

Constable., G., 'Medieval Charters as a Source for the History of the Crusades', in *Crusade and Settlement*, ed. P. W. Edbury (Cardiff, 1985), pp. 73–89.

—— *The Reformation of the Twelfth Century* (Cambridge, 1996).

Contamine, P., *War in the Middle Ages*, trans. M. Jones (Oxford, 1984).

Coss, P., *The Knight in Medieval England 1000–1400* (Stroud, 1993).

Cottineau, L. H., *Répertoire topo-bibliographique des abbayes et prieurés*, 1 vol. in 2 (Mâcon, 1935–37).

Crouch, D., *The Image of Aristocracy in Britain, 1000–1300* (London, 1992).

Dierkens, A., 'Réflexions sur le miracle au haut moyen âge', in *Miracles, prodiges et merveilles au moyen âge: XXVe Congrès de la Société des Historiens Médiévistes de l'Enseignement Supérieur Public (Orléans, juin 1994)* (Série Histoire Ancienne et Médiévale, 34; Paris, 1995), pp. 9–30.

Dubois, J., and Lemaître, J.-L., *Sources et méthodes de l'hagiographie médiévale* (Paris, 1993).

Duby, G., 'French Genealogical Literature', in his *The Chivalrous Society*, trans. C. Postan (London, 1977), pp. 149–57.

—— *The Three Orders: Feudal Society Imagined*, trans. A. Goldhammer (Chicago, 1980).

Dufour, J., *Les évêques d'Albi, de Cahors et de Rodez des origines à la fin du XIIe siècle* (Mémoires et documents d'histoire médiévale et de philologie, 3; Paris, 1989).

Dunbabin, J., *France in the Making 843–1180* (Oxford, 1985).

—— 'Discovering a Past for the French Aristocracy', *The Perception of the Past in Twelfth-Century Europe*, ed. P. Magdalino (London, 1992), pp. 1–14.

Finucane, R. C., 'The Use and Abuse of Medieval Miracles', *History*, 60 (1975), pp. 1–10.

—— *Miracles and Pilgrims: Popular Beliefs in Medieval England* (London, 1977).

—— 'Pilgrimage in Daily Life: Aspects of Medieval Communication Reflected in the Newly-Established Cult of Thomas Cantilupe (d.1282), its Dissemination and Effects upon Outlying Herefordshire Villages', in *Wallfahrt und Alltag in Mittelalter und frühen Neuzeit* (Veröffentlichungen des Instituts für Realienkunde des Mittelalters und der frühen Neuzeit, 14; Vienna, 1992), pp. 165–217.

—— *The Rescue of the Innocents: Endangered Children in Medieval Miracles* (London, 1997).

Fletcher, R. A., *Saint James's Catapult: The Life and Times of Diego Gelmírez of Santiago de Compostela* (Oxford, 1984).

Fliche, A., 'L'état toulousain', *Histoire des institutions françaises au moyen âge. I: Les institutions seigneuriales*, ed. F. Lot and R. Fawtier (Paris, 1957), pp. 71–99.

Flori, J., *Chevaliers et chevalerie au Moyen Age* (Paris, 1998).

Foreville, R., 'Les "Miracula S. Thomae Cantuariensis" ', *Actes du 97e Congrès National des Sociétés Savantes, 1972: Section de philologie et d'histoire jusqu'à 1610* (Paris, 1979), pp. 444–68.

Forsyth, I. H., *The Throne of Wisdom: Wood Sculptures of the Madonna in Romanesque France* (Princeton, 1972).

France, J., *Western Warfare in the Age of the Crusades 1000–1300* (London, 1999).

François, M. (ed.), *Le livre des miracles de Notre-Dame de Rocamadour* (2e Colloque de Rocamadour; Rocamadour, 1973).

Frank Jr., R. W., 'Pilgrimage and Sacral Power', *Journeys Toward God: Pilgrimage and Crusade*, ed. B. N. Sargent-Baur (Studies in Medieval Culture, 30; Kalamazoo, 1992), pp. 31–43.

Freedberg, D., *The Power of Images: Studies in the History and Theory of Response* (Chicago, 1989).

de Gaiffier, B., 'Les revendications de biens dans quelques documents hagiographiques du XIe siècle', *Analecta Bollandiana*, 50 (1932), pp. 123–38.

—— 'L'hagiographie et son public au XIe siècle', in *Miscellanea Historica in honorem Leonis van der Essen*, 1 vol. in 2 (Brussels and Paris, 1947), i.135–66.

—— 'Hagiographie et historiographie: Quelques aspects du problème', in *La storiografia altomedievale*, 2 vols. (Settimane di studio del centro italiano di studi sull'alto medioevo, 17; Spoleto, 1970), i.139–66.

Geary, P. J., *Furta Sacra: Thefts of Relics in the Central Middle Ages*, rev. edn (Princeton, 1990).

Genicot, L., *Les généalogies* (Typologie des sources du moyen âge occidental, 15; Turnhout, 1975).

Gillingham, J., 'The Unromantic Death of Richard I', *Speculum*, 54 (1979), pp. 18–41.

—— *Richard the Lionheart*, 2nd edn (London, 1989).

Given, J., *State and Society in Medieval Europe: Gwynedd and Languedoc under Outside Rule* (Ithaca, 1990).

Gold, P. S., *The Lady and the Virgin: Image, Attitude, and Experience in Twelfth-Century France* (Chicago, 1985).

Gonthier, D., and Le Bas, C., 'Analyse socio-économique de quelques recueils de miracles dans la Normandie du XIe au XIIIe siècle', *Annales de Normandie*, 24 (1974), pp. 3–36.

Goodich, M. E., *Violence and Miracle in the Fourteenth Century: Private Grief and Public Salvation* (Chicago, 1995).

Gordon, E. C., 'Child Health in the Middle Ages as Seen in the Miracles of Five English Saints, A.D.1150–1220', *Bulletin of the History of Medicine*, 60 (1986), pp. 502–22.

Grabois, A., *Le pèlerin occidental en Terre Sainte au Moyen Âge* (Bibliothèque du Moyen Âge, 13; Brussels, 1998).

Graef, H., *Mary: A History of Doctrine and Devotion*, rev. edn (London, 1985).

Green, J. A., *The Aristocracy of Norman England* (Cambridge, 1997).

Grundmann, H., 'Rotten und Brabanzonen: Söldner-Heere im 12. Jahrhundert', *Deutsches Archiv für Erforschung des Mittelalters*, 5 (1942), pp. 419–92.

Hamilton, B., 'Rebuilding Zion: The Holy Places of Jerusalem in the Twelfth Century', *Renaissance and Renewal in Christian History*, ed. D. Baker (Studies in Church History, 14; Oxford, 1977), pp. 105–16.

—— *The Latin Church in the Crusader States: The Secular Church* (London, 1980).

—— 'The Impact of Crusader Jerusalem on Western Christendom', *Catholic Historical Review*, 80 (1994), pp. 695–713.

Head, T., *Hagiography and the Cult of Saints: The Diocese of Orléans, 800–1200* (Cambridge, 1990).

Heinzelmann, M., *Translationsberichte und andere Quellen des Reliquienkultes* (Typologie des sources du moyen âge occidental, 33; Turnhout, 1979).

—— 'Une source de base de la littérature hagiographique latine: Le recueil de miracles', *Hagiographie, cultures et sociétés, IVe–XIIe siècles: Actes du Colloque organisé à Nanterre et à Paris (2–5 mai 1979)* (Paris, 1981), pp. 235–59.

Herbers, K., 'The Miracles of St. James', *The Codex Calixtinus and the Shrine of St. James*, ed. J. Williams and A. Stones (Jakobus-Studien, 3; Tübingen, 1992), pp. 11–35.

Higounet, C., 'Un grand chapitre de l'histoire du XIIe siècle: La rivalité des maisons de Toulouse et de Barcelone pour la prépondérance méridionale', *Mélanges Louis Halphen* (Paris, 1953), pp. 313–22.

Holtzmann, W., 'Quellen und Forschungen zur Geschichte Friedrich Barbarossas', *Neues Archiv der Gesellschaft für ältere deutsche Geschichtskunde*, 48 (1930), pp. 384–413.

Hubert, J., 'Le miracle de Déols et la trêve conclue en 1187 entre les rois de France et d'Angleterre', *Bibliothèque de l'Ecole des chartes*, 96 (1935), pp. 285–300.

Keen, M. H., *Chivalry* (New Haven, 1984).

Köbler, G., *Historisches Lexicon der Deutschen Länder* (Munich, 1992).

Köster, K., *Pilgerzeichen und Pilgermuscheln von mittelalterlichen Santiago-straßen: Saint-Léonard, Rocamadour, Saint-Gilles, Santiago de Compostela* (Ausgrabungen in Schleswig, Berichte und Studien, 2; Neumünster, 1983).

Koziol, G., 'Monks, Feuds, and the Making of Peace in Eleventh-Century Flanders', *The Peace of God: Social Violence and Religious Response in France around the Year 1000*, ed. T. Head and R. Landes (Ithaca, 1992), pp. 239–58.

Krötzl, C., *Pilger, Mirakel und Alltag: Formen des Verhaltens im skandinavischen Mittelalter (12.–15. Jahrhundert)* (Studia Historica, 46; Helsinki, 1994).

Labande, E.-R., 'Recherches sur les pèlerins dans l'Europe des XIe et XIIe siècles', *Cahiers de civilisation médiévale*, 1 (1958), pp. 159–69, 339–47.

—— '"Ad limina": le pèlerin médiéval au terme de sa démarche', *Mélanges offerts à René Crozet*, ed. P. Gallais and Y.-J. Riou, 1 vol. in 2 (Poitiers, 1966), i.283–91.

Lambert, M. D., *The Cathars* (Oxford, 1998).

Lartigaut, J., 'Nouvelles sociétés et nouvaux espaces (milieu Xe siècle–fin XIIe siècle)', *Histoire du Quercy*, ed. J. Lartigaut (Toulouse, 1993), pp. 91–106.

Latouche, R., 'Sainte-Foy de Conques et le problème d'or aux temps carolingiens', *Annales du Midi*, 68 (1956), pp. 209–15.

Lifshitz, F., 'Beyond Positivism and Genre: "Hagiographical" Texts as Historical Narrative', *Viator*, 25 (1994), pp. 95–113.

Lotter, F., 'Methodisches zur Gewinnung historischer Erkenntnisse aus hagiographischen Quellen', *Historische Zeitschrift*, 229 (1979), pp. 298–356.

Mason, E., ' "Rocamadour in Quercy above all Other Churches": The Healing of Henry II', *The Church and Healing*, ed. W. J. Shiels (Studies in Church History, 19; Oxford, 1982), pp. 39–54.

Mayer, H. E., 'Das syrische Erdbeben von 1170: Ein uneditierter Brief Königs Amalrichs von Jerusalem', *Deutsches Archiv für Erforschung des Mittelalters*, 45 (1989), pp. 474–84.

McCready, W. D., *Signs of Sanctity: Miracles in the Thought of Gregory the Great* (Toronto, 1989).

Morison, P., 'The Miraculous and French Society, circa 950–1150', unpublished D. Phil thesis (Oxford, 1984).

Morris, C., 'The *Gesta Francorum* as Narrative History', *Reading Medieval Studies*, 19 (1993), pp. 55–71.

Mundy, J. H., *Liberty and Political Power in Toulouse 1050–1230* (New York, 1954).

Niemeyer, G., 'Die Miracula S. Mariae Laudunensis des Abtes Hermann von Tournai: Verfasser und Entstehungszeit', *Deutsches Archiv für Erforschung des Mittelalters*, 27 (1971), pp. 135–74.

Parisse, M., *Noblesse et chevalerie en Lorraine médiévale: Les familles nobles du XIe au XIIIe siècle* (Nancy, 1982).

Paterson, L. M., *The World of the Troubadours: Medieval Occitan Society, c.1100–c.1300* (Cambridge, 1993).

Pernoud, R., ' "Le livre des miracles de Notre-Dame de Rocamadour": étude des manuscrits de 1172', *Le livre des miracles*, ed. François, pp. 9–23.

Philippart, G., *Les légendiers* (Typologie des sources du moyen âge occidental, 24–5; Turnhout, 1977).

Poly, J.-P., *La Provence et la société féodale (879–1166): Contribution à l'étude des structures dites féodales dans le Midi* (Paris, 1976).

Preiss, M., *Die politische Tätigkeit und Stellung der Cisterzienser im Schisma von 1159–1177* (Historische Studien, 248; Berlin, 1934).

Previté Orton, C. W., *The Early History of the House of Savoy (1000–1233)* (Cambridge, 1912).

Remensnyder, A. G., 'Un problème de cultures ou de culture? La statue-reliquaire et les *joca* de sainte Foy de Conques dans le *Liber miraculorum* de Bernard d'Angers', *Cahiers de civilisation médiévale*, 33 (1990), pp. 351–79.

—— *Remembering Kings Past: Monastic Foundation Legends in Medieval Southern France* (Ithaca, 1995).

Rendtel, C., *Hochmittelalterliche Mirakelberichte als Quelle zur Sozial- und Mentalitätsgeschichte und zur Geschichte der Heiligenverehrung untersucht aus Texten insbesondere aus Frankreich*, 1 vol. in 2 (Düsseldorf, 1985).

—— 'Wallfahrt und Konkurrenz im Spiegel hochmittelalterlicher Mirakel-berichte', in *Wallfahrt und Alltag in Mittelalter und früher Neuzeit* (Veröffentlichungen des Instituts für Realienkunde des Mittelalters und der frühen Neuzeit, 14; Vienna, 1992), pp. 115–31.

Riley-Smith, J. S. C., *The Knights of St John in Jerusalem and Cyprus c.1050–1310* (London, 1967).

—— *The First Crusaders, 1095–1131* (Cambridge, 1997).

Rocacher, J., *Rocamadour et son pèlerinage: étude historique et archéologique*, 2 vols. (Toulouse, 1979).

Rollason, D. W., 'The Miracles of St Benedict: A Window on Early Medieval France', in *Studies in Medieval History Presented to R. H. C. Davis*, ed. H. Mayr-Harting and R. I. Moore (London, 1985), pp. 73–90.

Rouche, M., 'Miracles, maladies et psychologie de la foi à l'époque carolingienne en Francie', in *Hagiographie, cultures et sociétés, IVe–XIIe siècles: Actes du Colloque organisé à Nanterre et à Paris (2–5 mai 1979)* (Paris, 1981), pp. 319–37.

Runciman, S., *A History of the Crusades, I: The First Crusade and the Foundation of the Kingdom of Jerusalem* (Cambridge, 1951).

Rupin, E., *Roc-Amadour: étude historique et archéologique* (Paris, 1904).

Sassier, Y., *Louis VII* (Paris, 1991).

Shideler, J. C., *A Medieval Catalan Noble Family: The Montcadas 1000–1230* (Berkeley, 1983).

Sigal, P.-A., 'Maladie, pèlerinage et guérison au XIIe siècle: Les miracles de saint Gibrien à Reims', *Annales: Économies, Sociétés, Civilisations*, 24 (1969), pp. 1522–39.

—— 'Un aspect du culte des saints: Le châtiment divin aux XIe et XIIe siècles

213

d'après la littérature hagiographique du Midi de la France', in *La religion populaire en Languedoc du XIIIe à la moitie du XIVe siècle* (Cahiers de Fanjeaux, 11; Toulouse, 1976), pp. 39–59.

——— 'Les voyages de reliques aux onzième et douzième siècles', in *Voyage, quête, pèlerinage dans la littérature et la civilisation médiévales* (Sénéfiance, 2; Aix-en-Provence, 1976), pp. 73–104.

——— 'Histoire et hagiographie: Les "Miracula" aux XIe et XIIe siècles', *Annales de Bretagne et des pays de l'Ouest,* 87 (1980), pp. 237–57.

——— 'L'ex-voto au Moyen-Age dans les régions du Nord-Ouest de la Méditerranée (XIIe–XVe siècles)', *Provence historique,* 33 (1983), pp. 13–31.

——— 'Miracle in vita et miracle posthume aux XIe et XIIe siècles', in *Histoire des miracles* (Publications du Centre de Recherches d'Histoire Religieuse et d'Histoire des Idées, 6; Angers, 1983), pp. 41–9.

——— 'Les différents types de pèlerinage au Moyen Age', *Wallfahrt kennt keine Grenzen,* ed. L. Kriss-Rettenbeck and G. Möhler (Munich and Zurich, 1984), pp. 76–86.

——— *L'homme et le miracle dans la France médiévale (XIe–XIIe siècle)* (Paris, 1985).

——— 'Le travail des hagiographes aux XIe et XIIe siècles: Sources d'information et méthodes de redaction', *Francia,* 15 (1987), pp. 149–82.

——— 'Reliques, pèlerinage et miracles dans l'église médiévale (XIe–XIIIe siècles)', *Revue d'histoire de l'église de France,* 76 (1990), pp. 193–211.

Signori, G., 'The Miracle Kitchen and its Ingredients: A Methodical and Critical Approach to Marian Shrine Wonders (10th to 13th Century)', *Hagiographica,* 3 (1996), pp. 277–303.

Spiegel, G. M., *The Chronicle Tradition of Saint-Denis: A Survey* (Medieval Classics: Texts and Studies, 10; Brookline, Mass., 1978).

——— 'History, Historicism, and the Social Logic of the Text in the Middle Ages', *Speculum,* 65 (1990), pp. 59–86.

Southern, R. W., *The Making of the Middle Ages* (London, 1953).

——— 'The English Origins of the "Miracles of the Virgin"', *Medieval and Renaissance Studies,* 4 (1958), pp. 176–216.

——— 'The Place of England in the Twelfth Century Renaissance', in his *Medieval Humanism and Other Studies* (Oxford, 1970), pp. 158–80.

Stock, B., *The Implications of Literacy: Written Language and Models of Interpretation in the Eleventh and Twelfth Centuries* (Princeton, 1983).

Strickland, M., *War and Chivalry: The Conduct and Perception of War in England and Normandy, 1066–1217* (Cambridge, 1996).

Sumption, J., *Pilgrimage: An Image of Mediaeval Religion* (London, 1975).

——— *The Albigensian Crusade* (London, 1978).

Tatlock, J. S. P., 'The English Journey of the Canons of Laon', *Speculum,* 8 (1933), pp. 454–85.

Tillmann, C., *Lexicon der deutschen Burgen und Schlösser,* 1 vol. in 4 (Stuttgart, 1958–61).

Usseglio, L., *I marchesi di Monferrato in Italia ed in Oriente durante i secoli xii e xiii*, 2 vols. (Biblioteca della Società Storica Subalpina, C ns 6; Casale Monferrato, 1926).

Van Dam, R., *Saints and their Miracles in Late Antique Gaul* (Princeton, 1993).

Vauchez, A., *La sainteté en Occident aux derniers siècles du moyen âge d'après les procès de canonisation et les documents hagiographiques*, 2nd edn (Bibliothèque des Écoles Françaises d'Athènes et de Rome, 241; Rome, 1988).

Vázquez de Parga, L., Lacarra, J. M., and Uría Ríu, J., *Las peregrinaciones a Santiago de Compostela*, 3 vols. (Madrid, 1948–49).

Vidier, A., *L'historiographie à Saint-Benoît-sur-Loire et les Miracles de saint Benoît* (Paris, 1965).

Vogel, C., 'Le pèlerinage pénitentiel', *Pellegrinaggi e culto dei Santi in Europa fino alla Ia Crociata* (Convegni del Centro di Studi sulla Spiritualità Medievale, 4; Todi, 1963), pp. 37–94.

Wakefield, W. L., *Heresy, Crusade and Inquisition in Southern France 1100–1250* (London, 1974).

Ward, B., *Miracles and the Medieval Mind: Theory, Record and Event 1000–1215*, rev. edn (Aldershot, 1987).

Warlop, E., *The Flemish Nobility before 1300*, trans. J. B. Ross and H. Vandermoere, 4 vols. (Courtrai, 1975).

Warner, M., *Alone of All Her Sex: The Myth and Cult of the Virgin Mary* (London, 1976).

Warren, W. L., *Henry II* (London, 1973).

Webb, D., *Pilgrims and Pilgrimage in the Medieval West* (London, 1999).

Wilson, S. (ed.), *Saints and their Cults: Studies in Religious Sociology, Folklore and History* (Cambridge, 1983).

INDEX

INDEX OF MIRACLES